What Your Colleagues Are Saying . . .

"Barry Gilmore and Gravity Goldberg have crafted a far-reaching, practical encyclopedia of teaching unhooked from any particular educational bias other than becoming a responsive, effective, powerful educator. Whoever you are, at whatever stage of your career, this book will help you to find new ways to engage, push, and support your students in any subject. Like a surgeon's assistant, these authors have found a way to present you with the exact tool you need at the moment you need it, as if they are standing over your shoulder as you teach, ready to say: *Look at what's happening; try this!* Just reading this book made me feel more empowered to teach."

—Kate Roberts
Literacy Consultant and Author
DIY Literacy and *Falling in Love With Close Reading*

"This is your go-to professional book for preparing students for today and their future! Learn the teaching moves, learning tools, collaborative structures, and reading and writing routines that develop students' creative, empathetic, problem-solving, and independent thinking while fostering trusting relationships. You'll find tips for getting started using assessments that inform instruction and intervention, suggestions for using the book, and charts that open each chapter showcasing all the teaching and learning methods at a glance!"

—Laura Robb
Teacher, Instructional Coach, and Author
Guided Practice for Reading Growth and *Read, Talk, Write*

"*Active Learning: 40 Teaching Methods to Engage Students in Every Class and Every Subject, Grades 6–12* is a brilliant book you will consistently reach for, reread, and talk about with others. Across each page, Barry Gilmore and Gravity Goldberg provide practical and actionable strategies for engaging the mind, body, heart, and soul of everyone in the learning community. While deeply grounded in research, this text clearly lays out classroom-ready ideas that enable practitioners to foster a strong sense of community interdependence while simultaneously promoting student independence. This professional text leaves readers more prepared to approach daily work with trust, confidence, and joy."

—Pam Koutrakos
Instructional Coach and Author
Word Study That Sticks, The Word Study That Sticks Companion,
and *Mentor Texts That Multitask*

"This book addresses a fundamental, yet sometimes overlooked, aspect of education: teaching students how to think. By breaking down the correlation between student behaviors and the *why* behind teaching practices, Barry Gilmore and Gravity Goldberg present practical methods to promote thinking in any classroom in a way that is accessible and actionable for new and veteran teachers. I highly recommend this book to any teacher who wants to center and grow their students' thinking."

—Carmen Lacherza
Supervisor of English Language Arts and ELL
Ramsey High School
Ramsey, NJ

"Barry Gilmore and Gravity Goldberg conceptualize 'gold standard' teaching methods through the lens of current educational research on cognition and motivation. It is a must-read for all teachers entering secondary education who are seeking a well-rounded tool kit of instructional practices. Moreover, this text is valuable for veteran teachers, who likely incorporate these teaching methods daily, but can now appreciate the purpose, foundation, and most effective implementation strategies to strengthen their practice."

—Dr. Brad Siegel
Superintendent of Schools
Upper Saddle River, NJ

"This is a very solid foundation text that I would hope to be used for new teachers and/or in new teacher training programs. I would have loved this type of easy-to-use manual as I planned lessons my first few years of teaching!"

—Theresa Walter
Teacher, Department Chairperson
Great Neck Public Schools
Great Neck, NY

ACTIVE LEARNING

For my daughters, Katy and Zoe Gilmore and Phoebe Fink-Gilmore. — Barry

For my mentors, teachers, and coaches. — Gravity

ACTIVE LEARNING

40 Teaching Methods to
Engage Students in Every
Class and Every Subject

Grades
6–12

BARRY GILMORE
GRAVITY GOLDBERG

FOR INFORMATION:

Corwin

A SAGE Company

2455 Teller Road

Thousand Oaks, California 91320

(800) 233-9936

www.corwin.com

SAGE Publications Ltd.

1 Oliver's Yard

55 City Road

London EC1Y 1SP

United Kingdom

SAGE Publications India Pvt. Ltd.

Unit No 323-333, Third Floor, F-Block

International Trade Tower Nehru Place

New Delhi 110 019

SAGE Publications Asia-Pacific Pte. Ltd.

18 Cross Street #10-10/11/12

China Square Central

Singapore 048423

Vice President and
    Editorial Director: Monica Eckman

Director and Publisher,
    Corwin Classroom: Lisa Luedeke

Associate Content
    Development Editor: Sarah Ross

Project Editor: Amy Schroller

Copy Editor: Melinda Masson

Typesetter: C&M Digitals (P) Ltd.

Proofreader: Dennis Webb

Cover Designer: Gail Buschman

Marketing Manager: Megan Naidl

Printed in the United Kingdom

Library of Congress Control Number: 2023935848

This book is printed on acid-free paper.

24 25 26 27 28 10 9 8 7 6 5 4 3 2 1

CONTENTS

For downloadable resources related to *Active Learning*,
visit the companion website at
resources.corwin.com/activelearning.

ACKNOWLEDGMENTS

Thank you to Barry Gilmore for being a profoundly thoughtful and caring human being who spent his career mentoring others. This book began as Barry's vision, and unfortunately, he passed away before it was completed. Until the end of his life, Barry worked to support teachers and students by sharing his insights and passion for learning. I am grateful this book has some of his final thoughts on creating classrooms that support students to think deeply.

Thank you to Lisa Luedeke—friend, colleague, and publisher—for all of the conversations and guidance. Lisa's leadership helped us map out the book even when Barry was unable to write. Somehow we were able to collaboratively plan, maintain our connection, and share some laughs together.

This book brought Wendy Murray, editor extraordinaire, back into my writing life, and I am grateful for her attention to detail, visionary thinking, and creativity. It is a clearer and more beautiful book because of her guidance.

I am grateful to my husband, John Altieri, who helped me carve out space to dedicate to this book. He also listened and offered ideas, cheered me on, and cooked hundreds of meals. Your support and belief in me and my work is a true gift.

My teammates Renee Houser, Dana Clark, Heather Frank, Brianne Annitti, Lily Howard Scott, Laura Sarsten, Margy Leininger, Julie McAuley, Christy Curran, and Sarah Fieledely inspire me in all the ways they show up for students and teachers. Every interaction with them offers an opportunity to learn more. Our conversations and collaborations offered rich soil for this book to grow. Most importantly, you each live the ideas of this work every day in classrooms around the country, and I am so grateful for you.

The educators with whom I partnered were always there with insightful questions and feedback along the way. The ideas in this book have been tested and revised due in large part to the following educators: Brooke Benavides, Carmen Lacherza, Courtney Rejent, Brennan Heffernan, Dan DeMartino, Andrew Matteo, Dana Silver, Alyssa Reyes, Steve Gebhart, Emma Petersen, Michelle Baldonado, Demi Aguirre, Lou Mardesich, Sharon James, Michelle Ponferrada, Matt Marone, Michele and Patrick Bulla, Rosanne Cavallo, Brad Siegel, and our Civic Education Think Tank, as well as educators from Nutley Middle and High School, Smith Middle School, Ramsey High School, Pearl River Middle and High School English

Department, San Pedro High School, Los Angeles District South cohort, and Hackensack Middle and High School.

I am forever grateful for the students who spoke up and challenged me and my colleagues to create classroom experiences that honored who they are and who they wanted to become. This book is really for you.

Thank you to the Corwin team: Sarah Ross, Amy Schroller, Megan Naidl, and Melinda Masson.

ABOUT THE AUTHORS

Barry Gilmore was the Middle School Head and later the Assistant Head of School for Teaching and Learning at Hutchison School in Memphis, Tennessee. A National Board Certified Teacher, he taught English and social studies for nearly 20 years. Barry is the author of seven education books and former president of the Tennessee Council of Teachers of English (TCTE). Awards for his teaching have come from the National Council of Teachers of English, TCTE, the U.S. Department of Education, and the Tennessee Holocaust Commission. He passed away in 2019 at the age of 50 and is dearly missed by his students, family, friends, and fellow faculty.

Gravity Goldberg is an international educational consultant and author of eight books on teaching. *Mindsets and Moves* (Corwin Literacy, 2015) put her on the world stage with its practical ways to cultivate student agency, leading to speaking engagements and foreign translations of her work. She has over 20 years of teaching experience, including positions as a science teacher, reading specialist, third-grade teacher, special educator, literacy coach, staff developer, assistant professor, educational consultant, and yoga teacher. Gravity holds a BA and MEd from Boston College and a doctorate in education from Teachers College, Columbia University. She is the founding director of Gravity Goldberg, LLC, a team that provides side-by-side coaching for teachers.

HOW TO USE THIS BOOK

This book is divided into seven sections and is meant to help support you with designing active learning experiences for students.

Introduction: The introduction is foundational and explains the rationale for why it is important to design with student thinking and relationships at the center. We suggest you read this first.

Sections 1–7: These sections can be read and applied in the classroom in any order. For example, if you want to focus on student collaboration, jump right into Section 4.

Methods: Each section is divided into methods. For example, Section 3: Learning Tools includes five methods: Multimodal Learning, Graphic Organizers, Thinking Routines, Memorization, and Reflection. You can choose any of these methods to focus on first; you do not need to read and implement them in the order they appear.

Opening Charts: Every section opens with a chart that helps you see all of the methods at a glance (see below). This is like a table of contents for the section and can help you decide where to turn first. These charts also provide our take on how each method can be leveraged to develop a particular kind of thinking (independent, creative, problem-solving, and empathetic).

WRITING ROUTINE	HOW STUDENTS MIGHT USE THE ROUTINE TO DEVELOP INDEPENDENT THINKING	HOW STUDENTS MIGHT USE THE ROUTINE TO DEVELOP CREATIVE THINKING	HOW STUDENTS MIGHT USE THE ROUTINE TO DEVELOP PROBLEM-SOLVING THINKING	HOW STUDENTS MIGHT USE THE ROUTINE TO DEVELOP EMPATHETIC THINKING
Planning for Writing Page 166	Plan in ways that work for them	Match the ways they plan for the audience and purpose	Adjust plans as challenges arise	Put themselves in the reader's shoes and plan in ways that will help them get their message across
Considering Audience Page 172	Choose an audience and purpose that matters to them	Match the ways they write to their audience	Use feedback to revise writing choices	Imagine what the audience wants and needs as they write
Studying Mentor Texts Page 177	Choose to use writing moves they found effective in others' writing	Select, combine, and organize writing moves in unique ways	Notice how authors have managed writing challenges with success	Understand others' perspective and process by noticing their writing choices
Developing Central Ideas for Essays Page 183	Develop their own idea about a topic or text	Generate an idea others may not have considered	Develop ideas for how to navigate a challenge	Understand their own perspective on a topic so they can understand others

Recurring Features: Within each section's methods you will find the following recurring features, which are noted by icons.

PART	WHAT IT'S FOR
Why?	Explains the *what* and *why* and may offer some examples
Quick Tips	Lists some helpful tips for both novice and veteran teachers
Getting Started	Offers concrete steps, tools, charts, and examples you can try right away
Heads Up	Advises you on what to be on the lookout for when you try this out and addresses common challenges and/or next steps
The Key Idea	Summarizes the method

Make this book an actionable tool by using it in the ways that best meet your student goals. Find places that confirm what you already do as some of the methods in this book are ones you likely use often. You can also find ideas that are familiar to you but offer some tips and tweaks that you may want to try out. Finally, seek out methods you have never tried and give them a go. We trust you will make choices that best support you and your students.

Introduction

What It Means to Actively Engage the Whole Mind

Take a look at any preschool-aged children and you'll see lots of activity. The climbing wall at a new playground provides opportunities for children to experience where their limits are, use their imaginations, and feel the joy of stretching toward something new. Children are constantly in motion, observing others, testing out what they can do, and asking friends to join in the fun. It is both taken-for-granted knowledge and research-based practice that help us recognize that young children need to be actively engaged in order to learn. Those same children grow taller and are now middle and high schoolers, and they still need the same elements in order to learn. Our goal for this book is to help you bring these elements into the classroom.

Research from neuroscience, cognitive psychology, and embodied cognition have shed a light on what many secondary teachers already knew intuitively—learning happens when students of all ages and all subjects are actively engaged. Being active might include physically moving our bodies, intellectually grappling with a problem, or feeling angst alongside a character. When students' brains and bodies are actively engaged, they develop more focused attention, experience the pleasure of learning, and develop the ability to understand others, leading to more connection and fulfillment.

Physically Active. Studies from embodied cognition found that tossing a ball from side to side leads to increases in new thinking (Beilock, 2015) and moderate exercise such as jumping and dancing helps students control their attention and boosts cognition (Chaddock et al., 2011). We are not suggesting students spend time playing catch and jumping around the classroom unless you are a physical education teacher, but it does show how important it is that students do not sit still all day long. Transitioning students during workshops from whole-group meeting areas to independent spaces and moving around the room in stations are two examples you will read more about in this book that call on students to physically move their bodies.

Intellectually Active. When students are actively engaged, they experience the pleasurable effects of learning with their brains releasing dopamine. The reward networks in students' brains activate in response to things that bring joy, and deactivate in response to things that reduce enjoyment (Waytz & Mason, 2013). Curiosity has shown to be a powerful reward. In one study participants read trivia questions and rated how curious they were about the answers. The stronger their desire to find out, the greater the activation in the reward network before they received an answer (Kang et al., 2009). When we create classrooms that foster curiosity, students' reward centers are more actively engaged. This can lead to deeper learning and also reinforce the desire to learn. Compelling essential questions and debatable lines of positionality are two examples from this book that create the context for curiosity to develop.

Emotionally Active. Cognitive empathy includes the ability to understand another person's perspective. Brain imaging studies found a number of brain regions that are activated in order to do this perspective taking. When students make inferences about others' mental states, they first use their awareness and effort to establish personal theories about others' psychological states, and then further adjust their theories during interactions (Carlson & Moses, 2001). The notion that people are born empathetic has been disproven. Empathy is a skill that is learned through active effort. When we incorporate more collaborative learning structures like the ones in Section 4 of this book, students get consistent practice and coaching in developing this ability.

Just like young children engage in play as a powerful learning tool, older children and teens benefit from active learning experiences. Active classrooms call upon students to test their limits, imagine possibilities, and collaborate with peers to innovate and create. When students are actively engaged, it can lead to deep thinking and independence of mind.

Develop Independence of Mind

As teachers, we don't actually know the details about the world we are preparing students for. We do our best to predict what higher education will look like, what jobs will be available, and what challenges need to be addressed. What we do know is that being a creative and deep thinker will help students no matter the details of their future. Whether our current students become citizens, scholars, or performers, what counts is that they will know *how* to think for themselves. We can help cultivate independence of mind through learning experiences that lead to thoughtful, active engagement.

As citizens, students can be supported to envision both the current and future contributions they can make. What gifts can they bring to their communities? What challenges can they take action on? How can they help build a beautiful future for themselves and others? Active citizenship entails using your voice to create change, knowing when to listen and step aside to support others, and building new systems that allow everyone to live a happy and healthy life.

As scholars, students can understand and find value in the pursuit of knowledge. They fall in love with learning, nurture passions, and develop inquiry mindsets. They may formally enroll in programs, or they may take on an apprenticeship to learn a trade or art. When we say *scholarship*, we mean it in the broadest sense. Scholars have a mindset for learning and growing, which does not necessarily have to be grounded in traditional coursework.

Classroom experiences can also develop performers. This may mean actors, artists, and even influencers, but it also refers to any action-oriented field. In this sense a performer is someone who can take meaningful action in the world. While scholars might study and accumulate knowledge, performers use that knowledge to teach, lead, mentor, and create.

Knowing students well enough to design experiences that are truly learner-focused humanizes the classroom. It acknowledges the individual preferences, personalities, and interests of students in an attempt to make classrooms work for them. When we seek to know our students as people and learners, we build relationships of trust and mutual respect. This seeking to really know others is something author Azar Nafisi (2022) explains is essential for developing independence of mind. Only when we seek connection by understanding others and their experiences will we be able to question our current beliefs, connect with others, and truly think. She explains, "We want to arm our children with this independence of mind that can stand up to terrible things that happen every day."

When a textbook publisher writes lesson plans, they may be filled with useful information and ideas, but they can never reach all of your students because the authors of those materials have never met your students. This does not mean we don't lean on resources and texts that meet curricular standards, but it does mean we make daily and moment-to-moment decisions about what tools, strategies, and structures will work for our students right now. Only you know that answer. Trust yourself and your students to be the guide in instructional decision making. Think about some of your past or current specific students.

- What does this student care about?

- What does this student want?

- What is this student afraid of?

- What gifts does this student have to offer?

- How does this student tend to think?

- How does this student define success?

When we design classroom experiences so that students think deeply, critically, and imaginatively, both within and across content areas, they become adults who think. According to researcher Tom Chatfield (quoted in Salmons, 2018), critical thinking "entails making good arguments and seeking good explanations. . . . Equally importantly, critical thinking is concerned with clarifying the limits of our knowledge—and with recognising the limitations built into our cognition and assumptions." Chatfield's description lays out a framework for a focus on arguments, explanations, and also metacognitive awareness and self-reflection on our own assumptions.

The following questions can help you reflect on the types of thinking your particular students will benefit from developing.

- What topics do we spend time thinking about?

- What are the current ways people think about these topics?

- What types of thinking might be missing?

- Whose thinking do we lean on in this course?

- Who else's thinking might we be missing?

- What kinds of thinking do students need to develop?

- Do I build in enough time for student thinking?

- What kinds of thinking do I tend to do?

- How does thinking develop across this domain?

In this book we will focus on four types of thinking as a framework to help us design learning experiences. While these types do not represent all learners and all learning, they can help guide the daily and yearly choices we make. The goal is not to use these types of thinking as boxes to be checked or to typecast learners. Instead, think of them as overarching ideas that can help shape instruction. For example, if you are designing a unit, ask yourself, "What types of thinking will students develop in this unit?" This can help you decide what matters most and what you ask students to lean into.

INDEPENDENT THINKING

Independent thinking is focused on forming one's own ideas based on experience, beliefs, and knowledge. When people learn to think independently, they form their own theories, decide what is and is not important, and draw conclusions that seem logical to them given what they know. Independent thinking is a vital part of being in society because it allows a person to live a meaningful life. If students do not learn how to think for themselves, they are more easily manipulated, make shortsighted decisions, and may miss opportunities for growth.

Independent thinking is a form of critical thinking. Vincent Ruggiero (2012) claims critical thinking "is searching for answers while reaching for meaning" (p. 4). He explains that critical thinkers typically:

- Acknowledge personal limitations

- See problems as exciting challenges

- Have understanding as a goal

- Use evidence to make judgments

- Are interested in others' ideas

- Are skeptical of extreme views

- Think before acting

- Keep an open mind

- Engage in active listening

Some ways to incorporate more independent thinking involve asking students to pose and answer their own questions; creating space for students to research, debate, and form their own claims about a topic; and making connections between what students have learned and how it may apply to their own lives.

Murawski (2014) explains, "Students who develop critical thinking skills often practice those skills well into later life. These skills may, in fact, literally change their lives forever. Developing critical thinking abilities translates to both academic and job success. Using these skills, students tend to expand the perspectives from which they view the world and increase their ability to navigate the important decisions in learning and in life" (p. 26). The goal of critical thinking is for students to live meaningful and independent lives. Don't get caught up in trying to figure out if a lesson is supporting independent thinking or critical thinking or both. It is not about labeling each type of thinking, and is about making sure students are thinking for themselves.

Take a few minutes to consider what independent thinking looks like in your content area.

- What are the dispositions and habits of mind independent thinkers carry?

- How do you support students' independent thinking?

- How do you get to know students as independent thinkers?

CREATIVE THINKING

In addition to independent thinking, we want students to develop creative thinking. By *creative* we mean the ability not just to make a piece of art or write a poem, but also to look at situations from multiple angles, to be open to new ideas, and to revise past thinking. This means students visualize and imagine new possibilities. According to psychologist Karen Nimmo (2020), creativity is the "ability to think in new directions."

In order to develop creative thinking, learners need to first be adept at the dominant ways of thinking within the discipline. For example, a biology student needs to know the ways biologists think, and a social studies student needs to know how a sociologist or historian thinks. Learners must understand the system that exists in order to eventually create outside of it. Students must learn the following in order to understand the overall system of thinking in a given discipline:

- The purpose or goal of the system

- The kinds of questions it answers or problems it solves

- The key concepts it generates

- The underlying assumptions it rests upon

- The implications embedded in it

- The point of view or way of seeing things it makes possible (Paul, 2004)

Creative thinking involves thinking "outside of the box." According to Giovanni Corazza's 2014 TEDx Talk, the box is made up of (a) what we know and (b) what we do not yet know. School tends to focus on what *other people* thought, discovered, and created. He claims we need to cross the border from what we do know to what we have not yet thought about to truly leave the box. This sort of creative thinking involves:

- Combining ideas in a new way

- Applying principles to a new system or context

- Looking for possible alternatives

- Including divergent information

- Trying out new metaphors

When supporting students to become creative thinkers, they need to understand the "box" or system of the discipline as well as be willing to step outside of it. This might mean we model how to think in disciplinary ways and encourage students to take intellectual risks by purposefully switching up parts of the system. For example, if we know that many history textbooks are written and edited with a chronological structure, what if we consider parallelism or missing voices or environmental impacts when looking at historical events? How might looking through this different lens lead to more creative thinking?

Take a few minutes to consider what creative thinking looks like in your content area.

- What are the dominant systems and ways of thinking that students must learn in this field?
- How do you encourage students to think outside of the box?
- How do you get to know students as creative thinkers?
- What obstacles might be getting in the way of creative thinking? How might you remove them?

PROBLEM-SOLVING THINKING

Our current world is full of what seems like impossible challenges. Questions involving ethics, mental health, economic opportunities, overall well-being, and survival on this planet keep many a scientist, theologian, parent, and teen awake at night. Plus there are the daily challenges for students, from how to keep the car from smelling like sports equipment, to how to wake up in time for the first period, to how to tell a friend they hurt your feelings. The ability to think in problem-solving ways can lead to both personal and community-based innovations.

Problem solving includes the ability to:

- Know the goal

- Name the challenge

- Consider options

- Identify potential roadblocks

- Try out a process

- Analyze outcomes

- Refine and revisit previous thinking

A key aspect of supporting problem-solving thinking is to focus on the result but not too much. When we help students focus on the process, we are supporting them in identifying where they went wrong. Knowing they were wrong is one aspect of changing course, but knowing where and why they were wrong helps them make a different choice next time. This might look like error analysis in a math or science class or critiquing a claim's evidence in a history class.

Carol Dweck's (2006) research on growth mindset is tied to a problem-solving approach. When students view their success as a result of the effort they put in, they are more likely to learn from failure, ask for feedback, and persevere when faced with challenges. As teachers, we can help support a growth mindset while also modeling problem-solving thinking. This might mean we model how we:

- Normalize struggle as a part of the learning process

- Reflect on what worked and didn't, and why

- Make a plan, try it out, and then get feedback from others

- Learn from failure and try again

Developing learning experiences that are problem-based is a highly supportive way to foster this form of thinking. Look at learning experiences and consider how authentic the problem is, think about how students might help with a larger challenge by contributing their unique ideas, and ask students what problems they want to help solve. A high school English teacher recently stated, "Teens today are not waiting for us adults to solve the world's problems. They are frustrated with us and are taking it on themselves."

> Take a few minutes to consider what problem-solving thinking looks like in your content area.
>
> - What are the big problems that students might help your field solve?
> - How do you design learning experiences that are problem-based?
> - How do you model a growth mindset?
> - How do you get to know students as problem solvers?

EMPATHETIC THINKING

The reason many of us cry when watching a sad scene in a movie is because we have mirror neurons. These neurons help us replay the emotional experience of others in our own nervous system so we have the same feelings ourselves. Seeing and feeling are connected (Niedenthal, 2007). In fact, the field of embodied cognition discovered that we understand others by replaying their behavior in our own motor system as if we are performing the behavior ourselves (Beilock, 2015). This is referred to as empathy. According to Theresa Wiseman's (1996) research, empathy includes:

- Perspective taking

- Staying out of judgment

- Recognizing emotion

- Communicating our understanding about the emotion

Brené Brown (2021) draws upon Wiseman's work and explains, "We need to dispel the myth that empathy is walking in someone else's shoes; rather than walking in your shoes, I need to learn how to listen to the story you tell about what it's like in your shoes and believe you even when it doesn't match my experiences" (p. 123). Empathy is a tool people use for compassion.

While some disciplines might seem to develop empathetic thinking more than others, we have the opportunity to support this kind of thinking all day long. We can model empathetic thinking when we:

- Read and respond to a character in a text

- Share a story about a historical figure or group

- Look at a problem from multiple perspectives

- Show compassion for ourselves as we experience struggle

- Listen to understand rather than listen to agree or disagree

- Refrain from judgment when we hear something that is different from our own lived experience

During this time of extremes in our country where almost everything is portrayed as polarized, we can lean more into empathetic thinking. Teaching students to be empathetic is not about getting them to agree with our worldview or to feel badly for someone (that is sympathy, not empathy), but is about developing dispositions that allow everyone to maintain their humanity. This may come up in class conversations, argument-based writing, and research presentations. No matter the context, we can choose to center and support an empathetic lens.

Take a few minutes to consider what empathetic thinking looks like in your content area.

- What does empathy sound like, look like, and feel like in the classroom?
- How do you design learning experiences that support empathetic thinking?
- How do you explicitly talk about and model empathy?
- How do you support students as empathetic thinkers?

While it can be helpful to look at each of the four types of thinking as a framework for designing learning experiences, these types are best thought of as guidelines and not four discrete goals; the lines between them often blur. Many times an experience incorporates multiple types of thinking. Sometimes it is hard to tell if it is one type or the other. Remember the goal is for students to think deeply and develop both content knowledge and strategies for learning. Put simply, the methods in this book will help you bolster both logic and creativity.

The following chart offers an at-a-glance summary of four types of thinking (Appendix A). Having clarity about desired student thinking helps make the day-to-day instructional method choices more purposeful.

Types of Thinking

TYPE OF THINKING	DESCRIPTION	WHY IT IS IMPORTANT
Independent thinking	Forming one's own ideas based on experience, beliefs, and knowledge	• Leads to academic and job success • Expands your understanding • Increases ability to navigate the important decisions in learning and in life • Less likely to be manipulated and make shortsighted decisions
Creative thinking	Thinking "outside of the box" by imagining innovative ideas	• Develops habits of mind • Encourages intellectual risk-taking • Values seeking alternatives • Opens up endless possibilities • Develops a hopeful outlook
Problem-solving thinking	Addressing challenges by developing possible solutions	• Values the process • Normalizes struggle • Supports a growth mindset • Positions students as contributors • Develops metacognition
Empathetic thinking	Seeking to understand others' experiences, feelings, and beliefs	• Develops compassion • Supports a nuanced view of the world • Humanizes others • Leads to less polarization • Opens up one's mind and heart

Create Trusting Relationships

According to psychologist Amy Cuddy (2015), the two most important elements in a strong relationship are warmth/trust and competence. While both of these elements are essential aspects of relationships, she and her research colleagues found that trust was most important. Cuddy explains,

> Why do we prioritize warmth over competence? Because from an evolutionary perspective, it is more crucial to our survival to know whether a person deserves our trust. If he doesn't, we'd better keep our distance, because he's potentially dangerous, especially if he is competent. We do value people who are capable, especially in circumstances where the trait is necessary, but we only notice that *after* we've judged their trustworthiness. (p. 72)

A teacher's job is literally to help develop competence—to teach students to think deeply and independently. And yet our other primary job is actually to build trust with our students. If we want them to take intellectual risks, test out ideas, and ask for feedback, they need to feel they are in a safe space. One way we help students feel safe is by showing them we are competent teachers, but research shows that before they are even thinking about our capabilities, they are asking, "Can I trust this person?"

Trusting relationships are developed in a number of ways over time. We can look at research from developmental psychology, positive psychology, and sociology to gain insight into key elements of trust.

CONSISTENCY

Dr. Bruce Perry, a world-renowned expert in trauma-informed therapy, explains that connection is vital for a sense of safety. Connections happen in an accumulation of small interactions. To keep showing up over and over again is how trust is built. For example, he quotes research that several 5- to 10-minute positive interactions have a bigger impact than meeting a therapist once a week for an hour (Perry & Winfrey, 2021). Every day, in each interaction, we can show students that we care, that we are here to support them, and that they are safe to learn. Connecting moments can accumulate in many forms whether they be during shared classroom experiences where you truly listen to a student's idea, a share-out where a student explains their thinking to the class, or a one-on-one conference where you take a few minutes to really get to know one student and offer feedback. The key component is consistent connections across time.

LOVE

bell hooks (2003) taught us that "Love is a combination of care, commitment, knowledge, responsibility, respect, and trust" (p. 88). This means we are committed to making choices in students' best interest, even though those choices may make us stray from plans or the comfort of the familiar. We also model how to take personal responsibility for our actions. Rather than focus on intent, we focus on impact. We ask, "How did my words and actions impact others?" When we show up for students from a place of love, they feel it, and it builds a culture of trust. They want to engage with us. For example, we might pause and show our love by really listening to students before jumping in with our own ideas, or we might build in celebratory moments where all students are given specific and timely feedback on the strengths they are contributing to the classroom community.

COLLABORATION

In *Big Potential*, Shawn Achor (2018) explains how collaboration and interdependence lead to greater success than trying to go it alone: "When we are brave enough to expand power to others, suddenly we find that a huge weight is lifted off our shoulders, increasing our power to lift even heavier loads. . . . We can all inspire others to dream more, learn more, do more, and become more, no matter what seat we are in" (p. 114). This means we intentionally work to make others better by adding to, cheering on, and supporting their ideas. Designing experiences around collaboration positions students as active contributors to each other's learning and cultivates a sense of interdependence. For example, after teaching students a handful of ways to collaborate, we might offer choices in the ways students want to work together and when. By offering choice we help students self-reflect on when it is and is not beneficial to collaborate along with how it can lead to even greater learning success.

BELIEFS

John Hattie's meta-analysis research found that collective teacher efficacy has the biggest impact on student learning (Waack, 2018). This means the beliefs that teachers carry have a bigger influence on student growth than any instructional element or tool. The good news is this does not require additional funding or professional development, but it does require intentional choices to align our beliefs and practices. When we have teacher efficacy, we see a direct correlation between what we choose to do as teachers and the learning that happens in the classroom. When a group of teachers come together and believe they can have a positive impact on student learning, they are more likely to be successful. This might look like co-planning a unit with your grade-level or department team and then taking time to look at assessments together, naming strengths and next steps.

For us, the benefit of cultivating trusting relationships with students is that our teaching becomes freer and fuller. With trust, we know students well enough to joke and laugh or have a hard conversation. Teaching and learning become multidimensional. And when we trust enough to be authentic, we engage our whole mind.

Choose Teaching Methods

It is estimated that teachers make close to 1,500 choices per day. One of the most important decisions is "What teaching methods will I use?" There really aren't right and wrong answers to this question if we are clear on our purpose. We can design learning experiences by tapping into our creativity and seeing our job as a set of choices that set up the conditions for students to learn and grow. As designers of learning experiences, we:

- Develop a clear vision

- Create classroom spaces where students feel safe and supported

- Focus on learning

- Plan for active engagement

- Build upon student strengths

- Ask for and use feedback

- Collaborate with students and colleagues

We make a series of choices—some long term and some short—about how we want students to feel, what we want them to think about, and the types of learning experiences they will engage in. We see the interconnectedness of each of these choices. Of course, none of us makes perfect choices and always hits the mark. As designers, we also get to change course, rethink a past practice, and revise our plans. This takes some of the pressure off and reminds us that we can always redesign something in a different way.

This book invites you to purposefully step into your role as a designer. It helps you look at key aspects of classroom life so student engagement and thinking are front and center. Each section is devoted to a different but complementary aspect of the classroom—instructional structures, teaching moves, learning tools, collaboration structures, reading and writing routines, and assessment opportunities. As you begin using the methods in this book, use the following table to help you get started. Of course, if you know exactly what methods you want to try, jump right in.

IF . . .	THEN . . .
Students have trouble getting started with their work	Begin with **Section 2** and think about which teaching methods (modeling, guided practice, coaching) might help them get started with more clarity. They may need more gradual release across all three methods before working independently.
Students are chatty, but don't yet know how to use conversations to develop their thinking	Harness their chattiness by trying ideas from **Section 1** such as shared experiences and simulations. Try out lines of positionality in **Section 4**.
Students are silent and don't participate in discussions	Begin with a few collaboration structures from **Section 4** and repeat them until students feel confident. Consider think-pair-share and sentence stems. Then move on to incorporating other structures.
Students choose not to read or struggle understanding readings	Carve out time in class to use reading routines from **Section 5**. Try incorporating close reading as a class shared experience and independent reading to build in more choice.
Students would benefit from support with their writing skill and engagement	Make time to teach writing and not just assign it. **Section 6** offers methods you can use across the year to make the process more concrete and actionable. Try using mentor text and teaching students how to plan for their writing with real audiences in mind.
Students would benefit from learning and study skills	Begin with **Section 3** and teach them learning tools to help with organizing, remembering, and synthesizing. Try offering choice in graphic organizers and teaching memorization strategies.
Students skim the surface and tend not to go deeper with their thinking	Consider beginning with **Section 3** and include more reflection time and teaching of thinking routines. Try out reading clubs from **Section 5** and teach students how to build ideas together.
You would like to get to know students' thinking better and need more information about the students as learners	Develop some assessment tools based on the ideas in **Section 7**. Try conferring with students and designing formative assessments that will show you what they already know and do.
You have some tried-and-true methods you already use and want to mix it up	Skim the opening section charts and choose a method you have not done in a while or have never tried.

Instructional Structures

Instructional structures help us design high-impact learning experiences. What unites the nine we discuss in this section is that they make our teaching goals transparent—and make our respect for learner engagement evident to students.

INSTRUCTIONAL STRUCTURE	WHY?	WHEN?
Do Nows Page 18	To activate students' prior knowledge, priming them for today's learning	At the start of class when students first come into the classroom
Unit Goals Page 21	To make learning targets explicit and clear for students and teachers	Introduce at the start of the unit, revisit throughout the unit, and then use to reflect at the end of the unit
Essential Questions Page 26	To create curiosity, encourage synthesis and application of learning	Introduce at the start of the unit, discuss in small groups and whole-class conversations throughout the unit, and use to reflect at the end of the unit
Shared Experiences Page 30	To develop knowledge and skills collaboratively and in an engaging way before asking students to apply knowledge and skills on their own	At the start of a unit or as a way to introduce new content or skills
Workshops Page 33	To support student independence and create an active learning environment	In the middle of a unit, use this structure across several days or weeks while students are working on projects and problems
Strategy Groups Page 39	To offer differentiated support to groups of students who all would benefit from learning a specific strategy	While the rest of the class is working independently
Stations Page 43	To offer review and new learning together, to best utilize the teachers in the room, and to break up a big topic into parts	In the beginning of a unit to build knowledge and skills, in the middle and end of the unit to review past learning and get extra practice
Simulations Page 49	To engage students in experiencing a problem, time, place, or perspective	When students have enough knowledge to apply it and then go deeper
Flipped Classrooms Page 53	To set students up to think, do, and create during class with support from peers and teachers	When students are not actively engaged in class time and need a shift

QUICK TIPS

- *Have Do Nows ready and posted* well before class begins to help yourself and students feel secure.

- *Keep Do Nows simple.* If an activity takes longer than five minutes to complete, it can be a lesson on its own.

- *Consider a "soft start"* version by playing calming music and offering a few minutes for quiet reflection on days where students may be experiencing high levels of anxiety.

Do Nows

WHY?

No doubt, instructional minutes are precious. The start of a class period often includes teachers taking attendance, signing absence forms, or tending to a dozen other demands. *Do Nows* are questions or brief activities students engage in as soon as they come into class—before or as the bell rings. Do Nows prompt students to work and think as you handle this other business. Because they are brief and engaging activities, Do Nows help to create a risk-free environment at the beginning of the lesson (Bonwell, 1995).

Consider these three examples:

- Mr. Carroll, a seventh-grade life science teacher, has a permanent spot on his board that lists an open-ended question such as "Why Do You Think This Happens?" Each day at the start of class students write a few sentences about the questions he posts, which range across topics from *animal extinction* to *benefits of research on cells.*

- Ms. Norton often asks tenth-grade English students to talk to a partner about their reactions to a reading and predictions about what might happen next based on what they know about the genre and characterization.

- Mr. Andrade, an art teacher, projects a renowned work of art on the screen as students enter the room; their task is to talk to a partner and guess as much as they can about the age and medium of the piece from context clues.

Some teachers call these engagements Warm-Ups, Do Firsts, or Bell Work. Regardless of the name, such opening activities can serve a number of teaching purposes:

- They provide review opportunities and help students access prior knowledge.

- They prepare students for the learning they are about to do.

- They send the message that the class is about active thinking and learning.

- They ease students into the topic.

- They provide opportunities for priming students with different types of thinking.

GETTING STARTED

Some teachers prefer the routine of starting class each day with the same introductory activity. Others use a variety of Do Nows as they see fit. Still others pin their opening activities to a day of the week: new vocabulary on Monday, essential question reflection on Tuesday, and so on. Your approach may depend on the age of your students or your teaching context, but if Do Nows are new to you, consider planning some sort of routine use that will be easy to maintain.

The following chart provides a list of activities for different purposes: reviewing previous material, preparing for new material, practicing different types of thinking, and paying attention to mindset and metacognition about learning. This last category, mindset, is easily overlooked, but it can be a particularly helpful way to engage easily distracted or overly stressed students. Notice how the variety of examples on this chart align to different types of thinking. For example, if you want to support empathetic thinking, you might choose to interview a partner, or if you want to support independent thinking, you might choose students setting goals for themselves.

Sample Do Nows

REVIEW PREVIOUS MATERIAL	PREPARE FOR NEW MATERIAL	PRACTICE SKILLS	MINDSET
Answer 2 or 3 review questions	Answer an open-ended question	Analyze a sentence, passage, or problem	Self-assess your progress in learning
Summarize a passage or topic	Summarize what you already know about a topic or text	Figure out new vocabulary from context clues	Respond to a quotation
Make a list	Look up a new term	Revise a written response or problem	Organize a notebook, desk, or planner
Define a term	Compare two topics or texts with a Venn diagram	Create a mnemonic	Set goals for learning
Fill in a chart	Read a new image or infographic	Discuss a problem with a partner	Meditate, stretch, or breathe
Identify a lingering question	Write down a question about a topic	Practice a specific skill or procedure	Make a to-do list
Solve a review problem	Interview a partner	Sort words, terms, or concepts	Write a note to the teacher
Review, mark, or categorize notes	Agree or disagree with a statement in writing or with a partner	Reread notes from the day before and jot down new ideas	Check in with your feelings or expectations

KEY IDEA

Start the learning as students enter the room. Plan opening activities intentionally to engage students with thinking right from the start.

HEADS UP

Avoid no-brainer activities. Search the internet for Do Nows and you'll quickly discover lists of fun icebreaker activities listed under the label "bellringer." There may be a place for playing a game or answering a riddle in school, but if the activity doesn't specifically further students' engagement in the curricular content, it's probably best to skip it.

Lack of clarity = chaos. Loosely planned activities can create a sense of unpredictability and cause students to feel unnerved and unfairly challenged by a confusing directive. Even if you don't always have students abide by an absolute routine for how class begins, students shouldn't be taken off guard. Use Do Nows to create a safe space for learning. Note here that noise is not the same as chaos: Do Nows hopefully generate talk and excitement and engage students in learning.

Is it too repetitive? If you do the same Do Now every day, students' brains start to tune it out. Instead of using the same Do Nows over and over again, elicit student feedback. Ask, "Which ones do you enjoy?" Watch to see which ones lead to engagement and a good buzz in the room. While it is helpful to have a consistent routine for how a Do Now goes, that routine should build in room for a variety of types of thinking and experiences.

Unit Goals

WHY?

Imagine you are driving a car on a long-distance trip. Your friend in the passenger seat is giving you directions, but has not told you where you are going. You are completely in the dark about your final destination. However, your driving will be assessed on whether or not you get there. At best you would feel anxious. You might feel angry because you are not clear where your friend wants you to go, and your relationship might suffer. If you become confused, you might even give up and declare you don't care about this trip anyhow. This can be students' experience in classrooms where goals are unclear.

Clear goals for each unit allow both teachers and students to know where they are going. Typically, a teacher works with their department colleagues to develop goals for each unit that build from grade level to grade level. This creates thinking-centered classrooms where students are supported to work and think in deeper and deeper ways across their educational experiences. In a four- to six-week unit teachers develop three to five goals so there is enough time for depth of thinking and mastery instead of covering topics and standards.

The goals align with standards but are not the standards themselves. A standard is an end-of-the-year benchmark for teachers. A goal is a learning target for students with sufficient challenge, written in language they can understand. If we share standards instead of goals for students, it is often like being given directions, while driving, in a different language that you do not understand. The following table shows how standards can be used to develop unit goals.

EXAMPLE OF STANDARDS FOCUSED ON WITHIN A UNIT (FOR TEACHERS)	EXAMPLE OF UNIT GOALS (FOR STUDENTS)
CCSS.ELA-LITERACY.RL.9-10.1 Cite strong and thorough textual evidence to support analysis of what the text says explicitly as well as inferences drawn from the text. CCSS.ELA-LITERACY.W.9-10.1 Write arguments to support claims in an analysis of substantive topics or texts, using valid reasoning and relevant and sufficient evidence.	• I can synthesize information across multiple texts. • I can design claims. • I can support claims with clear evidence while addressing other viewpoints.

(Continued)

QUICK TIPS

- *Get clear:* Make unit goals clear, simple, student-friendly, and public.

- *Communicate:* Discuss goals at the start of the unit and revisit them throughout the unit. Let students know which goal the day's focus aligns to, and be open to questions.

- *Use backward design:* First plan your goals for the course, then the unit, then the lesson.

- *Know students:* Design goals that students can attain and master, but that challenge them too.

(Continued)

EXAMPLE OF STANDARDS FOCUSED ON WITHIN A UNIT (FOR TEACHERS)	EXAMPLE OF UNIT GOALS (FOR STUDENTS)
CCSS.ELA-LITERACY.W.9-10.5 Develop and strengthen writing as needed by planning, revising, editing, rewriting, or trying a new approach, focusing on addressing what is most significant for a specific purpose and audience. (Editing for conventions should demonstrate command of Language standards 1–3 up to and including grades 9–10 here.) CCSS.ELA-LITERACY.W.9-10.9 Draw evidence from literary or informational texts to support analysis, reflection, and research.	• I can persuade the reader by using voice, structure, and precise language. • I can use grammar and conventions to convey ideas precisely and powerfully.

Unit goals don't guarantee uniformity in the classroom. That's an important point, so let's emphasize it: Two teachers can teach to the same goal on the same day, and the students may experience different learning. That's because other aspects of teaching matter a lot, including classroom activities, instructional choices and language, and even teacher–student relationships. What goals *can* do is provide some curriculum coherence (Westerberg, 2009). They can guide teachers—and students—so that everyone knows that what is being learned is important and relevant.

GETTING STARTED

So where to start? As with many things in education, start with the outcomes. Ask yourself:

- What are the essential learning outcomes for this course?

- What skills will students need to learn in each semester, grading period, or unit to achieve those outcomes?

- How do I order these goals logically so that students can master each as needed?

The visual that follows presents the link between goals, skills, and experiences as a flowchart:

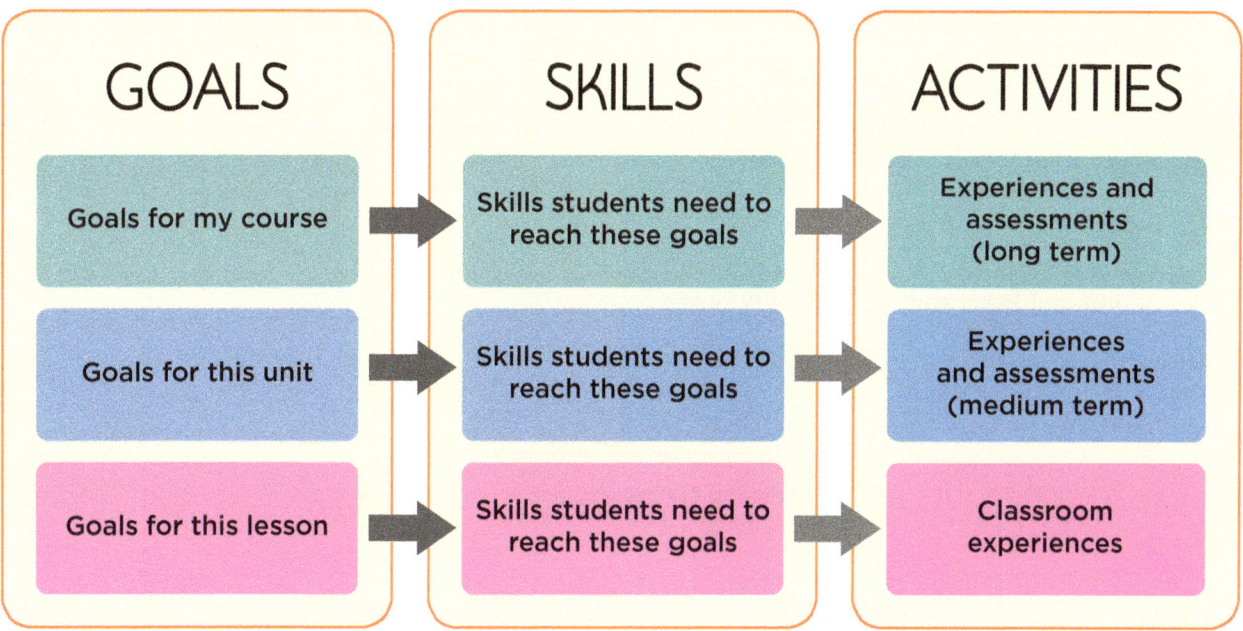

Some steps in designing a yearlong map follow. These will help you generate unit goals across the year.

1. Divide the school year into four- to six-week time periods (units).
2. Name the larger theme, topic, or concept that will be the focus of each unit.
3. Identify the standards you will focus on for each unit.
4. In your own words, list what students will know and be able to do by the end of the unit.
5. Turn that list of what they will know and be able to do into three to five student-friendly goals.

Here is an example from a high school social studies class.

STANDARDS	WHAT STUDENTS WILL KNOW AND BE ABLE TO DO	GOALS
History Standards: Explain how industrialization and urbanization affected class structure; family life; the daily lives of men, women, and children; and the environment.	**What Students Will Know:** • Power can shift within and between societies. • There are many ways that power can be acquired, exercised, or challenged.	• I can ask questions and make claims about the causes and results of revolutions. • I can analyze historical events and movements and their impact.

(Continued)

(Continued)

STANDARDS	WHAT STUDENTS WILL KNOW AND BE ABLE TO DO	GOALS
Analyze the extent to which racism was both a cause and a consequence of imperialism and evaluate the impact of imperialism from multiple perspectives. Analyze the impact of the policies of different European colonizers on Indigenous societies and explain the responses of these societies to imperialistic rule.	• People's identity and status impact their willingness to challenge power. • Access to ideas leads to revolutionary change. **What Students Will Be Able to Do:** • Develop questions and plan inquiry • Gather and evaluate sources • Seek diverse perspectives • Develop claims and use evidence	• I can describe who holds power and how it is used. • I can compare perspectives on historical events.

The following template can be used to develop your yearlong and unit maps. You can also find this template in Appendix B and on the book's companion website.

UNIT	TOPIC/FOCUS	STANDARDS	WHAT STUDENTS WILL KNOW AND BE ABLE TO DO	GOALS
1				
2				
3				
4				
5				
6				

HEADS UP

Make sure you are focusing goals on learning. Goals should encompass the important ideas and concepts students will take away, not just the task. The goal of the day should never be to "complete the worksheet on math symbols" or "complete problems one through ten" but rather could be to "understand the greater than, lesser than, and equals signs and how to use them."

Try not to focus on too many standards in one unit. An overabundance of standards and goals can make it difficult to gauge student learning (Popham, 2009). This is a problem for our education system as a whole, but can also become a problem in individual classrooms. Focus on standards that are absolutely essential to the learning of your students.

Check that the goals are not limiting learning. While too many standards can create problems, limiting instruction to only the day's standards also boxes in student learning unprofitably. Make room for students to explore ideas and connect to unexpected concepts or content.

KEY IDEA

Invite students into the learning process by telling them the unit goals. Carefully plan your goals by thinking about the standards and objectives for the entire year and then each unit. These unit goals will be used to plan daily lessons.

QUICK TIPS

- *Create questions that begin with "how" or "why"—as these are open-ended questions that activate higher-order thinking.*

- *Keep questions visible—post them on the board, at the top of syllabi, and online.*

- *Keep essential questions nonjudgmental ("To what extent might Hamlet be considered a hero?" rather than "How does Hamlet function as a hero?").*

Essential Questions

WHY?

Essential questions are open-ended, complex questions that guide both student learning and teacher planning (McTighe & Wiggins, 2013). They are the partners to unit goals. If the unit goal tells us what students will know and be able to do, the essential questions focus on the thinking that students can develop as they work toward the goals. If we want thinking-centered classrooms, then essential questions help engage students before, during, and at the end of each unit (and ideally beyond the course itself, into their lives). You can develop essential questions that support different kinds of thinking across the curriculum. For example, an essential question such as *How do we combat social injustice?* supports both creative and problem-solving thinking.

Goals and standards are meant to be attainable and defined; essential questions, on the other hand, are not meant to be answered easily or finally. Here are some examples of essential questions that might guide a unit or even an entire course:

- Why do human beings go to war?
- Is love innate or learned?
- How do we combat social injustice?
- How can we chart patterns in data to make predictions?
- How do humans impact their environment?
- How are new generations of artists affected by previous generations?

Used effectively, essential questions are both formative and summative for teachers when developing units. Teachers use such questions as they begin developing a unit or course to design potential end points—not so that students possess an absolute answer to the question, but so that they respond to the question thoughtfully and with evidence. As a unit unfolds, a strong question may also help guide teachers to choose particular activities, skills, and content and may ultimately determine the nature of assignments and assessments.

For students, essential questions create space for students to wonder, theorize, and then inquire. For the rest of the unit and oftentimes year, students keep coming back to the questions as their knowledge of the topic deepens. The questions help students focus on the big ideas and not get distracted by tiny details. We know we have posed compelling essential questions when students want to debate them and develop their thinking around them across time. In order to engage students, essential questions need to:

- Be open-ended
- Relate to students' lives

- Require analysis, synthesis, and some original thinking to answer
- Be debatable and leave space for multiple perspectives

GETTING STARTED

Draw on the core ideas and content of your discipline to develop essential questions. Look at state and national standards, and be inspired by your own passions and students' interests. You can also tap into the collective wisdom of a professional learning community; your colleagues bring a wealth of knowledge to the table—sometimes in the discipline you teach, and sometimes from other disciplines—as well as different life and professional experiences. Administrators, mentors, and professional networks online can also raise new directions for your questioning.

The following chart includes a list of essential questions developed by a group of middle and high school social studies teachers working together over several meetings. This list of questions may not be comprehensive, but it importantly represents the questions that were important to these teachers.

Essential Questions Generated by a Group of Social Studies Teachers, Grades 6–12

Questions for studying particular events or periods:

1. The *W* questions: What happened? Who was involved? When and where did it happen? Why is it important?
2. How is this experience different from my experience?
3. How did different people experience this change differently?
4. What would have changed the outcome, and how?
5. What aspects of this event or change are important to focus on? (Examples: wealth, resources, gender, ethnicity, geography, citizenship, minority/majority groups, migration, exploitation, imperialism, belief systems, conflict, acts of dissent, science and technology)

Questions for social studies courses:

1. How does studying history affect the way we act and think today?
2. What are the biggest changes in history, and why did they happen?
3. How does where and when people live affect how they live?
4. Who creates historical artifacts and documents, and why?
5. How do groups or people get or keep power?
6. How do groups in power balance or counterbalance the needs of individuals and the common good?
7. What is identity? How does my identity shape my understanding of history?
8. What does it mean to be a citizen? Of my local community? Of my country? Of the world?

Frame Questions Using Starting Words that Expand Thinking. Essential questions should not be easy to answer—avoid any question that prompts a simple "yes" or "no." To create open-ended questions that require thinking, try starting with phrases such as the following:

- How . . . ?

- Why . . . ?

- In what sense . . . ?

- To what extent . . . ?

- In what ways . . . ?

- What are the causes and consequences of . . . ?

- What factors create . . . ?

Use Essential Questions to Help Students Structure Arguments, Conduct Research, and Cite Evidence. Essential questions form the backbone of thoughtful argumentation. As your course or unit of study progresses, students should be more equipped to reach deeper for support and to make connections within and beyond a discipline. These questions should generate further study, not end it.

To support student thinking across an entire unit, keep the essential questions at the forefront of your teaching and learning. For example, at the start of the unit you can post the questions and offer a few minutes for students to jot down their initial ideas and predictions about them. This can lead to small-group and whole-group discussions. Each week of the unit you can connect the lessons to the essential questions and again offer time for jotting new ideas and discussing them with a small group. At the midpoint and end of the unit, you can ask students to look across their notes and think more deeply about the questions. Discuss the evolving ideas as a class. At the end of the unit the essential questions can be used for formal writing, presenting, and debates. Students can use all they learned and thought about across the unit to make an argument about at least one of the questions. This recursive use of an essential question provides students with opportunities to recognize how far their thinking and knowledge has grown, a boon to motivation and the student's developing identity as a learner.

Leaning on Essential Questions Across an Entire Unit

AT THE BEGINNING OF THE UNIT	MIDWAY THROUGH A UNIT	AT THE END OF A UNIT

• Students jot down initial ideas about the essential questions.
 	
• Students participate in small-group discussion around the questions.
 	
• Students have a whole-class discussion as the teacher scribes what they are hearing students share.
 	
• The teacher may add additional questions to the class essential questions that come from the student discussion.
	• The teacher begins each week (and possibly lesson) by connecting it to essential questions.
	
	• Students jot down what they now think about the essential questions. They may consider:
	
	  ○ What do I now know that I didn't know at the start of the unit?
	
	  ○ What misconceptions did I have?
	
	  ○ What am I wondering about now?
	
	• Students participate in small-group discussion around the questions.
		• Students debate an essential question.
		
		• Students write or present on an essential question.
		
		• Students have a whole-class discussion as the teacher scribes what they are hearing students share now, possibly comparing it to where they began.
		
		• Students share their curiosities based upon the essential questions that can be carried over into the next unit of study.

HEADS UP

Avoid writing questions that are too broad or too narrow. A question that is too broad (e.g., "Why is science important?") won't grab student interest or lead easily to specific activities. A too-narrow question (e.g., "Why do trees have rings inside?") may not create transferable, lifelong reflection.

Embrace other questions or ideas that rise up. Just because your essential question has to do with gender inequities in the 20th century doesn't mean you should shut down discussion or questions about, for instance, the role of the arts or shifts in political culture. Let students' questions drive the learning too.

Don't overuse the question. Use it recursively—but don't drive it home so far that it becomes a running gag in your classroom. Think of ways to reframe the question, or elements of it, to keep pushing student thinking.

KEY IDEA

Generate essential questions to propel and extend learning. Strong essential questions will aid in learning transfer by engaging students and deepening their understanding of big ideas and processes.

QUICK TIPS

Shared experiences should be joyful and engaging and also set students up to apply their learning to more independent practice later on. When designing the experiences, check that they:

- Connect to a relevant and timely question
- Draw upon past learning and new challenges
- Are challenging enough to require a team effort but not so hard it feels overwhelming
- Allow all students to bring their strengths to contribute
- Match the type of thinking in the unit goals

A few ideas for shared experiences include:

- Firsthand research (interviews and surveys) to understand a topic
- Reading and discussing a topic or text together
- Designing possible solutions together
- Checking out math educator Dan Meyer's (n.d.) TED Talk *Math Class Needs a Makeover*

Shared Experiences

WHY?

In his book *Big Potential: How Transforming the Pursuit of Success Raises Our Achievement, Happiness, and Well-Being*, Shawn Achor (2018), a best-selling author and researcher, explains how positive peer pressure can lead to great successes: "Just as being around negative, unmotivated people drains our energy and potential, surrounding ourselves with positive, engaged, motivated, and creative people causes our positivity, engagement, motivation and creativity to multiply" (p. 70). He goes on to explain the research studies on the impact of feeling supported when facing a challenge. Researchers found that if you are looking at a hill and judging how steep it is, you will judge it to be 10 to 20 percent less steep simply by having a friend standing next to you than if you were facing it alone. The researchers concluded that the presence of someone you trust to support you changes your actual perception of the intensity of the challenge.

What does the steepness of a hill have to do with algebra, history, or biology learning? Well, many students perceive the challenge in class to be too "steep." It can be overwhelming to begin a new unit on your own, especially if you lack the confidence to believe in your own ability to be successful. By creating engaging and high-success shared experiences early on in a unit, students often feel more prepared to face the challenges that will come later when working independently. Throughout the unit you can support different types of thinking by coming back to previous shared experiences and taking a next step together. For example, early on in the unit a teacher asks the class to work together on figuring out how much lumber is needed to build community garden beds. Later in the unit they can revisit this shared experience and work together to make a budget. These two experiences become landmarks the entire class can come back to when working on independent projects.

Shared experiences can build community, develop student confidence, and spark students' curiosity. A shared experience is one where we (students and teachers alike) are sharing the thinking, the learning, and the work.

GETTING STARTED

Assuming you have your unit goals and essential questions posted and students have already discussed them, it is helpful to create a shared experience that gets them doing the thinking of the unit right away.

1. Think backwards. What do you want students to be able to do on their own by the end of the unit? This is the time to do the same work now *with students.*

2. Break down the end goal of what you want students to be able to do into a series of steps. This can become the outline of the process you and the students will go through together. You just named the destinations on your journey.

3. Go through the same process with students. Your role is not to teach them how yet, but do be a co-learner with them. You are another social scientist, mathematician, or reader working alongside students.

4. Refer back to the shared experience later in the unit. This will help students build confidence and more concretely understand what they are being asked to do on their own.

The following chart shows an example of the three steps of the shared experience.

TEACHER'S STEPS WHEN PLANNING	SOCIAL STUDIES EXAMPLE
1. Think backwards.	Students will be able to compare two primary sources from the beginning of World War II and form a claim about the multiple perspectives of the time.
2. Break down the goal into steps.	• Read and analyze each primary source's perspective. • Develop a claim after evaluating two different primary sources. • Use formal writing to support the claim with textual evidence.
3. Go through the steps together with students.	Spend a week going through the shared experience together. Day 1: Read primary sources A and B together and take notes together. Day 2: Discuss possible claims together in small groups and then share them out. The teacher scribes them into one list. Day 3: Discuss which possible claim has the most evidence and bullet out the evidence to go with it. Students contribute the ideas, and the teacher mostly scribes. Day 4: Outline the argument together, and students go off in small groups to talk through and rehearse for the writing. The teacher and students refer to a list of formal language stems to help them while orally rehearsing for what to write down.

(Continued)

KEY IDEA

By beginning a unit with shared experiences, students have opportunities for success and confidence boosting from the start. This can propel them, feeling ready to tackle the challenges, into more independent learning. Become a co-learner with students and share the work and thinking so there is space for them to engage right away.

(Continued)

TEACHER'S STEPS WHEN PLANNING	SOCIAL STUDIES EXAMPLE
	Day 5: The teacher scribes as the students explain what they would write. The teacher writes exactly what students say, and they all work together to revise it as they go.
4. Refer to the shared experience later in the unit.	Now that students have had an experience going through the process together, they can refer back to the parts over and over again as needed. • Post and share all of the parts of the process for students to refer to. • When it is time for students to do the same work on their own with a different set of texts, remind them what they already did for confidence boosting. • Use the examples you created together in the shared experience as models.

HEADS UP

Design a shared experience that is not the exact same prompt or texts that students will work with later on in the unit. In the previous example with social studies primary texts, the shared experience texts and prompt would not be the exact same as the ones students would be using on their own in the unit. The process transfers, but it is not about copying the exact thinking.

Keep students in the driver's seat. The teacher's role can be tricky here. Yes, we do know a lot and can easily take over the thinking for students. Try using a new text or prompt or question you have never taught before so you can truly be a co-learner with students.

Privilege risk-taking over "right." Students can be intimidated to try something new without a lot of teaching first if they are afraid they will do it wrong. Don't make shared experiences high stakes. If you must grade them, focus on student engagement as the goal and not content knowledge just yet. Make intellectual risk-taking and creative thinking and collaboration the focus of your assessments and feedback instead of getting it "right."

Workshops

WHY?

One of the oldest forms of teaching is the apprenticeship model. Back before formalized school, if you wanted to learn a trade, you would apprentice in a workshop—observing, practicing, and getting feedback. Many sports teams and art programs use a version of this model today.

Think about a common soccer practice structure. After a warm-up, the coach models a drill and explains why it will be helpful. Then the players head off, balls at their feet, to practice. While they practice, the coach observes, offers quick tips, and maybe blows the whistle to pause and offer clarification. Then they continue, applying what they just learned. At the end of the practice of that drill, the coach may ask a player to demonstrate the move effectively for the entire team before a water break.

A workshop model in schools has a similar structure. It starts with a 10- to 15-minute whole-class minilesson. The teacher models a strategy. It is followed by a larger chunk of practice time, usually 20 to 30 minutes, to learn by doing. While the students practice, the teacher meets individually or in small groups to confer with students and offers feedback and coaching. The workshop ends with reflection and sharing where students teach one another what they learned and tried (Calkins, 2000).

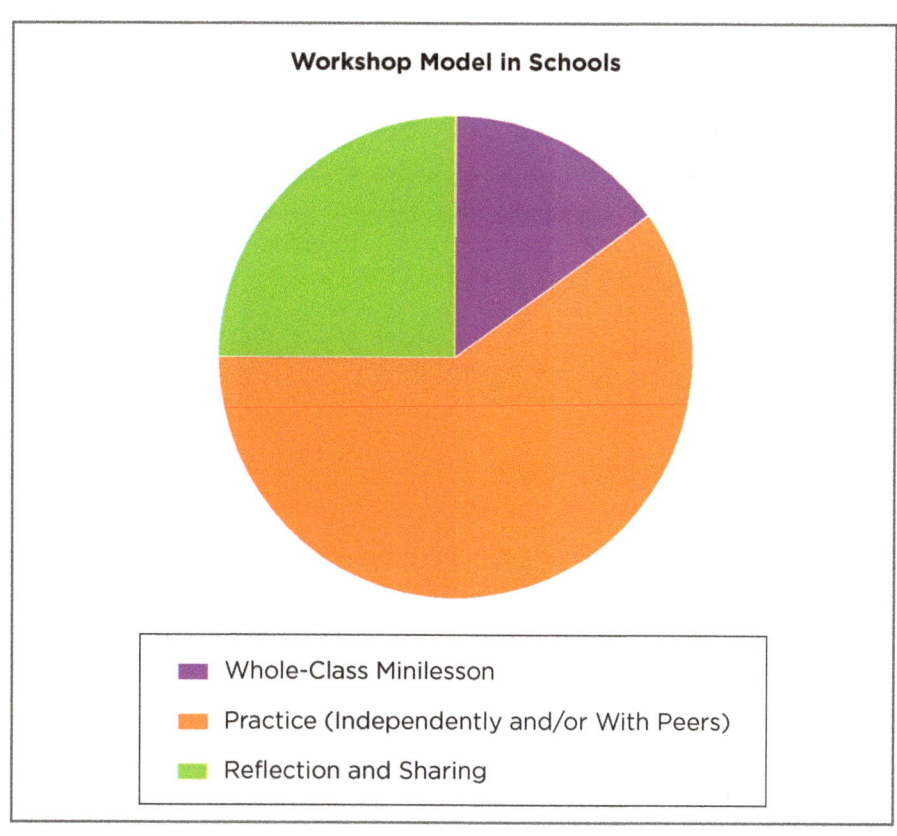

Workshop Model in Schools

- Whole-Class Minilesson
- Practice (Independently and/or With Peers)
- Reflection and Sharing

This structure is based on the research that we learn by doing, not simply by watching others or by hearing what others have already learned. Brian Cambourne (1988) researched and developed the conditions for learning, and most, if not all, align with the workshop model. He claims that in order for deep learning to happen we need the right conditions.

CONDITION FOR LEARNING	HOW IT ALIGNS WITH THE WORKSHOP MODEL
Demonstration	**Minilesson** At the start of the workshop the teacher demonstrates a strategy during a minilesson.
Engagement	**Practice** After the minilesson students practice. They learn from practicing and need enough time to actually use what they learned.
Expectation	**Teacher Mindset** During the practice the teacher expects the students will be able to learn. It might not happen right away and may require more modeling and coaching, but having expectations that learning will occur is key.
Responsibility	**Student Ownership** During the practice the students take responsibility for their own learning. They make choices, invest in trying, and are open to feedback. They believe that the effort will pay off.
Approximation	**Low Stakes** Part of learning something new is approximating it first. No one masters something right away. Create a context where we expect and celebrate approximations as the stepping stones to mastery.
Response	**Conferences** While students are practicing, the teacher meets individually or in small groups to offer feedback and coaching. These conferences allow students to get more personalized instruction in real time. (See page 198 for more on conferences.)

Source: Adapted from Cambourne, B. (1988). *The whole story: Natural learning and the acquisition of literacy in the classroom.* Scholastic.

Since the practice part of the workshop consumes the biggest chunk of time, it is important to make sure it is intentional. Ericsson and Pool (2016) have studied what makes deliberate and meaningful practice, and the following qualities should be designed into our workshops:

- Most practice should happen independently and not with others.

- There need to be clear goals.

- The practice itself needs to adjust for difficulty, building in sophistication across time.

- Learners need immediate feedback and reflection.

- Learners need a coach for individualized practice with opportunities for repetition and gradual refinement.

Workshops are also great places for students to integrate different types of thinking across days. For example, a psychology class is researching strategies for living a happier life. They might participate in a series of workshops all week long. On day one, they set a question that is personally relevant in relation to the class study such as how to develop happiness despite living in a community with housing insecurity (independent thinking). On day two, they read about psychology strategies that address their question using empathetic thinking to understand its theory and perspective. On the third day, they narrow down to a single strategy or combination of strategies they would recommend and explain why (problem-solving thinking). Days four and five might be focused on creatively developing a plan and reflecting on its effectiveness for actually implementing the strategies.

This is an example from an English class that shows multiple minilesson topics collected onto one chart.

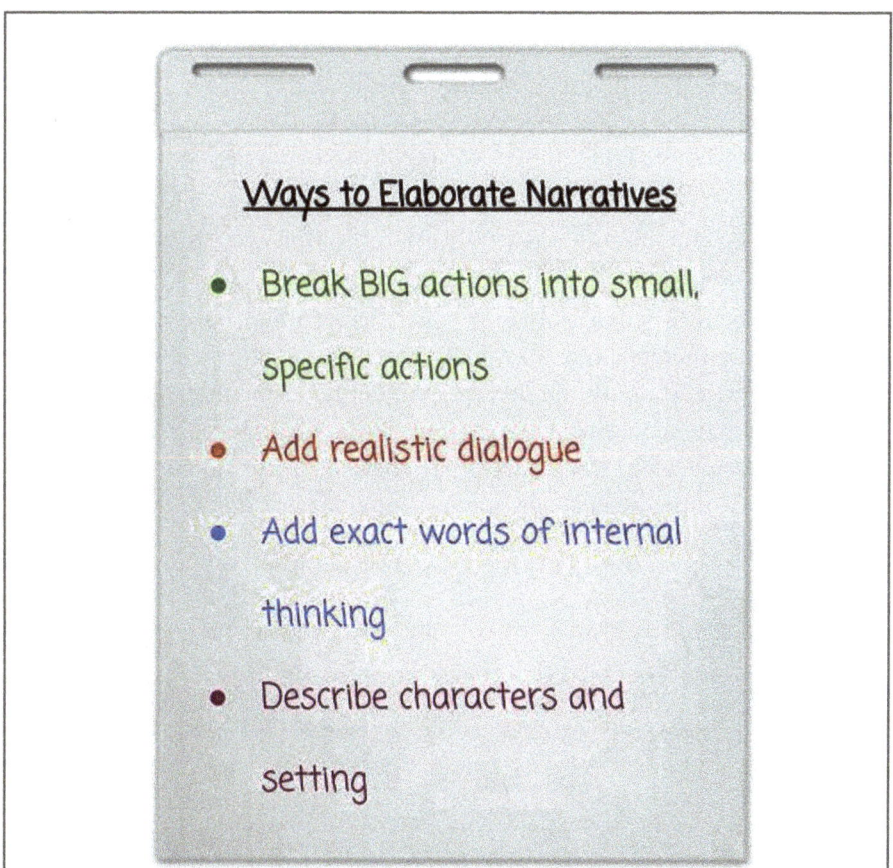

GETTING STARTED

Not everything can be taught in a workshop model. First, get clear on what your goals are and whether a workshop structure might be the right fit. Workshops are best for developing independence, for teaching and applying strategies, and for when students are engaged in longer projects. Workshops are not ideal for delivering new content or single lesson plans. Teachers tend to use a workshop model for several days in a row when students are working on readings, writing, or research or solving a multiday complex problem.

1. **Plan the minilesson.** Use the goals of the unit to decide on the focus of the minilesson. Then plan the minilesson by doing the work yourself. What strategies helped you? What were your steps? Jot down your steps so you can model them later for students. A minilesson is basically a how-to. Prepare to show students how to do something. Some examples include:

   • How to form a claim

   • How to preview a problem

   • How to decide if a source is credible

   • How to match your language to the audience

   • How to check your work

   • How to identify an author's perspective

A sample minilesson can be found in Appendix C.

2. **Plan for the practice time.** Even though students will be doing the work after the minilesson, make sure you consider what that practice time will look like. What choices do they have? What does effective practice look like? Make this clear or at least discuss this with students. If students are used to completing tasks and being "done," you will need to show them options for how to use their time. Here is one sample chart that a teacher made to support students during the practice time during a writing workshop.

Writers Keep Writing

When Collecting Entries . . .
- Continue an entry from day(s) before
- Start a new entry
- Go back and revise an entry

When Planning for a Draft . . .
- Try out multiple structures
- Refer back to mentor texts and plan out what you will try
- Try a few possible leads
- Get feedback and revise your next plan

When Drafting . . .
- Use your plan to get the entire draft down
- Try out craft moves
- Revise as you go

When Revising . . .
- Get feedback
- Ask "what if" and try out other ways it could go
- Add, delete, and move parts around

3. **Prepare for conferring with students.** Once students are independently working, you can move around the room and offer feedback and coaching. More will be shared on conferring in Section 7. For now, get a clipboard and schedule who you will meet with each day. For example, look across the week and jot down student names for each day you intend to meet with them. A second part of preparing for conferences is to carry your own modeling tools with you. Whatever you used to model in the minilesson can be used to show students examples of a process during conferences too. Oftentimes students benefit from seeing a mini demonstration in a smaller group tailored to their needs.

KEY IDEA

When we use a workshop model structure, we set students up to learn *how* to do something. Demonstrating in a minilesson and then giving students lots of time to practice allows them to develop skill and move from approximation toward mastery. The practice time also gives you time to personalize your instruction with feedback during conferences.

4. **Plan for the reflection and sharing.** Consider how you want to wrap up the workshop. Typically, teachers give students time to meet either with a partner or in a small group to share what they did and learned. This builds in some peer accountability and helps students learn from one another. Other times the teacher will ask a student or two to share what they did with the entire class. Ask the students' permission before putting them on the spot. This can help build confidence in students and offers even more examples for the rest of the class beyond the one you modeled yourself.

5. **Rely on ongoing assessment.** You typically don't need to give formative assessments during workshop weeks because conferring gives you an in-depth look at students' strengths and next steps. If you keep notes on what you are learning about students during conferences, that can give you some of the most impactful assessment data.

HEADS UP

Students may struggle with stamina. If they are not used to having a large chunk of work time, gradually build up the minutes. Start with just a few minutes of practice time and add a few minutes each day.

Minimize dependence. If you find yourself unable to confer because students keep raising their hands for help, keep a list of the things they think they need you for. Then teach a minilesson on how they can problem solve those things on their own. Students may need to be shown how to be independent. You may also want to make sure you are keeping the stakes low and not accidentally sending the message that you expect mastery before approximation.

Offer options. Provide some choices during practice time so students can develop ownership and move at their own pace. Make sure there are at least three options for how they may be spending the practice time so they don't think they are done too soon.

Strategy Groups

WHY?

While we know whole-class lessons expose all students to the same teaching, we also know that students have different strengths and needs. Strategy groups are small-group lessons that help us differentiate instruction by matching the strategy we teach to the students who are ready to learn it (Tomlinson, 2008). All students can benefit from this small-group structure whether they are not yet meeting expectations or are exceeding them.

We tend to have so much formative assessment data about our students' strengths and needs, and yet if we don't use it to inform our groupings and instruction, it can feel like a waste of time and energy to even collect it. So, use that information to form groups of students who are ready for the same next step.

The rest of the students are engaged in independent work while you meet with the strategy groups. A strategy group can be used when the rest of the students are reading, writing, working on problems, or involved in the practice portion of a workshop. Differentiating our teaching with strategy groups is helpful for a number of reasons:

- We get to know students better in smaller groups and can build stronger relationships by letting them know we created this lesson just for them.

- We can teach foundational skills to the students who need them and not waste the time of other students who don't.

- We can extend learning for those who have already mastered our whole-class lessons and are ready for a challenge.

- Sometimes students can self-select a strategy group when they self-reflect and decide they would like more support in an area. This builds ownership and engagement in the strategy group because they enrolled in it themselves.

GETTING STARTED

Prepare for the strategy groups by mining assessment data and observations. Choose a clear focus and sort students into groups. Look at patterns across students when planning the groupings. A form like the one that follows—basically a set of boxes where you can place students' names with similar next steps—can be helpful. See Appendix D or this book's companion website for a blank copy of this grid.

QUICK TIPS

- Don't put more than five students in one strategy group, or it becomes too large to really coach them all.

- Plan on meeting with a few groups in one period, but note not everyone in the class will get a strategy group each period. Try to get to all of the students across the unit.

- Sometimes what seems like it will be one strategy group ends up being a series of lessons. If that happens, you can meet with the same students a few times and go deeper into the work each time.

The following example was created as the teacher moved around the room and looked at students' research process. As students seemed to need a next step, the teacher added their name to the grid. The goals of the unit guided what each group's focus was.

Focus: creating a compelling research question	**Focus:** using relevant and credible sources of information
Students:	**Students:**
Melanie	Tammi
Antoni	Andres
Jon	

Focus: paraphrasing information in own words	**Focus:** synthesizing information across more than one text
Students:	**Students:**
Malcolm	Su
Jenny	Vince
Samantha T.	Rosie
Tyrone	

Make sure you are clear on the strategy you are teaching and not just the content. A strategy is a procedure for how to do something. A strategy is a series of steps that help break down a skill into clear parts. The following chart shows examples of strategies that can be taught to small groups. Take some time with your colleagues to develop strategies together, and know you can use many of these across disciplines so students get extra practice and reinforcement.

FOCUS SKILL (WHAT)	STRATEGY (HOW-TO)
Decoding a multisyllable word	1. Pause when you find a word you cannot decode. 2. Break the word into parts. Do you see a part (prefix, root, suffix, etc.) you do know? 3. Say the sounds of each part one by one. 4. Put all of the parts together until it sounds right.
Understanding the parts of a problem	1. Read the problem all the way through and ask yourself, "What do I think this problem is asking me to do?" 2. Read it again, part by part. Jot down the key action each part wants you to do (predict, correlate, analyze, etc.). 3. Make a plan for yourself that includes all of the parts of the problem with the action words you will take.

FOCUS SKILL (WHAT)	STRATEGY (HOW-TO)
Taking notes as you read	1. Get clear on your purpose for reading. 2. Preview the text and think about what type of text it is (story, article, directions, op-ed, etc.). 3. Set up a note-taking system that matches the purpose and text. Some examples include:
Actively listening to a partner	1. Turn your body toward the person who is talking and if comfortable look at them while they speak. 2. Pause and repeat back what you heard before adding your own thoughts. You might say, "So I heard you say . . ." or "To be clear, what you mean is . . ." 3. Then add your own ideas once you are sure you understood what the partner said.

Teach the strategy group with an I-go, we-go, you-go structure. Once you are ready to teach the strategy lesson, it is helpful to use the gradual release of responsibility. First, you model the strategy by telling and showing the students how to do it. Then, try the strategy together with students. Finally, set them up to practice on their own. The entire group should take around 10 to 15 minutes. If it is taking longer than that, it may be better off as a series of strategy groups where you teach one part at a time across a few sessions.

One way to differentiate instruction is to form small groups and teach them strategies that meet them where they are. These strategy groups can both reteach and extend learning. By modeling, practicing together, and then practicing on their own they are more likely to transfer the strategy beyond this one lesson.

HEADS UP

Set independence expectations. You can't focus on a strategy group if the rest of the class keeps interrupting you. Make sure the students who are not in the group are engaged in meaningful work they can do on their own. For more ideas see the previous section on the workshop model.

Don't be a superhero. Teachers new to strategy groups sometimes try to use entirely new materials and wind up feeling as though they're working overtime. Keep it simple for yourself and students by using the same materials you model with in your whole-class lessons in the strategy groups. You can refer back to a text you read to the whole class to model a strategy in a small group.

Divide and conquer. If the strategy you are teaching is complicated, it can help to plan a two-part group. In the first part model with an everyday topic that may not be related to the content of the course. Let students have a high-success experience. Then in part two you can model and practice the same strategy in more content-related materials.

Stations

WHY?

Stations are an instructional structure that chunks learning experiences into parts, and students rotate around the stations in small groups. Most of the time students end up working at each station (not all in one day), but by working for 15 to 20 minutes at one before moving to the next it allows them to focus on one aspect of learning at a time. The teacher is typically located at one of the stations, and the rest are for independent learning and/or small-group collaboration.

If you are in a co-taught classroom, each teacher can choose a station to support. Usually, these are the stations that require the most difficult or newer learning. In fact, station teaching is a commonly used co-teaching structure because it creates the space for both teachers to teach rather than one who tends to be consistently in a supportive role. It can maximize the impact that two teachers have in one classroom. Just make sure the groupings are not based on who has an individualized education program (IEP) and who does not as that actually gets in the way of creating an inclusive classroom learning environment (Friend, 2013). Groupings are flexible and based on ongoing formative assessment of students.

There are many reasons why using stations in the classroom is helpful even if you are not in a special education setting. They allow teachers to move through several concepts and learning experiences and usually make for a highly engaging period where the time seems to fly by. Station teaching is usually chosen when teachers want to differentiate as the stations can have varying levels of texts, complexity, and teacher support. Sometimes teachers choose stations so that at least one station is a review and practice while others may focus on new content or strategies. This helps balance the need to practice past learning and keep moving forward.

Look at your upcoming unit and consider how stations might be helpful. Following are some scenarios that lend themselves to stations:

- If you are in a unit that focuses on a process such as researching a topic, reading and responding to documents, or working through a multistep problem, each station can focus on one part at a time.

- If you are in a unit that focuses on hands-on learning such as experiments, making models, or simulations, stations can be helpful because you won't have every student working with materials at the exact same time.

- If the unit calls upon students to do a lot of reading of shorter texts, each text can be a station, and students can rotate through them.

QUICK TIPS

- Use the unit goals to generate ideas for possible stations. What do you want students to be able to do by the end of the unit? Consider stations that help them get practice with that skill across the unit.

- When circumstances call for remote and hybrid learning, digital stations may be used, and many teachers who have tried them realize they are a great structure to keep. Using Google Classroom or another digital sharing platform, teachers create a document for each station. Students then either work on one station per period or are expected to rotate through two or three per day.

- Make sure the time allotted for each station is adequate but not so much that students can lose focus. Try out the station yourself and then add on a few minutes to see how long it might take.

- Use a work board schedule to show students who is in each group and what stations they will get to each day. Students' names go in the boxes.

Eventually, they will read them all but are not overwhelmed with being handed a packet or link to five texts all at once.

- If half of the class needs review and extra practice in a concept and the rest does not, you can create some review and some new material stations, and not everyone needs to get to each one. Everyone is engaged but not necessarily in the same station experiences across the period(s).

An example of one station per day across the week follows:

WORK BOARD SCHEDULE	STATION A: READ ABOUT TYPES OF CHEMICAL REACTIONS	STATION B: VIEW THE VIDEO OF A CHEMICAL REACTION	STATION C: LIST EXAMPLES OF CHEMICAL REACTIONS AND THEIR TYPES	STATION D: DISCUSS YOUR BIG IDEAS AND QUESTIONS ABOUT CHEMICAL REACTIONS USING UNIT-SPECIFIC VOCABULARY
Monday	Day 1 Introduce all of the stations and groupings to the entire class			
Tuesday	Group 1	Group 2	Group 3	Group 4
Wednesday	Group 4	Group 1	Group 2	Group 3
Thursday	Group 3	Group 4	Group 1	Group 2
Friday	Group 2	Group 3	Group 4	Group 1

An example of rotating stations within a class period follows:

	STATION A: READ ABOUT TYPES OF CHEMICAL REACTIONS	STATION B: VIEW THE VIDEO OF A CHEMICAL REACTION	STATION C: LIST EXAMPLES OF CHEMICAL REACTIONS AND THEIR TYPES
9:00–9:20	Group 1	Group 2	Group 3
9:25–9:45	Group 3	Group 1	Group 2
9:50–10:10	Group 2	Group 3	Group 1

GETTING STARTED

Design stations that align with unit goals and allow for differentiation. The goals of stations are both to engage students in learning experiences and to either review past concepts and skills or explore new concepts and skills. You can use the following chart to help you make some choices.

IF . . .	THEN . . .	STATION EXAMPLES
You want to offer practice in a previously taught skill.	• Create a reminder chart that goes with the skill. • Set up a context for students to practice it more.	**Editing Practice** Reread your piece and use the comma chart to help you. Remember to use **commas** • When listing • When joining two independent clauses • After an introduction

You want to reteach a concept or skill.	• Remind students of the concept by referring back to previous teaching.
	
	• Model.
	
	• Offer a quick practice time with teacher support.
	
	(Note: A teacher would be at this station.)
		Reading a Primary Source Document
		
		1. Look at the title, author, and date.
		2. Preview the document's features (visuals, headings, language).
		3. Begin reading and pause after each chunk.
		4. Consider:
		  a. Why was this written?
		  b. When was this written?
		  c. Who was it for?

You want students to explore new concepts.	• Post the essential question that aligns with the station. • Give students something to read, view, listen to, or do. • Ask them to talk and/or jot down their new learning and questions.	**Inquiry** Essential Question: How does the amount of available water impact our environments? • View this video. • Look at this infographic. • Jot down your learning and questions. | MY THINKING	MY QUESTIONS | |---|---| | | |
Students are working through a process.	• Chart the process for all students to see. • Create a station for each part of the process. • The teacher supports the part of the process that is most new or challenging for students.	**Researching a Topic** • Station A: Finding sources • Station B: Reading and taking notes • Station C: Rereading notes across texts and forming possible claims • Station D: Sharing your findings with others

Decide Which Stations Will be Independent and Which Will Have Teachers. After designing the stations, make sure there are enough that can be done independently without you. Stations that are based on extra practice or inquiry often can be done without a teacher as long as there are clear charts and examples for students to refer to. Teachers are essential at stations that require modeling of new material or reteaching of past concepts and skills. If there are two teachers in the classroom, you can have one review station with one teacher and one new material station with the other teacher.

Make a Schedule. Make sure you have enough time for students to rotate through the stations. Make a schedule and post it so that both teachers and students can see it. Use timers if students are expected to rotate through multiple stations within one class period. Allow for a few minutes of transition time between stations too.

It can be important for students to get up and move their bodies during a class period, especially if your periods are a double block. By asking students to get up and move to a different part of the room for each station, you give them that brain and body movement break.

If you have a shorter class period and students who struggle with transitioning, you can have them stay in one area for the entire period, and instead the station rotates (not the students). This is when digital stations are helpful so the students can simply click on a new document to begin the next one. While this option is tempting because there are fewer transitions, consider if students might be more productively engaged toward the second half of class if they had that opportunity for movement. In many cases, they need that to focus all period long.

Introduce the Stations to Students. When stations are new to students, make sure you explain and model each one for them. Some teachers take the Monday of a new week to introduce the stations, and then the rest of the week the students get to work in them. Once you use stations more regularly, you can simply explain the station and get the students going. It can be helpful to have some predictable types of stations you use across units in the year so students know what to do and get the predictability. For example, maybe every unit has some sort of inquiry station and extra practice station. While you will have to review what students will inquire into and what the extra practice will be, you won't have to teach them how to be in those types of stations.

KEY IDEA

When learning experiences are structured as stations that students rotate through, teachers can differentiate and support smaller groups, and students can engage by focusing their attention on one aspect of learning at a time.

HEADS UP

Stay attuned to pacing. Make sure you give students enough to do in a station so they are not sitting and waiting for the station to end. This creates wasted time.

Shake up static groupings. The groups of students should be flexible and change. This is not about ability grouping. When at all possible, group students in heterogeneous groups. If you need them to be grouped with those at similar skill levels once in a while, look closely at formative assessments to form groups.

Counter disengagement with pillars of joy. Part of being engaged is finding joy in what you do. Joy doesn't have to mean getting rid of rigor. It means we tap into what the research on joyful learning has shown us. It means we create contexts where the happiness pillars are present. According to Dr. Katie Cunningham (2019), these pillars include connection, choice, challenge, play, story, discovery, and movement. How might you incorporate some or most of these into the stations?

Simulations

WHY?

Have you ever acted out a scenario with a friend or family member before the real event? Whether prepping for a work presentation, delivering a eulogy, or picking a spot for a first date, many important events in our lives include a dress rehearsal, and with good reason. The low-stakes quality of simulations allows us to take risks, learn from mistakes, and get live experience as opposed to imagining how it might go in our heads. Students also learn well from simulations when asked to assume the characteristics of another person, character, or figure in order to better understand motives and behaviors.

Simulations are not the same as role plays but share many characteristics (Chilcott, 1996). Role-playing calls on students to act out something that has already happened with a predetermined end point. The purpose is usually to help students understand a scenario and develop deeper awareness of the factors around it. This helps students develop empathy and understanding of what it would be like to walk in someone else's shoes. A simulation asks students to determine the end point and does not provide them with the outcome ahead of time. Part of the simulation is working to form a conclusion or create a solution based on the information and context. Simulations and role plays work best when students are actively engaged and willing to participate.

According to R. Garry Shirts (n.d.), simulations tend to engage learners when at least one of the following is in place. The simulation:

- Includes seeing the world through other people's eyes

- Calls on learners to integrate tasks and use multiple skills in tandem

- Develops systems thinking by helping learners see the whole process

- Creates cognitive dissonance by helping learners recognize when actions and beliefs are not yet aligned

Research tells us many students thrive during simulations.

- We have known for decades that role play has a positive effect on overall learning (Blank, 1985; DeNeve & Heppner, 1997).

- Role play prompts students to reflect on what they know and to draw information together from various areas of learning (Alden, 1999; Oberhofer, 1999; Sutcliffe, 2002).

- A meta-analysis of 145 higher education studies found that simulation-based learning had a large overall positive effect (Chernikova et al., 2020).

QUICK TIPS

- Susan Cain's 2013 book, *Quiet: The Power of Introverts in a World That Can't Stop Talking,* focuses on the power of introverts in a society that emphasizes extroversion as a virtue. Since around one third of students you teach are likely to have introverted tendencies, it's worth exploring how Cain's points might be reflected in your own classroom.

- Prepare for simulations as a whole class with small-group discussion. Give students a chance to gather information and present at the same time.

- During simulations, if you are not participating in an active role, stay attentive and coach those students who may need extra support.

- Consider following up simulation activities with writing. You might have students reframe the stances they took in class or take another position entirely; either way, writing offers a chance to reinforce both argumentation skills and empathy.

Part of implementing this structure, then, is reflection on your own goals, how much time these activities are worth in pursuing those goals, and your own student group and how they will respond. Fortunately, there are many ways to incorporate simulations in your class, ranging from brief episodes to weeks-long units.

GETTING STARTED

Some role-play exercises take more teacher planning time and effort than others. It's not teacher effort we want to see, however; student effort is the goal. The point at which a teacher is working harder than the students to make a simulation work is the point at which the activity probably isn't increasing learning.

The following table outlines a few possible simulation exercises, divided into those that likely take one class period or less and those that could easily extend to multiple classes.

TIME REQUIRED	ACTIVITY	EXAMPLE
One class period or less	Individual writing	In English class, students write from the point of view of more than one character. How would different characters react in key scenes?
	Act out a scene	After completing preparatory work such as close reading, students get into groups and plan and perform a scene from a novel or play or historical event, then explain their choices and interpretation.
	Interviews and panels	A history teacher places four students in chairs before the class, each representing a different historical figure. The rest of the class questions the panel, who answer using their knowledge and notes.
	Case studies	In science class, students read a case study that explores a legal case (e.g., involving Indigenous fishing rights vs. a government's move to avoid overfishing). Then, for discussion in small groups, each student in the group is assigned a role (e.g., an activist, a marine biologist, a commercial fishing company, a politician, and a representative from an Indigenous group in the region).
Multiple class periods	Formal debate	In art class, the teacher uses formal rules for debate to prompt discussion about whether the U.S. government should fund arts programs. Students are assigned to teams and follow protocols regarding time limits and the purpose of the argument. A first class is spent on planning and a second on the actual debate.
	Simulations	A Model United Nations simulation is an excellent example of a long-term simulation. Such activities usually take longer because they require a great deal of planning time and teamwork. With new virtual reality, some schools have invested in VR equipment that allows students to virtually travel to different places and see what it would be like to be in a different time and place. This can be helpful in really creating contexts for other simulated experiences.

Choosing the right activity for your class means considering how well all of these factors contribute to the learning of your students. There's little doubt that any simulation exercise will raise excitement in the class, but excitement without learning is not our goal.

You can also consider not just *how much* planning an activity will take, but how you will plan. If you have never facilitated a mock trial, debate, or large-scale simulation, planning will take time as well as learning on your own. In such cases, it may be worth using student groups to learn and teach fellow classmates how to participate.

Where Role Play and Simulations Work. Given that engaging simulations may take a good deal of teacher planning time to do well, it's worth paying attention to when and how to orchestrate such activities. Here are a few of the contexts in which it might be particularly worthwhile to try out a role-playing activity:

- **In world languages classes and for use with students learning English:** It's been long established that role-play exercises, such as practicing an informal conversation, should be a mainstay for students learning a language, including English (Rojas & Villafuerte, 2018).

- **With unsympathetic characters or historical figures:** Take advantage of opportunities to build empathy and comprehension through role-playing tasks that prompt students to portray all characters, but particularly those who do not elicit natural sympathy.

- **Complex systems and associations:** The United Nations, the North Atlantic Treaty Organization (NATO), Congress, or the federal courts might all fall into this category. Barry once had an extremely successful class unit of about three days simulating the work of the House of Commons in the United Kingdom.

- **Ethical dilemmas in science or other classes:** Assigning roles in order to debate dilemmas such as censoring a library book or the place of government in overseeing science research can serve as ripe scenarios for role play in the classroom.

Follow Up After Simulations. While participation may constitute one aspect of assessment in simulations, the focus of assessment should relate to the learning outcomes you want students to achieve. Of course, these activities themselves can also serve as formative assessment. As you think about assessing role play and simulations, you may also consider the variety of follow-up assignments that might benefit students *after* the activity is complete:

- Further writing

- Further research

KEY IDEA

Simulations can be effective ways for students to transfer and consolidate information, apply skills, and develop empathy.

- Constructing a visual

- Self-assessment with criteria

- Teacher assessment with criteria

HEADS UP

Do not allow role-play scenarios to oversimplify real constructs or people. Characters, historical figures, ethical issues, and organizations are complex by nature. A good simulation session sometimes has to simplify these elements in order to work, but that simplification shouldn't be permanent. Look for ways to ensure that students understand the complexity of the points of view—especially human character traits—they portray.

Repeat a simulation structure across the year or across disciplines. If you are going to put the energy into teaching students a simulation structure, it's worthwhile to use it more than once. By doing a debate a few times or acting out scenes, for example, students often get much better, and their thinking develops more deeply with some repeated practice. Another way to plan for repeated practice is to work with colleagues from other disciplines to use similar simulations across subjects.

Know where *not* to use role play. Be especially careful about role play that asks students to explore people's cruelty, particularly events that might raise personal connections such as the Holocaust or the civil rights movement. These role-play assignments can lead quickly to power imbalances, racial or ethnic issues, or comments that unwittingly cause others to feel affronted. This is not to say that we don't teach students about these pivotal moments in history—of course we should; student role play just isn't a good forum for these topics.

Flipped Classrooms

WHY?

After decades of students sitting in lecture halls at the college level listening to the same material that they just read about for homework, some professors realized they needed to invert the typical classroom model on its head. Eric Muzar, a Harvard physics professor, noticed that students' learning, problem-solving, and reasoning skills improved when they actively interacted with the material in class (Bates et al., 2017). Similarly, two Colorado high school teachers, Jon Bergmann and Aaron Sams (2012), began recording their slide lectures in the early 2000s and asking students to listen to them for homework. This way students could come into class ready to do the hands-on learning of using the material they just listened to at home.

Flipping the classroom is a "pedagogical approach in which direct instruction moves from the group learning space to the individual learning space, and the resulting group space is transformed into a dynamic, interactive learning environment where the educator guides students as they apply concepts and engage creatively in the subject matter" (Flipped Learning Network, 2014). According to the Flipped Learning Network (2014), using the flipped classroom model inverts Bloom's taxonomy so that the more complex aspects of learning happen in school. Students in this model are asked to read and listen to recordings ahead of time. This is the remembering and understanding elements of Bloom's taxonomy. Then the students come into class to work on the applying and analyzing aspects. After class they work on the levels of evaluating and creating. Flipped classroom experiences are especially helpful when you want to support creative and problem-solving thinking if you set up the context around an inquiry question.

In their book, *Flip Your Classroom: Reach Every Student in Every Class Every Day*, Bergmann and Sams (2012) discuss reasons why teachers should consider the flipped classroom model. Flipping:

- Allows students to pause and rewind their teacher
- Compels teachers to know their students better
- Increases student-to-student interaction in class
- Is conducive to authentic differentiation
- Supports frequently absent students and teachers

During the COVID-19-era remote and hybrid learning, many teachers stumbled upon aspects of this model and began to try it out. They made videos of new learning material and posted it for students to view during asynchronous time. When they did have synchronous class time (in person or via a video meeting), students engaged with the material via Jamboard,

QUICK TIPS

- Posting the materials that students need to read, listen to, or view before class allows students to move at their own pace. For example, by posting the materials on Friday for what students will need to be ready for the following Wednesday in class, you give students time and autonomy to get their work done within the constraints of their often busy schedules.

- Don't feel the need to make a video for everything. You can look at your unit maps and really prioritize what is essential and requires a video.

- Consider all of the ways people learn in today's context. It doesn't have to just be teacher-made videos that students view before class. You can use podcasts, articles, videos, infographics, excerpts from books, photographs, and more. Vary the types of information you ask students to view and read before class.

- Tie everything back to the essential questions and goals of the unit. What in-classroom experiences will likely help students apply and analyze information that is important in this particular unit?

breakout room discussions, and collaborative projects. I know many teachers and students struggled with engagement during this remote learning time, but having a collection of videos for students to view is one of the takeaways that many teachers were excited to leave with. If you and your colleagues have a YouTube channel or Google Classroom full of videos, you may be able to use them in a flipped classroom instructional context.

GETTING STARTED

Decide: To begin, decide which lessons from the unit map you will flip. These are likely lessons that are highly focused on content that students could learn from listening or viewing without a lot of modeling and extra explanation. They might also be introductory lessons that help students know just enough to get curious, but don't expect mastery just yet. If you are in a process-based unit, it may be a lesson that introduces each new part of the process.

Curate: Take some time to curate a set of texts that students can listen to, read, or view before class. It can be helpful to curate this set with colleagues. Know your class and think about what is going to be both engaging and accessible for them to understand. For example, giving students a college-level article might not work for all students, so you would likely want to pair it with a video or infographic. What follows is an example of a Padlet created by some teachers around an essential question about voting. You can see there are links to a variety of types of texts. Padlet is a free and useful digital tool for organizing the text sets.

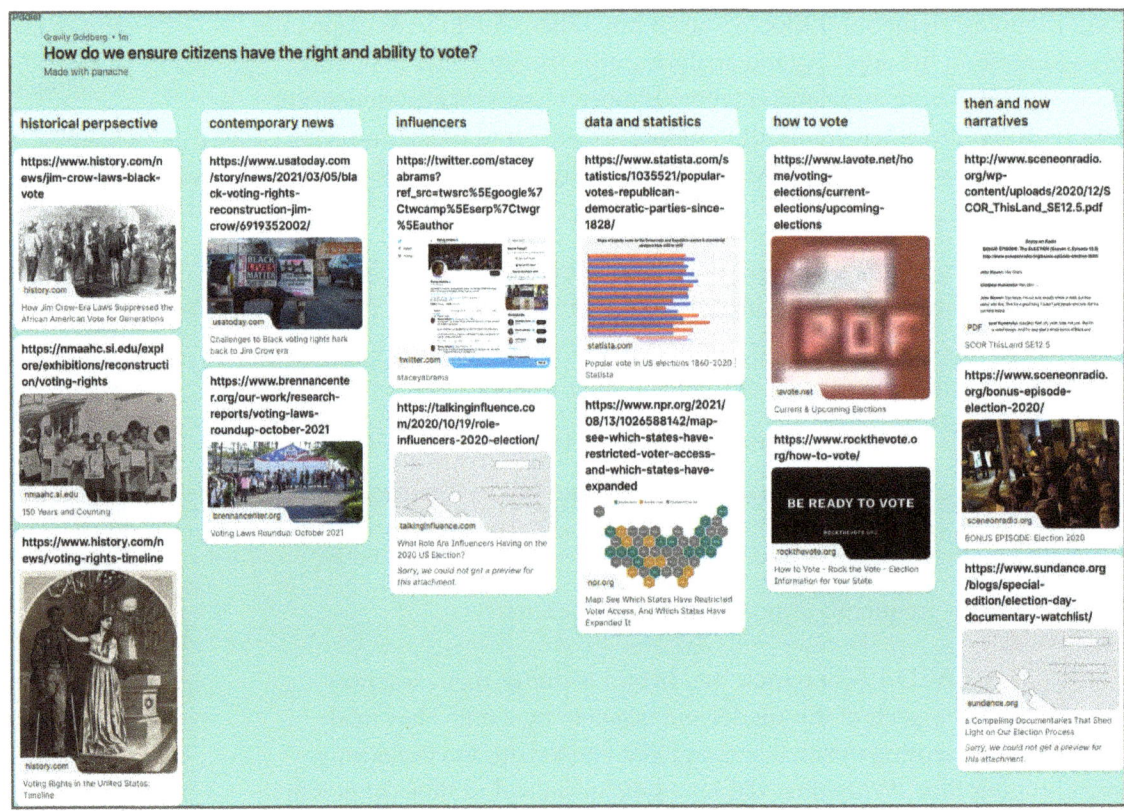

Communicate: So much of what engages students in a flipped classroom is the autonomy they have to move at their own pace. In order for that to happen, teachers need to be fully transparent and communicate when materials need to be read and viewed in order to participate in class experiences. One example of a weekly communication planner follows.

WEEK OF	ESSENTIAL QUESTION	AT-HOME LEARNING	IN-CLASS LEARNING EXPERIENCES
October 21	How do we ensure citizens have the right and ability to vote?	[Link to the text set.] Read, view, or listen to at least three texts from the category your group chose by Thursday.	**October 24: Thursday** Part 1: Meet with your group to discuss your reactions, ideas, and questions about the texts you read. Come with notes written down. Part 2: Regroup and meet in groups with those who read different texts than you. Discuss common themes and questions. Add them to a class Jamboard. **October 25: Friday (double period)** Part 1: Make a claim about how to go about ensuring citizens have the right and ability to vote based on what you have read and learned. Jot down your evidence for this claim. Part 2: Meet in small groups with those who have a similar claim to prepare for a debate simulation. Work together to generate a strong argument. Part 3: Participate in a debate simulation in small groups.

KEY IDEA

Choosing to use a flipped classroom across the year can maximize classroom learning time. It also helps students engage with the materials and creates space for teachers to listen and coach as students grapple with concepts.

HEADS UP

Locally source. Simply putting students in front of the computer to watch a video is not the same as having a flipped classroom. The learning really happens when students come to class ready to discuss, explore, collaborate, and make. The viewing and reading ahead of time is a primer to get students curious and to help them build background knowledge they can use in class. Relying too heavily on videos from others, such as Khan Academy, can turn students off and miss the mark. It is almost always better for teachers to make their own videos for their own students.

Keep it succinct, but make it memorable. It is so easy to use technology to audio record with slides. Try out Screencastify.com as it is popular with many teachers. But make sure you are not just talking over slides for too long as your presentation will likely never be viewed all the way through by students. Keep it short (three minutes or less) and use stories and examples to make the content come to life.

Pace for point of need. If you are asking students to view and read materials before class, make sure they are relevant and useful in class. Once students realize that doing the reading and viewing pays off, they will more likely keep doing it. If they don't see the value, they simply will skip that at-home portion.

Teaching Moves

In this section we explain teaching moves that align with the gradual release of responsibility model (Pearson & Gallagher, 1983). This model moves from the most amount of teacher support to the least. Some refer to it as the I-go, we-go, you-go model to describe who is doing most of the work in each phase. The following chart shows an overview of what you'll learn in the rest of the section.

TEACHING MOVES	WHICH PART OF THE GRADUAL RELEASE?	WHAT IS THE TEACHER DOING?	WHAT ARE THE STUDENTS DOING?
Modeling Page 58	I Go	Showing a strategy for how to do something	Watching and listening
Guided Practice Page 62	We Go	Co-collaborating with students on performing a process	Trying it out together and following the steps the teacher takes them through
Coaching Page 66	You Go	Prompting and offering quick feedback	Independently practicing and using the coaching feedback given by the teacher

QUICK TIPS

- *Plan and practice modeling.* You may be surprised at the information you personally need to think about before sharing it with a class. Mine your own process and use it to show students what you do.

- *Model at a moderate pace.* Expert teachers don't move too slowly or too quickly for the class to maintain interest.

- *Reflect.* After modeling a skill or content area, reflect. What worked? What didn't? Make notes for the future.

Modeling

WHY?

We learn most things in two connected ways: We see it done, then we try it out. There are also times, of course, when we're told information or when we discover a process entirely on our own. Most learning, however, unfolds through demonstration and practice. Think, for instance, of these examples:

- You watch a cooking show, then make the dish yourself.

- You listen to someone greet a relative in French, then practice the greeting.

- Your friend shows you how to change one tire, then you change the next one.

"Being a model is much more than telling students what I would do or what I did do. . . . Being a model means I explain a strategy I use, I demonstrate it by using the strategy in front of the students, and then I name what I did and when I choose to use it" (Goldberg, 2015, p. 37). It is all about showing and not just telling.

When students see us model, it is a form of direct instruction that allows them to see, hear, and understand how someone who is already proficient thinks. It makes the process of learning less magical and more concrete. It also makes the learning less daunting because it breaks down the steps into parts. As long as our modeling is active and not too long, it also creates an invitation for students to try the strategy on their own.

Modeling is the first part of the gradual release of responsibility model. It is the most heavy on teacher support because the students' job is really just to watch and listen. Later on they can apply and practice what they see, but during the actual modeling it really is the teacher show.

Who is doing the work?	I go
What teaching move are we using?	Modeling
What are students doing?	Watching and listening (to apply and practice later)

Modeling is effective when it focuses on a strategy for learning or a type of thinking and not simply directions for completing an activity. For example, modeling how to pay close attention to the verbs in the steps of a recipe helps students understand the difference between *bake* and *broil*. By slowing down your reading process and thinking aloud, you can show the way you think as you read. Another example is modeling how you scan a website to determine whether it is an e-commerce site that is trying to sell you something, a personal opinion site like a blog, or a scholarly site associated with a university. When you take time to model how you figure out the type of site it is, you are showing students a process they can apply as needed on their own.

GETTING STARTED

There are three main teacher actions for effective modeling. You can see these in all contexts from cooking shows to gaming tutorial videos. Modeling that sets students up to apply the learning includes setting the context, showing the steps, and naming the steps.

Set the Context: Before modeling it is essential to tell students what you will be modeling and why you will be modeling it. Ideally, this is tied to a unit goal and also a common challenge that students face. For example, you may tell students, "I am modeling this for you today because it will help us with our unit goal by _____." Or you might say, "Because so many of you have been asking for support with _____, today I am going to model how I _____." If we don't tell students what we are modeling and why, it can be really confusing and honestly boring for students to sit and just watch us work.

Language That Sets the Context

STATE THE *WHAT*	STATE THE *WHY*
"Today we are going to focus on _____ goal."	*"Because we are working on _____ goal"*
"I'm going to model for you how I _____."	*"Many of you have asked for help with _____"*
"The skill I am going to show you today is _____."	*"In order for us to accomplish _____"*
"Watch how I _____."	*"In this class and in your life outside of class it can be helpful to _____"*

Show the Steps: After setting the context you can actually do the work in front of students. Break down the focus into a series of steps that students can watch you move through. Possibly create a chart of the steps for students to have a visual representation to refer back to.

Here is a sample set of steps for looking at the impact of an author's word choices that the teacher posted while modeling one way to identify the author's perspective. This helps students deepen their empathetic thinking by showing them that considering word choice is important.

As you read . . .

1. **Pause** at words and phrases that make an impact.

2. **Think** about what they might mean.

3. **Jot** it down.

While modeling, it is also important to think aloud as you make choices and handle challenges. This means the teacher in this example had their own text and note-taking tool to show the steps. They made the metacognitive process visible by doing the work and explaining what they were doing in live time.

AUTHOR'S WORD CHOICES	IMPACT AND MEANING

Name the Steps: After showing the steps, it is important to name what you just did. This is because many students benefit from repetition but also because while you were modeling they may have missed a part and been focused on the content of what you were showing instead of also noticing the steps. Some summarizing language can be helpful such as "So the steps I just showed you were . . ." It can be especially helpful to pick a phrase and use it every time you model and name the steps so it becomes a sort of signal for students to focus and possibly even take some notes.

HEADS UP

Self-reflect. It can be challenging to know if you are actually modeling. The following chart shows what modeling is and what it is not. We often use this chart with teachers when we are learning to model as a reference point we can use together. It can be easy to move away from modeling and into something else. This "something else" that is not modeling might sound like assigning, guessing the teacher's thinking, or prompting.

MODELING IS . . .	MODELING IS *NOT* . . .
• Breaking down a skill into steps • Showing *how to* do something • Thinking aloud as you do the work yourself	• Telling students what to do • Telling what you would do in the future • Asking students what to do

Source: Goldberg (2015).

KEY IDEA

Modeling helps students see the steps that go into a learning process. When a teacher chooses to model, it is a form of direct instruction that supports not just what to do but also how to do it.

Slow down. Oftentimes our own proficiency and fluency with a skill makes it difficult for us to slow it down and really model the nuanced parts. When something becomes automatic, we may not know how we do it—we just do. Working with colleagues to co-plan our modeling can slow us down enough to actually notice the moves we make and to help us break them down into steps for students. Another way to study our own process is to try a skill in new content or with a new text so we are a bit disfluent. This not only helps us recognize the steps we take as learners but also helps us develop empathy for our students who are almost always learning something brand new.

Observe students. If you notice several students skip a step in the process you've modeled, that's of course a sign you need to reteach it. Look for patterns across time. When is your modeling most successful in terms of students being able to do something? Do students tend to do better when a process has fewer than four steps?

QUICK TIPS

- *Plan.* Be intentional about when you engage in guided practice. Keep the entire gradual release of responsibility framework in mind. Consider how soon after you model you will ask students to try it with you.

- *Decide the scope.* Choose whether the guided practice will be the whole class trying it together, small groups, or individuals. Depending on the skill, you may choose any of these options.

- *Kid watch.* Guided practice is a form of assessment as well as a teaching opportunity. Use the time to notice strengths and name them for students. You can also note challenges and do some mini teaching as students work to help them get back on track.

Guided Practice

WHY?

We can think of teacher modeling as a soccer coach stopping a practice and showing the players how to do a skill. The coach has the ball at their feet, and all eyes are on the coach. Guided practice occurs when the coach invites players to try it with them. The players have the ball at their feet, but the coach is still on the field and taking them through the steps.

In the classroom, guided practice includes any exercise in which students try out a skill for themselves with the direct involvement of the teacher as a mentor taking them through the steps. Guided practice typically happens after teacher modeling—either directly after or soon after. Using the gradual release of responsibility model, think of guided practice as the we-go portion of the approach. There is a partnership between the teacher and students.

Who is doing the work?	We go
What teaching move are we using?	Guided practice
What are students doing?	Trying something out with guidance and support through the steps

Oftentimes after modeling, we may believe students are ready to immediately begin trying out the new learning on their own. While some may be ready after a short model, many benefit from guided practice before going off to do the learning totally on their own. This is why the we-go portion of the gradual release is so important. It does all of the following:

- Builds student confidence to have a high-success experience

- Offers an opportunity for quick formative assessment while students try it out

- Helps the teacher clarify any parts that students seem to be confused about

- Creates momentum for students to be engaged enough to want to keep going on their own

- Supports executive functioning

Guided practice is tied to Lev Vygotsky's (1978) theory of the *zone of proximal development* (ZPD). The ZPD has come to represent the learning that a student can do with guidance—in other words, material that is neither too hard nor too easy to master. Douglas Fisher and Nancy Frey (2010), in their book *Guided Instruction*, connect the ZPD to *scaffolding*, the tools teachers use to guide students to greater learning. Fisher and Frey contend that while classrooms should be active, they should not be devoid of guidance from the teacher. Keeping both the ZPD and scaffolding in mind can help you differentiate in your classroom to assist every learner.

An example of guided practice that supports creative thinking includes a ninth-grade English class learning about rhetoric by bringing in favorite song lyrics. As each student reads their lyrics, the teacher takes them through the thinking steps in a guided way. He guides them to read the title and notice the word choice and tone. Then he guides them to read the whole song and circle language choices that reveal something about the author's thinking. He continues to guide them through a process that ends with a discussion about rhetorical devices and their purpose. By going through this guided practice, students are more likely to be successful doing similar types of thinking on their own, not just on song lyrics.

GETTING STARTED

Decide on the type of guided practice that will be supportive of student learning. Whole-class guided practice is most supportive followed by small-group and individual practice. The following chart helps you think through which type will best meet your students' needs.

TYPE OF GUIDED PRACTICE	WHEN TO CHOOSE IT	WHAT IT MIGHT SOUND LIKE
Whole class	• The skill is brand new to students. • You can quickly take them through the steps to save time. • Students need more self-confidence to get started.	"Let's all practice these steps together. First . . . Then . . . Next . . ."
Small group	• The skill is something students have tried before. • You can use a chart to show the steps without having to verbally take them through each one. • Students can work together to clarify and collaborate on the steps.	"Look at this chart and use it to help you remember the steps. Work in your group on each step and help each other as needed."
Individual	• The skill is familiar to students. • Students have various levels of proficiency with the skill and need different amounts of support. • Students are willing to get started on their own.	"Today as you practice on your own I will be meeting with you one-on-one to offer support. Don't forget our class chart of the steps and the example you have from the last time you did this. Take those out and use them as a reference."

Refer to a visual of the steps as you guide students. Make the chart clear and simple to use like a recipe with fewer words. This is often the same visual you used when you modeled, but now it is being used as a reference for students.

PREPARING TO SOLVE A COMPLEX PROBLEM

1. Read the entire problem. Ask yourself, "What do I think this problem is about?"

2. Read it again and underline verbs (the actions you need to take).

3. Jot down the steps you will take to answer all its parts.

Graphics from iStock: Dimitris 66, Andrii Shelenkov, and Hiranmay Baidya

As students practice, the teacher's job has three parts: notice, reinforce strengths, and support challenges.

TEACHER'S JOB	WHAT IT LOOKS LIKE AND SOUNDS LIKE
Notice	• Observing students as they work • Listening to their conversations • Looking at their work • Asking questions about their thinking
Reinforce	• Naming student strengths • Explaining how what a student is doing is helpful • Reminding students to use that same helpful strategy again
Support	• Naming a challenge the student is facing • Pointing to a chart or example that may be helpful • Offering a tip or suggestion • Modeling a part of the process again quickly

HEADS UP

How much? Students often do not need large amounts of time with guided practice. Use your observations during guided practice to decide when to move on. As long as students have had some high-success experiences, they are ready to try it on their own. Guided practice is not a time to expect mastery.

How often? Making space for guided practice almost every time you teach something new is helpful. Plan on following up most if not all of your modeling with some time for guided practice, even if it is just a few minutes.

How to mix it up? As with so much in teaching, being responsive to students is key. Put students in a variety of partnerships and small groups for guided practice. Keep seeing who learns best from whom, and why.

KEY IDEA

After teacher modeling it is helpful to build in time for guided practice. When students are supported through the steps of new learning, it helps them feel more prepared for independent practice and application later on.

- *Pause.* Don't begin coaching right away when students are moving into independent practice. This can create learned helplessness when students believe if they just wait a few minutes a teacher will come and do the work for them. Give students enough time to start on their own and get into the work before beginning.

- *Explain.* If students are new to getting more individual coaching, it is helpful to explain to them what it is and why you are using it. Having a chart of the gradual release of responsibility model up in the room and pointing to the part students will be working on that day can be clarifying and help students understand the framework and expectations.

Coaching

WHY?

Once students have had the opportunity to see a teacher model and participate in guided practice, they are likely ready for independent practice and coaching. Using the soccer example from the previous section, coaching occurs when the coach steps off the field and offers feedback from the sideline and during pauses in the practice. Coaching happens during the you-go portion of the gradual release of responsibility model.

Who is doing the work?	You go
What teaching move are we using?	Independent practice
What are students doing?	Applying learning on their own and getting support as they practice

The phases of gradual release can happen within a single lesson or across days. For example, you might model how you plan to solve a problem (I go). Then, immediately after, you might guide students to practice the same steps with a very similar problem (we go). In this same lesson you might ask students to use the same steps on their own with a similar problem (you go), and you are mostly watching and standing ready to assist *if* they need it. In this example the variables don't change much, so the progression from I go, to we go, to you go could all happen in just a few minutes in the first half of class. Another way to frame this progression is across days instead of within a single period. In this example, on day one the teacher would model. On day two the class or small groups would participate in guided practice. On day three the students would be set up to practice independently.

An example of a coaching session comes from an eighth-grade Spanish teacher. She met with pairs of students as they participated in a conversation describing a photo they were looking at. Their goal was to describe a building's architecture. The class had already seen this model and had guided practice, so they were ready to try it on their own. The teacher was not a part of the conversation, but did sit close by and listen. When students got stuck, she either pointed to a reference tool for them to try or, if that didn't help, offered a reminder strategy. She was supporting students only when they really needed it and only with the least amount of words so she didn't end up taking over the conversation. After two minutes she moved on to the next pair and repeated her coaching. While she did not get to each student, she was able to support several students and noted who she would want to circle back with next time.

	I GO	WE GO	YOU GO
What is the teacher doing?	Modeling	Guided practice	Coaching
What are students doing?	Watching and listening	Trying it out together and following the steps that the teacher takes them through	Independently practicing and using the coaching feedback given by the teacher

- *Equip yourself.* Having a clipboard handy when coaching can help you feel like a coach and also enable you to carry tools with you as you sit down with students. You might carry the following:

  o A class list to keep track of which students you have coached

  o Copies of charts or examples you have used with the whole class that you might want to show students or offer to them to use

  o Language prompts that you might use depending on your coaching focus

  o Note-taking forms to collect formative assessment information about what you are learning about students

  o Your own work you can use as an example to show students as needed

GETTING STARTED

Personal Goal Setting: Independent practice begins with a clear goal in mind. Make sure students know what they are independently working toward. This may be decided by the teacher or class but can also be decided by the student. This sort of personal goal setting can happen when students have had enough guided practice to have a sense of where their strengths and needs are. For example, maybe the whole class is working on collecting evidence to support a claim, but each student has their own goal around the part of this work that they want to grow. Maybe one student has a goal to read multiple texts when collecting evidence, and another student has a goal of organizing evidence.

Consider asking students to digitally share their personal learning goals during independent practice using Jamboard or Google Docs so you can see them. This can also lead later on to peer feedback and collaboration, which will be discussed in Section 6.

GOAL	WHY I CHOSE THIS	HOW I WILL WORK TOWARD IT	I WOULD LIKE SUPPORT WITH . . .

Teach Students How to Ask for Coaching: For coaching to be effective, students need to understand their role. They do not sit and receive and instead are the leaders who ask for what they need. This requires students to (a) be aware of their needs and (b) know how to ask for support. It is worth taking some time early in the year to model these two skills. Students' sense of self-advocacy as learners is critical; it's a mindset that will benefit them throughout schooling and life, and too few students feel they can do it.

Develop Self-Awareness of Needs

Offer regular and consistent time for students to reflect. This might be part of a Do Now or an end-of-the-period quiet few minutes to think and jot. You can project a slide or chart that can be used often, and students can choose what to reflect upon. A few questions can help:

- What did I learn today?

- What challenge did I face today?

- What next step am I ready for?

- What am I confused about?

- What kind of information would help me?

- What is working? What is not working?

Get Clear on the Type of Support You Want

Once students know what they want support with, they can think about how they want to be supported. A chart like the one that follows can be a helpful tool for students who are new to asking for support.

TYPE OF SUPPORT	HOW WE MIGHT ASK FOR SUPPORT
Clarification	"Can I clarify expectations with you?" "I understand _____. But can you say more about _____?" "Can you show me an example of _____?"
New strategy	"I've already tried _____. I need a strategy for _____." "_____ part is challenging for me. I need another way to try it." "Can I show you what I have tried? How else might I approach this?"
Action plan	"I am not sure how to get started." "I understand the goal, but am not sure how to break it down into parts." "Can we make a list of what needs to be done together?"
Confidence	"When it gets challenging, I sort of shut down. I need to know what to keep doing more of." "Am I on the right track? How can I know for myself?" "My inner voice tells me I can't do this. What else might I say to myself?"

Just having a chart in the room won't be enough. Model how you get clear on the support you need.

Schedule Coaching Time: In order to support students as they work independently, you will want to rotate who you coach. One way is to group together students with similar goals, and another is to work one-on-one with students. If a project is taking place over several days or weeks, it works well to begin with individual coaching sessions and then follow up with students in small groups with similar next steps. If you don't have that much time, you can group students by goal and coach them as groups.

Option A: Use formative assessment information to form the groups by instructional focus.

Focus:	Focus:	Focus:
Students: • •	Students: • •	Students: • •
Focus:	Focus:	Focus:
Students: • •	Students: • •	Students:

Option B: Use student-created goals to form groups.

- Look at student-created goals and color-code who has similar goals.

Goal: Students: • •	Goal: Students: • •	Goal: Students: • •
Goal: Students: • •	Goal: Students: • •	Goal: Students: • •

Option C: Students sign up for the group they want coaching with.

- Set the expectation that everyone signs up for one group, but offer students a choice of which group they think would benefit them most.

	MONDAY	TUESDAY	WEDNESDAY	THURSDAY	FRIDAY
Coaching Focus					
Student Sign-Ups					

HEADS UP

Normalize it. Convey that everyone, teachers and adults too, needs supportive coaching. You might even point out that professional athletes and executives have coaches, and they are literally the best in the field. Help students see coaching as an opportunity to learn and grow.

Guide, don't grade. Sometimes we think we are coaching, but we are really evaluating. Evaluation can actually get in the way of authentic feedback opportunities if the student feels threatened that this will all be graded. Coaching is not a time to grade and is a time to support. Reflect on your language and mindset to make sure coaching is not feeling like an oral quiz to students or to you.

Watch, respond, pivot. When offering coaching feedback, observe how it's being received, and respond accordingly. Sure, students may say they want one type of support, but it doesn't mean you always stick to one type. If you see a student needs a confidence boost too, a cheerleading comment about their perseverance can really help.

KEY IDEA

Learners all benefit from supportive coaching opportunities. By carving out time to meet students where they are and offering very targeted tips, students see you as a mentor who can be trusted to help them grow.

Learning Tools

3

Learning tools scaffold students as they learn to stretch themselves and do more complex thinking. These tools also help both teachers and students deliberately *develop* a type of thinking to apply. In this section we explore ways to support different kinds of thinking by introducing and supporting students' use of learning tools.

TOOL	HOW STUDENTS MIGHT USE THE TOOL TO DEVELOP INDEPENDENT THINKING	HOW STUDENTS MIGHT USE THE TOOL TO DEVELOP CREATIVE THINKING	HOW STUDENTS MIGHT USE THE TOOL TO DEVELOP PROBLEM-SOLVING THINKING	HOW STUDENTS MIGHT USE THE TOOL TO DEVELOP EMPATHETIC THINKING
Multimodal Learning Page 73	Select their own modality for learning that works for them	Develop their own multimodal tools or combine them in new ways	Use multimodal tools to tackle challenges or look at a problem in a new way	Examine an idea through a different modality to understand a different angle
Graphic Organizers Page 78	Select their own graphic organizers that match their goals/purposes	Develop their own graphic organizers or use them in new ways	Use graphic organizers to break a problem into parts and then put the parts together with a new organizer	Compare graphic organizers with peers to understand there are different ways of thinking about a topic

(Continued)

71

(Continued)

TOOL	HOW STUDENTS MIGHT USE THE TOOL TO DEVELOP INDEPENDENT THINKING	HOW STUDENTS MIGHT USE THE TOOL TO DEVELOP CREATIVE THINKING	HOW STUDENTS MIGHT USE THE TOOL TO DEVELOP PROBLEM-SOLVING THINKING	HOW STUDENTS MIGHT USE THE TOOL TO DEVELOP EMPATHETIC THINKING
Thinking Routines Page 85	Select thinking routines that match their goals/purposes	Integrate multiple thinking routines or create their own	Use thinking routines to work through a challenge bit by bit	Look at a challenge from a different angle using thinking routines
Memorization Page 90	Select cues that match their memorization purpose	Develop their own cues that help with memory retrieval	Decide on which memorized information will help with the problem	Compare cues with peers to understand there are different ways to encode and access information
Reflection Page 95	Select their own ways to reflect that match their process	Intentionally reflect throughout a learning process to see what they might want to create next	When feeling stuck, reflect on what is and is not working	Share reflections with peers to understand we all learn in our own ways and can also learn from one another

Multimodal Learning

WHY?

Learning involves all five senses. Neuroscientific research is shedding more light on why this is so, proving what teachers have known intuitively for a long time: Teaching with a mix of visual, tactile, and auditory strategies is effective. Some researchers posit that multimodal approaches work because they help to solidify understanding in a person's long-term memory, while others think it has more to do with the fact that involving more senses leads to more engaging, memorable learning. The learning "sticks" because a person has been motivated to attend to it for sufficient time.

Other researchers focus on the interplay of movement and language. In the embodied theory of cognition (Glenberg, 2011) all cognitive processes are based on bodily and neural processes of perception, action, and emotion. Glenberg (2011) contends that language is understood by our brains *simulating* the situation described by the language. A word or words drive the brain into perceptual action and stir emotional states that arise during the real situation. For example, studies have indicated that the same part of the brain that is used to physically kick a ball is activated when someone reads the word *kick* (Glenberg, 2011). Think about how this might impact the types of thinking your students are doing when they try to solve problems. Problem-solving thinking involves understanding each part or variable on its own and how it impacts the problem itself. Tapping into visual and kinesthetic modalities supports this simulation aspect of learning that is required for this sort of depth of understanding.

In one review of 129 studies in which teachers used visual approaches such as pictographs and sketches with one class but not with another, the class exposed to nonlinguistic strategies displayed gains in achievement equal to 17 percentile points (Haystead & Marzano, 2009). Another study found that acting out a story boosted students' understanding by 50 percent compared to those who simply reread (Glenberg, 2011). Similar studies have been replicated in math as well.

Harnessing the power of multimodal learning doesn't mean you offer a steady parade of pictures and dances. For example, you can model and encourage students to use nonlinguistic tools and actions in the midst of learning. Drawing and graphics on the board; using your body language and facial expressions; showing various ways to take notes with more than words—even simple gestures can each embed concepts and skills more deeply than verbal transmission alone. "What comes out in gestures adds new information to our repertoire of thoughts—information that is often more easily expressed and remembered when it is conveyed with our hands. It's also information we may not yet know we have in our mind" (Beilock, 2015, p. 91).

QUICK TIPS

- *Tailor the modality.* Watch for any concept or process that has more than three main aspects. Ask yourself: What part of this content lends itself to being introduced (and practiced) with a visual or kinesthetic approach?

- *Embrace less-is-more moves.* If you use movement to teach, do so efficiently, sometimes relying on hand or finger gestures rather than whole-body responses.

- *Plan your presentation of material.* Working in advance helps you make it more visually stimulating and engaging. This might mean making a visual in live time in front of the students to show your process. Or you might plan on sharing artifacts or manipulatives.

- *Involve kinesthetic moments for students.* Incorporate movement into the class period for students too. Have students been sitting the entire time? What movement might be helpful right now?

GETTING STARTED

Following are some examples of how you can shift verbal approaches toward visual and movement.

VERBAL APPROACH	VISUAL APPROACH
• Complex fractions: *Students are presented with a definition: "A complex fraction is a fraction where the numerator or the denominator is also a fraction."*	• Complex fractions: *Students work a problem by filling in a visual layout:*
• Foreign policy approaches of the first four U.S. presidents: *Students read four paragraphs of text, one about each president's foreign policy.*	• Foreign policy approaches: *Students make a notes sheet with four boxes, one for each president.*

VISUAL PRESENTATION BY TEACHER	MOVEMENT
• Complex fractions: *The teacher draws an illustration to demonstrate the concept.* $\frac{1}{4}$ Cup $+$ $\frac{1}{2}$ Cup $=$? 	• Complex fractions: *Students use actual measuring cups filled with water or sand to practice combining fractions with one another.*
• Foreign policy approaches: *Instead of just making a list on the board, the teacher uses a timeline to demonstrate the sequential nature of change in foreign policy.* Washington Adams Jefferson Madison 	• Foreign policy approaches: *The teacher uses a discussion exercise in which students move to different parts of the room to signify their own feelings about foreign policy as it relates to postcolonial issues— whether they are isolationists, interventionists, or neutral, for instance.*

Encourage Student Thinking in Multimodal Ways. Graphic organizers are one of the most commonly used tools for students to represent their learning. When designed and used well, they are powerful supports, helping students organize information, understand it, and deepen their unique thinking about it. What remote and hybrid learning has taught us, though, is that simply giving students a digital graphic organizer to fill out is not that different from handing them a worksheet. Why? Because they remain in a passive stance. Instead, we want to use organizers—or any multimodal tool—in ways that compel learners to *act* on information. We want them to synthesize in visual and auditory ways so raw information morphs into a long-lasting insight or point of view. We want to make sure, whatever the mode, that it scaffolds students to make connections between facts and ideas.

Following are a few ways students can represent their learning beyond traditional written response:

- Talk to a partner

- Make a short video

- Animate a slide

- Create a model

- Draw an example

- Organize and explain connections between ideas and objects

- Act out a scene

In an eighth-grade English class, a teacher noticed students were struggling to revise their work. To get them engaged in the process, she tapped the social dimension of writing for an audience. She gave them options for sharing how they revised their writing. Students could work on their own or with others.

> Highlight revisions and explain *what* and *why* using any of the following:
>
> - Written comments (using Google Docs)
> - Audio (using the MoteApp extension)
> - Narrated slides (using Screencastify)
> - Video recording of a partner conversation showing the revisions made
> - Live explanation during office hours in a conference

Incorporate Manipulatives. Math classes in the lower grades often include cubes, place value tables, base ten blocks, fraction tiles, pattern blocks, and so on. In other content areas we can also include manipulatives. A manipulative is any tool that can make an abstract idea more concrete, often leading to more visual, auditory, and kinesthetic processing. The table that follows shows examples of secondary manipulatives that can be used purposefully across the content areas and curriculum.

MANIPULATIVE	EXAMPLES
Sticky notes	• Jot down ideas and then sort and categorize them to see connections and make comparisons. • Identify key events and then line them up to create a timeline. • Jot down thinking and then with a partner make a Venn diagram, affixing the sticky notes based on negotiated understandings.
Blocks	• In conversations, each student puts down a block when they speak. Groups try to build a conversation by stacking blocks as they add on. • Use blocks to group evidence for both sides of an argument and then look at the groupings to make a claim. • Use blocks to represent a quantity or subject and create three-dimensional bar graphs.
Play dough	• Create a model with a basic sculpture. • Visualize and then build a scene, setting, or place. • Practice a revision mindset by adding to, taking off, or moving parts of a sculpture.
Paper clips	• Divide up the clips into categories as a way to show quantities or frequency. • Connect ideas by creating clip chains or showing disconnection by breaking the chain. • Bend them into shapes to show the arc of a story.
Hands	• Explain a sequence by touching each finger as you move across your hand. • Act out a concept with gestures. • Show the relationship between ideas (hands).

HEADS UP

Focus on understanding. Drawing, moving, painting, constructing, speaking—these various modalities are avenues for students to build understandings, not ends in themselves. So, avoid grading students on the execution and instead provide feedback on their depth of understanding.

Know the myth of learning styles. The notion that each person is especially gifted in one mode (whether visual, kinesthetic, verbal, etc.) has been disproven. It's best to offer students options for representing their learning. Doing so doesn't mean you always offer a menu of modalities, either. There are times when you do want to focus on verbal and written communication. The goal is to teach in ways that develop students' strengths across the board.

Build in reflection. Give students regular time to reflect upon their process and their product. Doing so invites them to discover which modalities they tend to favor, and in what contexts.

KEY IDEA

Building in more visual, auditory, and kinesthetic approaches to teaching and learning helps students become flexible and versatile as learners, able to use a variety of tools for developing understanding.

QUICK TIPS

- *Be explicit.* Teach students to use graphic organizers through modeling and explicit explanations.

- *Emphasize efficiency.* Show students how to jot notes quickly. Are complete sentences necessary? What kinds of information are worth jotting down?

- *Go for a plethora of types and purposes.* Don't assume the graphic organizer that you prefer is also your students' preference. Show a few options and keep adding to a growing class chart of organizers so students can create the ones that work best for them. A chart such as the one at the top of page 79 can become a helpful reference for students.

Graphic Organizers

WHY?

Take a look at the examples that follow and notice how including a visual representation can help with understanding.

NARRATIVE EXPLANATION	VISUAL REPRESENTATION
The plot of a story begins with exposition. Then, rising action heightens the plot until one reaches the climax. Following the climax, falling action gradually leads to a story ending with a resolution.	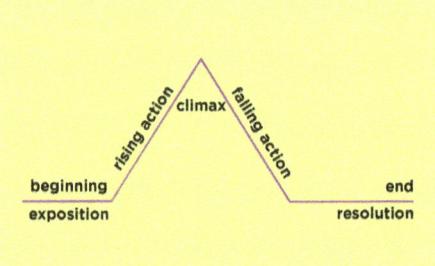

The visual representation makes intuitive sense, engages curiosity, and helps us to remember information. It's a good example of a graphic organizer. In the classroom, a teacher might begin by thinking aloud about how to analyze a particular novel students have read, projecting the organizer onto a SMART Board. Students could then contribute additional ideas, or perhaps work in partnerships or groups to continue thinking through a work of literature. Students would then have this classic story structure visual that they could then adapt and embellish as they wish. For example, they could use it as readers, and they could use it as fiction writers.

Research across disciplines has shown that in general, when graphic organizers are incorporated into instruction, student learning improves (Hall & Strangman, 2002). Graphic organizers work best when the learner makes choices about when and how to use them. You might want to deliver a few minilessons on various types of organizers and discuss their potential purposes (see some examples as follows). Co-create an anchor chart that students can refer to over time. For example:

I can create a graphic organizer to:

- Remember information
- Record my thinking
- Organize information
- Prepare for conversations

Through this shared work with graphic organizers, students develop a sense for "good fits" between the tool and the type of thinking involved. For example, if a student is trying to understand the water cycle, they may sketch and label a model. If a student is reading an article and watching a video on the same topic to compare information, they may make a Venn diagram. If a student is preparing for a class debate, they may want to organize information in a T-chart with side A and side B and then highlight key ideas. Purpose always drives the graphic organizer process; otherwise, it leads to little understanding and future use.

GRAPHIC ORGANIZER	WHEN AND WHY I MIGHT CHOOSE THIS

GETTING STARTED

Know some options for graphic organizers and when you might use one. The following table shows many examples that you can model across time.

WHAT IT LOOKS LIKE	HOW TO USE IT	SUBJECT-AREA EXAMPLES
Venn diagram	Use a *Venn diagram* to compare and contrast two or more ideas or concepts.	*Examples to compare or contrast:* • Merit of ways of solving math problems • Literary characters • Historical movements • Types of organisms
T-chart	*T-charts* are effective for breaking down main ideas and details, causes and effects, or other related concepts.	*Examples of related concepts:* • Causes and effects of historical change • Rhetorical devices used in a passage and examples from a particular text • Types of conversations in a world language and particular vocabulary that could be used in each

(Continued)

(Continued)

WHAT IT LOOKS LIKE	HOW TO USE IT	SUBJECT-AREA EXAMPLES
Concept map	Use *concept maps* to brainstorm details about a central idea or concept.	*Examples of uses for concept maps:* • Elements of a genre • Reasons human beings migrate • Effects of stimuli on the human body • Ways a painter might use light in their work
KWL chart **KWL** What I Know / What I Want to Know / What I Learned	*KWL* charts, which ask for reflection about what students know, want to know, and have learned, are often used for either formative or summative assessment during a lesson. There are many subtle variations of these charts.	*Examples of use of KWL charts:* • Activating prior knowledge about the location of states or nations • Generating questions for further study, such as "Why are these borders where they are?" • Measuring knowledge at the end of a unit to conduct a self-assessment
Flowchart	*Flowcharts* help to structure ideas in a logical order, emphasizing transitions, evidence, and organization.	*Examples for using flowcharts:* • Planning a narrative writing piece • Outlining steps in a scientific process (e.g., the mutation of cells) • Ordering the steps of historical events • Reminders for solving a math problem with multiple steps

WHAT IT LOOKS LIKE	HOW TO USE IT	SUBJECT-AREA EXAMPLES
Cycle	Use *cycles* for concepts that return to a beginning step or for situations that repeat themselves.	*Examples for using cycles:* • Exploring the water cycle in science • Cycles of doing research using secondary sources • Economic policies across time
Tree	Somewhat like a concept map, *trees* prompt students to delve deeper into ideas and content by "zooming in" on details and making more nuanced distinctions.	*Examples of activities using trees:* • Questions one might ask about a historical event • Ideas about character or figure based on a detail from the text • Details about why and how plants grow
Timeline	*Timelines* help students place events in a recognizable order.	*Examples of using timelines:* • Putting events in order in history class to determine cause and effect • Mapping the timeline of a story or novel, especially one told out of chronological order • Tracking changes in thinking about scientific phenomena such as the shape of the Earth or the development of map projections

These types of graphic organizers provide an overview of some classic ones, but we encourage you and students to use them as springboards to create your own.

If students are stuck always using the same type of thinking, try introducing a new organizer that could scaffold new moves in their thinking processes so they notice and evaluate information differently. For example, this student is using a concept map to record what they are learning about Malala Yousafzai. The student seems to be thinking about each fact on its own.

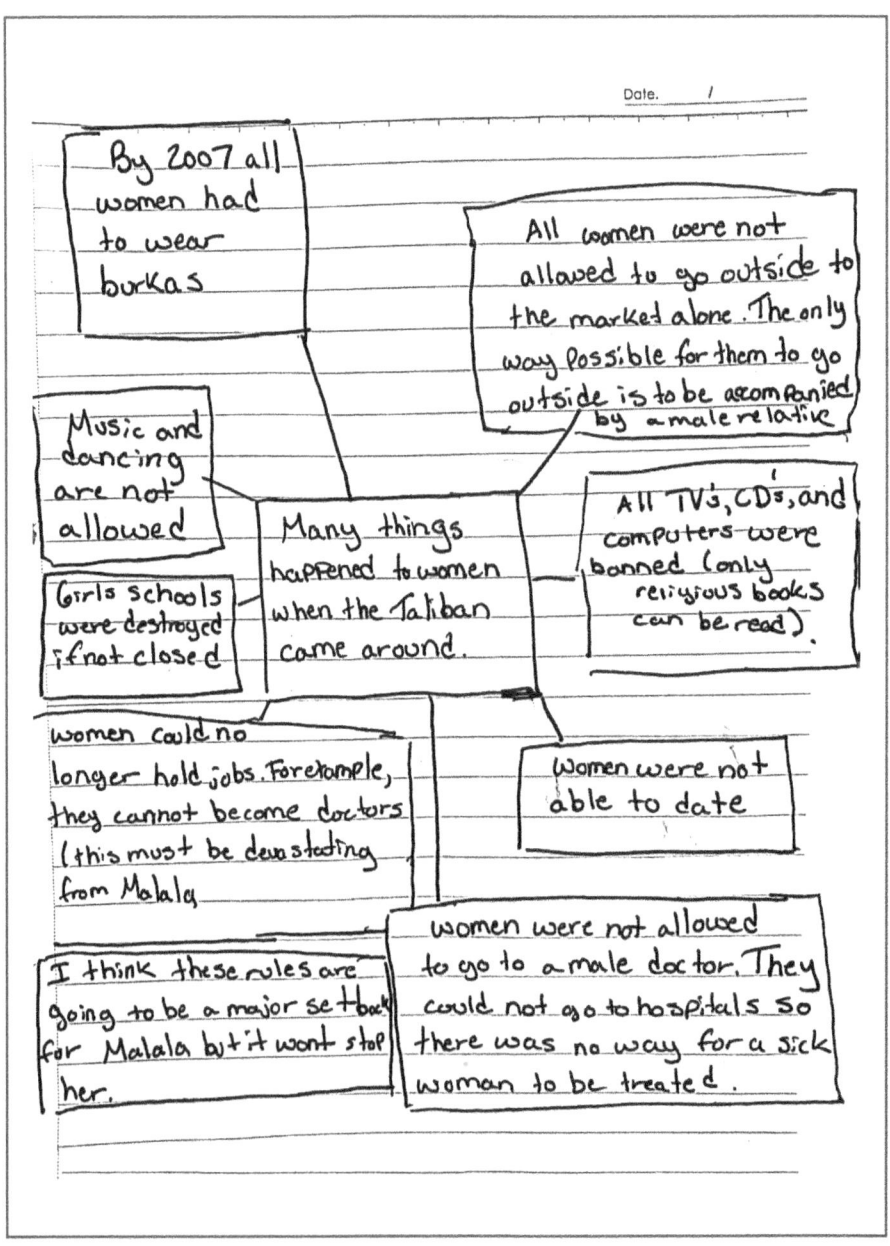

A student's thinking can be extended using this same type of organizer, as shown in the next example featuring Ruth Bader Ginsburg, by adding in arrows that show which facts go together and then giving each grouping a category heading. This can support the student to see connections between facts and work toward building bigger ideas based on each category of information. The teacher can show a model and then coach the student to try it.

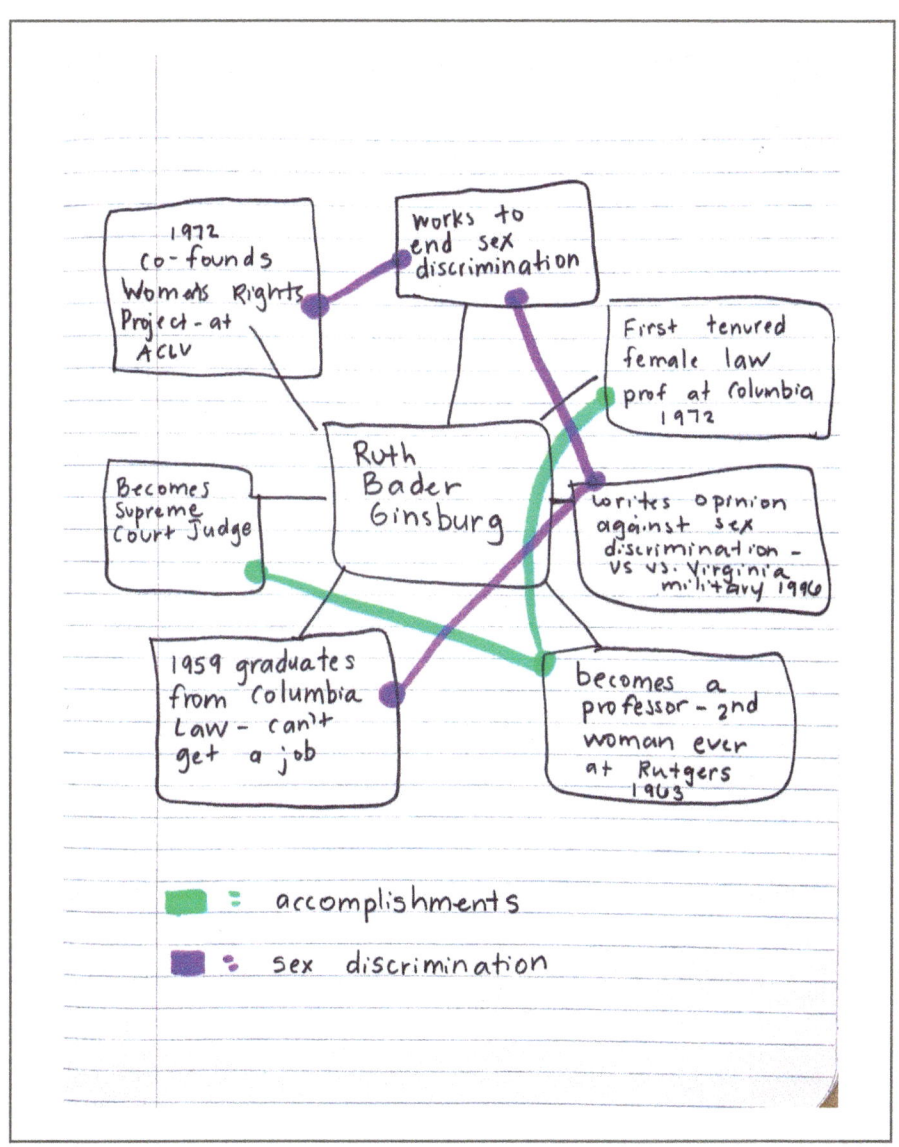

Connect Graphic Organizers to Discussions. Encourage student discussions before, during, and after creating graphic organizers. Doing so allows for peers to hear one another's thinking and deepens everyone's knowledge of the content.

- Before creating a graphic organizer, invite students to explain their goal and why they chose the format they did. Peers can ask questions and comment.

- While students use a graphic organizer, they can pause and share their thinking with a partner or small group. This allows students to problem solve and learn from each other.

- As a whole class or in small groups, invite students to share their finished graphic organizer. Circulate, listen to discussions, prompt, or ask questions to deepen students' thinking if necessary.

- Teachers can meet with students to discuss their organizers and use them as formative assessment windows into students' understanding.

- Build in time for students to revisit, revise, and add on to graphic organizers as they learn more across time. This makes the organizer a learning tool rather than a "one and done" assignment.

HEADS UP

Invite students to invent their own organizers and share. Oftentimes the best organizers are ones that learners invent themselves. This might incorporate aspects of previously used organizers in new and creative ways. Then post students' examples (with permission) so others can try them too.

Suggest organizer formats and let students choose. The whole class does not need to use a single organizer format. Invite choice and then include time for reflection so students can determine if the choice they made was helpful or not.

Include digital tools that bring audio and video elements into graphic organizers. Consider apps and Google extensions, such as Mote, that allow users to audio record and save a note. Or students might hyperlink a video into their organizers to include another example.

Thinking Routines

WHY?

Barry observed a Latin class in which students were learning to create the comparative and superlative forms of adjectives, such as *good*, *better*, and *best* or *fast*, *faster*, and *fastest*. Here's an excerpt from the conversation:

Natalie:	Wait, if the original word is just *pulcher*, why does *pulcherrimus* have an extra *r*?
Mrs. Roman:	All of these forms have a double consonant. It's a good way to recognize them.
Natalie:	Yeah, I'm never going to remember that.
Mrs. Roman:	There are also a few special forms, like *bonus*. That one just has its own special words, and you'll just have to memorize them. It goes *bonus, melior, optimus*.
Jonathan:	Like Optimus Prime in the movies!
Mrs. Roman:	Tell me about Optimus Prime.
Jonathan:	He's the biggest Transformer.
Mrs. Roman:	Okay, well, *optimus* means best, so that works. There's actually a special form for biggest, too. It's *maximus*.
Natalie:	[Sighs heavily].
Hailey:	So the special ones are big, small, good, and bad, right?
Mrs. Roman:	That's right.
Hailey:	I think of those as my family. Dad is big, my sister is small, I'm good, and my brother is bad.
Natalie:	Ha! That makes a lot of sense!

What interested him about this exchange was that both Jonathan and Hailey intuitively accessed cognitive approaches that helped them learn, while Natalie simply shut down until such a structure was presented to her. Jonathan and Hailey "steered" their cognition along neural pathways so it could be stored in long-term memory.

Thinking routines are tools that guide this process of memory-making. They are verbal or graphic constructs that help students make cognitive connections between concepts or ideas. Thinking structures actually train

QUICK TIPS

- *Notice.* Watch for thinking routines to pop up during class and point them out—students use them naturally quite often.

- *Use the routines verbally and in writing.* Purposefully use thinking routines to stimulate discussion or writing assignments.

- *Name.* Point out your thinking routines for students so that they can repeat the process as needed. Remember, the goal of these activities is to model structures students can bring to other content as needed.

students to think in certain ways. By presenting explicit, narrow models for connecting ideas, we build scaffoldings for students such as Natalie that they can reuse in future learning. If we were to formalize Jonathan and Hailey's thinking routines, they might look like this:

> I can remember . . . because it reminds me of . . .

GETTING STARTED

You've probably learned or taught in a classroom where some students make leaps others don't—where some students leap from cause to effect, follow a process, or make a connection that other students fail to see. One benefit of thinking routines—which could also be called patterns of thinking, mental moves, cognitive routines, or a host of other names—is that they help such students learn to replicate that line of cognition in the future. But they also just work as good teaching methods for an entire class.

The most robust work on these structures probably comes from Project Zero at the Harvard Graduate School of Education (n.d.), which labels them *visible thinking*. (You can find out more at Project Zero's website, www.visiblethinkingpz.org.) Project Zero's routines include those that are probably familiar to you, such as *think-pair-share* or *I used to think. . . . Now I think*, in addition to less common structures. Based not just on Project Zero's work but beyond, the following table includes some thinking routines you might see in the classroom, even though students don't always explicitly use these words.

These thinking patterns are quite common; they're what we think of as the low-hanging fruit of thinking patterns. Accessible, useful, sure—but we want to guide students to use more advanced thinking routines as well. To do this, model them explicitly, and provide collaborative practice with them so students begin to use them on their own. For some rich, engaging examples, we can turn to Harvard's Project Zero site and highlight just a few of their thinking routines you might use in class.

THINKING ROUTINE	STUDENT EXAMPLE
I learned that/I remember . . . Therefore, I think . . .	"I remember all of the states because I learned that song that lists them all back in fifth grade."
I connect . . . to . . .	"This poem always reminds me of my favorite TV show because it's got the same mood."
When I combine X and Y, I get Z.	"So to solve a two-step equation, I have to know both how to balance the two sides of the equation and how to simplify the answer after that."
X must have thought/felt . . . so I can think/feel . . .	"I bet that Alexander Hamilton was really confused about how to vote; I've felt that way during student council elections."
All . . . are . . . , so . . . must be . . .	"All the recipes in this cookbook are gluten free, so the author must believe gluten should be avoided."
X happens when Y happens. So if X is happening, Y must be happening.	"Every experiment we've tried shows that the outside of a wheel spins faster than the inside, so that must be why I feel faster when I ride an animal on the carousel near the outside rim."
So far, X always = Y. So X always equals Y (deductive).	"I checked eight houses on my block, and they all have a basement, so I think that all of the houses built on that block have basements."

Source: Adapted from Harvard's Project Zero, www.visiblethinkingpz.org

Thinking Routines to Model Explicitly

ROUTINE	DESCRIPTION	EXAMPLE
Compass Points	Divide the board or other space into four "compass points": • North = Need to know • East = Excited • South = Suggestion • West = Worrisome While considering the topic at hand, each student completes a sticky note or adds a comment for each compass point. The class then reads results and discusses or writes about them.	
Tug of War	Draw a line with opposing points of view or a "fairness dilemma" at either end. Students fill out notes for either end to identify the "pulls" for either end, as well as the "tugs" that lead them individually to agree with one side. After reading the notes, pose discussion questions, including a "What if?" question, to the class.	
Color, Symbol, Image	Choose a topic or aspect of a topic being studied. Then make individual charts that identify a color, a symbol, and an image for that topic, along with explanations of why each student made the choices they did. Post and read these and then discuss.	
Circle of Viewpoints	Each student creates a circle with three sections: • I am thinking of . . . from the point of view of . . . • I think this because . . . • A question I have from this point of view is . . . This exercise invites empathy and stretches student thinking.	
I used to think . . . Now I think . . .	Deceptively simple, this routine is both quick and useful. Simply ask students to focus on what has changed about their thinking on a topic. Invite the rest of the class to read the responses silently and then discuss.	

As you can see, many of these activities lean toward the use of sticky notes or poster-sized paper. You'll also notice that the advanced routines tend to be useful when working with tough questions in a content area.

There are many more advanced structures available to you at Harvard's Project Zero site. You can also come up with your own thinking routines based on the thinking and consideration you want students to undertake. Student responses can remain posted for multiple class periods to give each class time to consider and revisit responses.

Don't forget that the goal of using such structures—both the simpler and advanced forms—is to solidify student thinking in the short term, but also to give students tools they can use in the long term, including, for instance:

- Self-reliance in building logical lines of thought

- Ways of examining multiple sides of an issue or question

- Engagement in thinking about particular dilemmas or difficult questions

KEY IDEA

Thinking routines help students learn to structure logical trains of thought and to expand their approaches to difficult topics and content areas. Teach them explicitly so that students can carry them forward and apply them to further content areas as they learn.

HEADS UP

Don't forget the discussion. Build in some form of discussion and thus allow students to stretch their thinking and engage the thinking of others. This can be with a partner, small group, or whole class.

Focus on the thinking more than the routine. The goal is to deepen understanding and thinking, not the routine itself. If students are able to think without the routine that was modeled, they have still met the goal.

Make sure thinking routines are used with meaningful content. Thinking routines don't work if the goal is literal recall or memorization. Make sure the goal being worked on is one that involves deep thinking such as synthesis of ideas or understanding multiple perspectives.

QUICK TIPS

- *Make it snappy.* Keep memorization tasks short and make sure they are truly useful to students.

- *Consider fluency.* When deciding whether or not to ask students to memorize something, consider if this is necessary to be fluent in a given content area. Is the information something that can just be googled as needed, or does the learner need to use the information often? For example, a musician may not need to memorize the name of the composer who wrote a song they want to play on the piano, but they do need to memorize the notes on the piano to know how to play it.

- *Encourage student mnemonics.* Have students create their own strategies on the spot in class so they are more meaningful and also set them up for more independence later on.

Memorization

WHY?

Psychologists distinguish between three stages of memorization—encoding, storage, and retrieval (Melton, 1963). Encoding refers to the initial learning of information. Storage refers to the ability to hold onto information over time. Retrieval refers to being able to access information as needed. When someone struggles to remember information, it can be helpful to consider at which stage the challenge arose.

While all of us are constantly encoding information, the most important or emotionally charged information tends to stick. This is why memorizing without understanding doesn't work. Students need to recode and not just encode in order to convert the information they read or hear about into something that makes sense to them. Many of the other tools in this section can help students recode information and develop their own meaning from it such as developing their own graphic organizers, using thinking routines, and reflecting on learning. In order to move from this first stage of encoding/recoding, students need to think and not just rotely try to recall.

Neurobiologists have found that experiences leave "memory traces" in our brains. This is why active experiences are so important: so learners aren't merely reading or listening to information passively all the time. These memory traces create physical changes in the nervous system that represent our experience. But, memory traces are not verbatim transcripts or video-like recordings. They are consolidated and then reconstructed with more recent information. For example, if we try to recall the characters' names in a book we read a year ago, the other characters we have read since then can interfere with our ability to accurately recall.

Cues help our brains more easily and intentionally gain access to information. For example, you may not be able to access a name on your own, but given three choices you can recognize the correct one. When trying to memorize information, you can create cues, but they should match the content and also be distinct enough from other cues that they will work. A cue can be a word, an image, a smell, a sound, or any combination that helps your brain.

All of this research implies we can support students' memorization in three main ways.

- Teach for understanding so all information is contextualized.
- Create meaningful learning experiences so students can process, think about, and understand the information.
- Help students create cues to retrieve information.

While the first two ways listed are woven throughout this book, the third, creating cues, is the focus of the following pages.

GETTING STARTED

The following are three tips for teachers who want to help students learn *how* to access stored information using cues.

Teach Mnemonic Strategies Explicitly. Mnemonics, those quick tricks for planting information in one's memory, are often used in the classroom without being named as such (think "Thirty days have September, April, June, and November"). It's helpful for students to learn when and why they are using mnemonic devices; later on, they'll make better choices on their own about learning material by applying specific devices.

Research tells us that the best mnemonic devices are brief, connected to the material being learned, and humorous where possible (Mocko et al., 2017). Such devices not only help students remember; they also reduce anxiety about learning. Keep in mind, however, that memorizing material using a mnemonic is not the same as *understanding* that material. A student who can instantly recall the names of the original 13 colonies may not be able to explain why that list is important or, indeed, what a colony is.

With these parameters in mind, the following table includes the 10 mnemonic strategies that most research has agreed are most effective, popular, and simple. Note that many of the verbal strategies are closely related in type but not exactly the same.

DEVICE	WHAT IT IS	EXAMPLES
Same-Letter Starts	Using starting letters of words only to remember simple information	• To remember the directions of the y- and x-axis of a graph, think "y is yawning, and x is exhausted." • "Mnemonics" make you go "hmmm," while "pneumonia" makes you go "plll."
Acronym	Using a series of starting letters to form a word	• HOMES: the five Great Lakes (Huron, Ontario, Michigan, Erie, Superior) • ROYGBIV: the spectrum of colors (red, orange, yellow, green, blue, indigo, violet)
Acrostic	Making a new sentence using the starting letters of material	• "Every good boy does fine" (E, G, B, D, F): the notes on the treble staff in music • "Please excuse my dear Aunt Sally" (parentheses, exponents, multiply, divide, add, subtract): the order of operations in math

(Continued)

(Continued)

DEVICE	WHAT IT IS	EXAMPLES
Visual Strategies	Conjuring or drawing a mental image as a way to remember information	• A capitol has a dome (shaped like an *o*), but a capital does not • A Bactrian camel's back is shaped like the letter *B*, while a dromedary camel's back is shaped like a *D*
Rhyming	Creating direct rhymes or short poems to connect material and memorization tools	• "*I* before *e* except after *c,* or when sounding like *a* as in *neighbor* or *weigh*": the common spelling rule • "In fourteen hundred ninety-two, Columbus sailed the ocean blue": the year of Columbus's famous voyage
Song	Setting material to music in order to remember it	• The ABC song: the song used almost universally to remember the 26 letters of the English alphabet • Any of the cartoon songs from the *Schoolhouse Rock!* series
Word Within a Word	Finding one word within another that helps to remember its meaning	• The perimeter of a shape runs around its *rim* • The principal is your *pal*, the principle is not
The Spelling Trick	Using a specific aspect of a word to remember how to spell the word correctly	• I scream "Eee!" as I run by the cemetery: a device for remembering that all vowels in *cemetery* are the letter *e* • It is not necessary to use two *c*s at the start of the word *necessary*
Simple Movement	Remembering information using very simple motions, often with body parts	• Using the knuckles and grooves between knuckles to remember the months with 31 days • If you extend your left hand with the thumb perpendicular to the fingers, it makes a correctly formed *L*, while your right does not
Chunking	Breaking longer information into three or fewer parts for memorization	• Remembering the first nine numbers of pi (3.141592653) as a common telephone number: (314)-159-2653 • Remembering how to spell *Antarctica* by breaking it into separate words: *Ant arc tic a*

Teach Visually. One way to help students memorize is to teach in ways that incorporate visuals. In addition to the section on multimodal learning, you can consider the following:

- Drawing stick figures on the board while teaching a poem or story

- Making lists on the board instead of writing single words

- Making a two-column chart instead of simply writing a list

- Using a timeline

- Connecting material you write on the board with clear arrows or other visual cues

- Including a relevant picture in digital slides

Use the Power of Emotions. A team of researchers investigated the impact of emotions on memorizing information. They asked participants to take part in a test, in which they were rapidly presented with different words. Each word was printed in a different color, and participants were asked to name the color as they read them. Later they were asked to recall the words. MacKay et al. (2004) found that taboo words that elicited an emotional response were recalled more frequently than words that carried less emotion. This along with other studies has prompted psychologists to claim, "When we are led to experience feelings of delight, anger or other states of mind, vivid recollections are often more possible than during everyday situations in which we feel little or no emotional attachment to an event" (Psychologist World, n.d.).

Yet another reason to make sure students are engaged during our classes is that they are more likely to remember what they learned. Consider how you can create a classroom environment where students experience joy and emotional investment through the texts they read, their interactions with peers, and the authenticity and relevance of the curriculum itself. While we cannot entirely take away stress and hardship in students' lives, we can make our classrooms highly relevant, supportive places to be. When students are bored, stressed, and emotionally checked out, they remember less. Let's help them literally remember more by actively drawing them into the curriculum.

KEY IDEA

Students can benefit from memorizing some material. Teach students *how* to use cues to retrieve information that is important enough to commit to memory.

HEADS UP

Memorization is not the end goal. The overall goal of teaching is to help students understand material by making connections, considering nuances, and thinking deeply.

Assign memorization with caution. Memory work will always disadvantage certain students, especially those with learning differences. It's vital that you consider when, why, and how much memorization to assign.

Include students in deciding what is important to memorize. If we teachers, who are already experts in our content, are always the ones deciding what is important, students don't learn this skill. Model and then offer time for students to decide which information is worth memorizing and which is not. This is a skill that they can take with them beyond your classroom.

Reflection

WHY?

Decades ago John Dewey famously claimed, "We do not learn from experience . . . We learn from reflecting on experience." Reflection is essential for creating independent learners who can make choices, learn from those choices, and develop a growth mindset. Taking the time to make reflection a part of the classroom routine makes it much more student-focused. Jennifer Porter (2017) has written for the *Harvard Business Review*, "Reflection gives the brain an opportunity to pause amidst the chaos, untangle and sort through observations and experiences, consider multiple possible interpretations, and create meaning. This meaning becomes learning, which can then inform future mindsets and actions."

In order for students to reflect in ways that positively impact learning, they need to be clear on the goal they are working toward and what success looks like. Reflection requires some preparation as well as quiet contemplation. It is also important to have a supportive community to help you feel safe.

Think of reflection as having a before, during, and after phase.

Before Reflecting	• Know and name a goal you are working toward. • Know and name what success looks like and sounds like.
During Reflection	• Consider the goal and look back at your work. • Ask yourself some questions. • Sit quietly and think and maybe write.
After Reflecting	• Possibly share with someone. • Use reflection to name next steps.

GETTING STARTED

It's important to fully anchor reflection into the day. Create reflection routines so it's not perceived as an afterthought, or students will not take it seriously. It takes time and practice and a safe environment for students to honestly reflect on strengths and next steps. These routines can include:

- When reflection happens (daily, weekly, set points during a unit)

- How reflection happens (thinking, reviewing past work, writing, talking to a partner)

- Who reflection happens with (teacher, peer, by yourself)

QUICK TIPS

- *Use reflection liberally and with variation.* Reflection can happen in quick, regular routines such as the last three minutes of class or every Friday. Reflection can also take on more extended time such as before a unit begins, midway through a unit, or at the end of the unit.

- *Model it.* When you think aloud as you reflect, students come to see that reflection is a natural part of engaged learning at every age and in every content area.

- *Make it goal-oriented.* Tie reflection to unit goals and/or students' personal goals so they have a clear purpose for why they are self-reflecting.

Provide Examples of Self-Reflection Questions.

Educator and instructional coach John Altieri (personal communication, December 16, 2020) shared the following set of questions he uses with students and teachers.

Self-Reflection Questions

- What did I learn today?

- What questions do I have about today's work?

- How does today's experience remind me of something I have worked on before?

- What strategy do I now have that I didn't have before?

- Why was the work I did today helpful?

- What was the biggest challenge for me today? What did I do that helped?

- What caused me to have an aha moment or realization?

- How did I solve a problem today?

- What helps me get started or persevere during challenges?

- What advice would I give myself before starting my work next time?

- What did I want to avoid in my work today? Why?

- What would happen if _____?

- What tools do I need?

Before handing out these questions to students, consider adding in one or two each session so the list of reflection questions grows across time. You will also want to model how you think through and choose the ones you think about so students see the thoughtful process you go through.

Offer Language Stems. Sometimes the hardest part of reflecting is getting started. For many students it is helpful to have some language stems they can use to begin. This is not an assignment where they must use these phrases and is meant to be a tool they can use if needed. Some examples include:

- Something that made me think today was . . .

- I wonder what would happen if . . .

- Today I learned . . .

- I am confused about . . .

- I still don't understand . . .

- I was surprised by . . .

- I noticed . . .

- I observed . . .

- _____ really helped my learning today because . . .

- The most important thing to remember about _____ is . . .

- One thing I learned about _____ is . . .

- New questions I have are . . .

- I'd like to learn more about . . .

- I am proud of how I . . .

Use Self-Reflection to Ask for Feedback. Once students are familiar and comfortable with self-reflection, they can use it to ask for and offer feedback. Students can use their reflections to get clear on what kind of tools, strategies, and clarity they need next. This makes it much easier to ask for what they need. Partners who are listening to their peers share their reflections can offer feedback and ideas that can help them with next steps. Ideally, reflection leads to action and is not solely a philosophical exercise. A quick exit ticket or formative assessment via Google Forms can help you as the teacher check in with how students' reflections are going. For example, you might give students a few minutes to consider the following.

Self -Reflection Survey

Name

Your Answer _____

What goal are you working toward?

Your Answer _____

What is your reflection on progress toward that goal?

Your Answer _____

What is one next step you are going to take? Why?

Your Answer _____

KEY IDEA

Building in consistent time for self-reflection helps students get clarity on where they are and where they are going. It also helps engage students in being open to feedback and next steps.

HEADS UP

Support partnerships that work. In classes where students might feel particularly vulnerable with self reflection, it can help for them to have a consistent partner they can build trust with over time. Keep the partners consistent, and the relationship can grow to one where authentic reflection begins to happen.

Avoid inserting yourself in the process. Do not grade student reflections on whether or not you agree with their self-assessment. This is a form of artificial reflection and can really damage a relationship with students. You may have a different perspective on where the student is in relation to your goals, but that does not mean the student is wrong. It does mean that the success criteria for what learning looks like and sounds like has not been clear enough for the student, and more time and examples can be given.

Offer some choice in how students reflect. Some students prefer to talk it through with a partner while others prefer writing quietly on their own. The goal is reflection, not the modality it happens in.

Collaboration Structures

4

Understanding can deepen when students work together to investigate ideas, build and challenge ideas, and share their insights with others. When we intentionally support student collaboration, peer-to-peer learning can thrive. The following table shows how collaboration structures can support student thinking.

COLLABORATION STRUCTURE	HOW STUDENTS MIGHT USE THE TOOL TO DEVELOP INDEPENDENT THINKING	HOW STUDENTS MIGHT USE THE TOOL TO DEVELOP CREATIVE THINKING	HOW STUDENTS MIGHT USE THE TOOL TO DEVELOP PROBLEM-SOLVING THINKING	HOW STUDENTS MIGHT USE THE TOOL TO DEVELOP EMPATHETIC THINKING
Discussion Stems Page 101	Stems can help students share their thinking in conversation	Stems can push students to think in new ways	Stems can help students name a challenge and talk through it	Stems can help students acknowledge other perspectives and experiences
Think-Pair-Share Page 105	The "think" phase creates space for independence	By going through all three phases students create more clarity and depth of thinking	The "pair" phase allows students to work through challenges together	The "share" phase allows students to hear multiple ideas on the same topic
Lines of Positionality Page 109	Students make a claim supported by evidence	Students interpret information in a variety of ways and understand the spectrum of thinking	Students consider compelling challenges, claims, or phenomena when forming their stance	Students consider evidence and reasoning of others and may shift their claims

(Continued)

(Continued)

COLLABORATION STRUCTURE	HOW STUDENTS MIGHT USE THE TOOL TO DEVELOP INDEPENDENT THINKING	HOW STUDENTS MIGHT USE THE TOOL TO DEVELOP CREATIVE THINKING	HOW STUDENTS MIGHT USE THE TOOL TO DEVELOP PROBLEM-SOLVING THINKING	HOW STUDENTS MIGHT USE THE TOOL TO DEVELOP EMPATHETIC THINKING
Fishbowls Page 114	Students have the opportunity to develop both listening and speaking skills.	Students respond in the moment with new ideas and reactions.	Students decide when to speak, when to listen, and when to step in or out.	Students hear a variety of interpretations and ideas.
Jigsaw Page 117	Students become the expert in one aspect of a topic.	Students work to see connections and synthesize information across topics.	Students work together and on their own to decide what is most important.	Students share connections and disconnections across a topic or experience.
Silent Conversations Page 122	Students begin with their own original ideas.	Students get written reactions they can use to revisit, revise, or get clarity on their original ideas.	Students use evidence and reasoning to decide on what is most important to jot down.	Students see a variety of perspectives and may even change their own thinking.
Share-Outs Page 126	The sharing student serves as a teacher to others who can take something that was shared and use it in their own work.	Students can teach one another unique or new ways of thinking.	Students can bring solutions or challenges to the group.	Students build relationships based on supporting one another and seeing the common ideas, strategies, and challenges learners face.

Discussion Stems

WHY?

Thoughtful, interactive conversation is a learned skill. As students mature and advance through the grades in school, they naturally learn some discussion skills through imitation and practice in and out of the academic setting. Most students, however, greatly benefit from explicit teacher demonstration and practice of speaking and listening skills. In fact, when you fast-forward to high school debate clubs and think about the deliberate tools and strategies involved in rhetoric, it becomes all the more evident that productive, enlightening academic exchanges are a learned skill—and one of the most highly prized skills we can instill in students.

Discussion stems (what we might also call *sentence starters*) offer students easy-to-follow models that elevate discourse. They train students to think logically, reason, and support their ideas with evidence so listeners can follow their thought process. The sentence starters also provide students with bridging language that invites others to jump in and express support of, disagree with, or suggest an augmentation to another's view. The goal of using such stems is to make them, eventually, a natural part of student conversation. Practice and repetition can reinforce the value of the stems, but over the course of a year or of multiple years of learning, we hope to remove scaffolding such as reminders or handouts and simply hear these phrases enter the discussion routines of students.

You can also introduce specific stems that align with the types of thinking students are ready to develop. For example, if students would benefit from thinking more creatively and taking an intellectual risk, you might introduce the stem, "Maybe . . ." While it seems like such a basic word, it often opens up the conversation and the thinking to include alternative ideas.

In writing, sentence starters have been shown to help students structure thinking and focus on key elements (Institute of Education Sciences, 2016). You'll notice a similar effect in discussions if you introduce stems, provide opportunities to practice, and then provide opportunities for students to incorporate the stems throughout the year.

QUICK TIPS

- *Pace and practice.* Introduce discussion stems a few at a time and allow time for students to try them and get comfortable using them.

- *Model.* Use the stems yourself in your conversations.

- *Make visible.* Post the stems on anchor charts so students can refer to them as they talk.

- *Encourage paraphrasing.* Students may use their own wording if that makes them more comfortable.

GETTING STARTED

Set norms for your discussions up front. Before you begin the first discussion of the year, you should capture at least a few ideas from the class. You might ask, "How do we talk to and listen to one another?" List these on an anchor chart so that you can refer back to them, and treat the list as an evolving document, one to which you and your students can add as your discussions progress.

Start with a group of stems, then add. Instead of offering your students a wide array of stems to begin, start with a few, practice, and then add more. We suggest in particular giving students starters for introducing ideas, agreeing and disagreeing, and providing concluding thoughts or ideas as a first round for practice. Other stems can be added in subsequent conversations with explicit examples and practices.

Use partners or small groups to set up practice. Try having students use the stems initially with one or two others. Provide students with a short text and ask them to discuss a particular aspect of it. Or, without a text, pose an engaging issue students have been studying. It can also work well to display a visual problem of some kind and ask groups to discuss how to solve it.

Allot two minutes for quick preparation before students enter a full conversation. It helps students feel prepared to talk if they have a moment or two to think and possibly jot down an idea before being expected to enter the conversation. Students can use a stem to jot down an idea on a sticky note so they can remember what they might want to say.

Organize stems into categories. When offering stems, you can sort them into categories for what they do. An example of beginning stems follows.

ADDING ON	CHALLENGING IDEAS	CLARIFYING	REVISING IDEAS
Tell me more about that.	I disagree with ____ because . . .	What I heard you say was . . .	Could it also be . . . ?
What do you think?	That's a good point; however, . . .	Is it your position that . . . ?	Have we also considered . . . ?
To add on . . .	What if . . . ?	To be clear, are you saying that . . . ?	I used to think . . . but now I think . . .
Another example is . . .	Let's look at this from another perspective . . .	I'm confused when you say ____. Can you say more?	Let's focus on a different angle . . .

As you overhear students using stems that others would benefit from using, you can ask them to add the stems to a class chart. Over time the chart of stems can get quite large, so organization helps students know where to look. The following resource is color-coded so students can refer to it quickly even though it has several possible stems to choose from.

Introducing

Ideas:

I think . . .

I believe that . . .

In my opinion . . .

First, we need to consider . . .

Research:

The main point of this piece is . . .

I discovered that . . .

Based on my reading, I think . . .

Author _____ argues that . . .

Inference

This suggests to me that . . .

This could mean that . . .

I assume that . . .

Using Evidence

Ideas:

On page _____ it says that . . .

The text says . . .

My experience is that . . .

One statistic to consider is . . .

We might want to reread this part . . .

It's worth looking at . . .

I think this is proven by . . .

Extending

Connections:

This reminds me of . . .

This is similar to . . .

Another place this occurs is . . .

I'd like to contrast this with . . .

This is relevant because . . .

I want to add to that point . . .

Inquiries:

I'd like to know more about . . .

I wonder if . . .

I still have a question about . . .

One thing we haven't considered is . . .

We should find out if . . .

Responding

Clarification:

Do you mean that . . . ?

Could you repeat your point?

I'm confused by . . .

What does the evidence say?

Agreement and Disagreement:

I agree/disagree with . . .

I want to piggyback on that idea by . . .

I like this idea because . . .

I'm struggling with the idea that . . .

I see your point, but . . .

Paraphrase:

So you're suggesting that . . . ?

I want to repeat the idea that . . .

Another to say this might be . . .

Probing:

If that's true, then . . .

Part of that idea is . . .

Why are we assuming that . . . ?

Summarizing

Summary and Synthesis:

To bring this all together . . .

A big takeaway for me is . . .

I'm drawing the conclusion that . . .

Conclusion

My last thought is . . .

I've learned that . . .

I used to think _____

but not I think _____

KEY IDEA

Supporting students with sentence stems offers a concrete scaffold for how to begin a conversation, add on, challenge, and then offer alternative ideas. By offering this tool, teachers allow students to focus on the content of their ideas without getting stuck in how to begin saying them.

Gauge the moment when students move beyond stems. Keep in mind that some students may prefer the security of using a discussion stem while others prefer to not use the stems or to rephrase them in their own words. As long as each student is productively participating in conversation, don't compel everyone to use the stems. Generally, though, for all students, there comes a time when using the exact wording of a stem becomes an "autopilot" move, and that's when to switch it up with a new set of stems or stop focusing on them altogether.

Reinforce the purpose of stems by showing how they connect to writing. The structure of a conversation guided by stems can often mirror the structure of writing. Model and then give students time to use what they learned from stems in conversations by applying it in their writing.

HEADS UP

Use stems to get at big ideas. A discussion stem is only as good as the idea that follows it. At first students may practice talking by using the stems without much content (e.g., "I agree with Jill because I think she made a good point"). Over time, however, push students to use evidence and questioning to explore concepts deeply. Encourage the use of stems that focus on ideas that will elicit multiple points of view or possibilities of interpretation such as "Can we look at this idea in a different way?" or "What about considering ___ when we look at this idea?"

Encourage authenticity. You can vary the audience and purpose of discussions so students get practice recognizing when language is and is not appropriate for the context. For example, students might simulate a context like talking to an elected official or interviewing for a job. Encourage the use of language that matches the context students are speaking in. This can also be a time to use simulations (see Section 1, page 49).

Model and then step back. Sometimes in an effort to help a conversation get off the ground we stay too long and end up doing most of the work. If you choose to model, step into the discussion and then make sure you step back out so students can take back over. Use that time to listen and get some formative assessment information instead of accidentally taking over the conversation.

Think-Pair-Share

WHY?

Think-pair-share (Lyman, 1981) is a learning strategy that encourages active engagement. Here's an example: A science teacher lists several items on the board. She asks the class to take about 30 seconds to think about whether these items would best be measured by mass, weight, or volume. Then, students turn and confer with their table partners. Finally, she points to one group or partnership at a time and asks them to share their thoughts with the class.

The technique serves several purposes:

- It allows every student to process information.

- It can be done in super-quick bursts of half a minute or extended to a few minutes, but it's always brief and efficient.

- It compels every student to participate in a low-risk way.

- It creates space for students to prepare for a fuller, whole-class discussion by first practicing with a partner.

The chart that follows shows an overview of the three-step process and what the teacher is doing in each part.

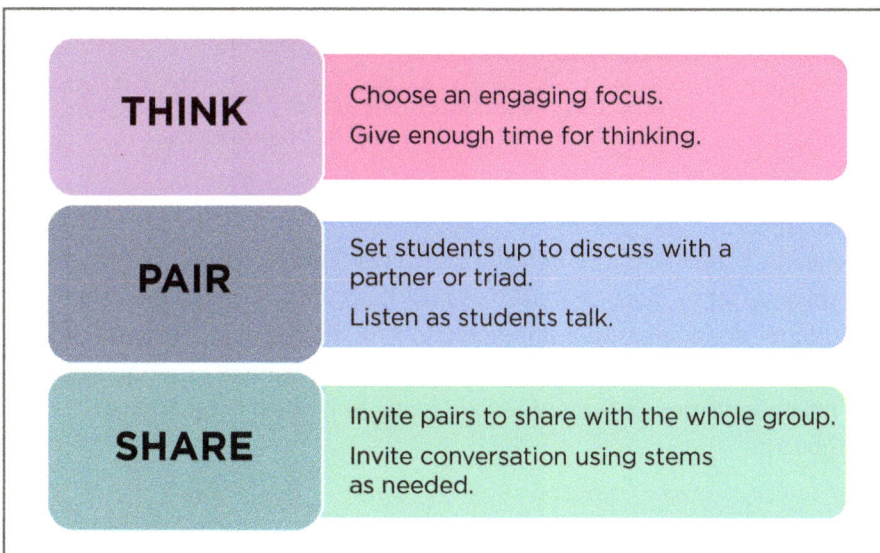

THINK	Choose an engaging focus. Give enough time for thinking.
PAIR	Set students up to discuss with a partner or triad. Listen as students talk.
SHARE	Invite pairs to share with the whole group. Invite conversation using stems as needed.

QUICK TIPS

- *Create comfort.* Group students thoughtfully with someone they will feel safe sharing with.

- *Mix it up.* As variations, try write-pair-share, draw-pair-share, or read-pair-share.

- *Listen and learn.* While students pair up, you can tune in to conversations as a form of formative assessment to see what they are thinking.

GETTING STARTED

Think:

Choose an engaging focus. As you plan, look for specific focuses that may lend themselves to the think-pair-share approach. Here are a few examples of material that works well with this strategy. Notice each type focuses on a different type of thinking.

TYPE	EXAMPLES
Lists	*Name some similarities between the American Revolution and the French Revolution.*
	What could you measure in your kitchen at home using the formula for volume?
	List the figurative devices you might look for in a poem.
	What are some factors that might cause a species to become extinct?
Open-ended questions	*Why do we value some works of art more than other works of art?*
	How does the work of engineers make a difference in your life every day?
	Why are love triangles such a popular device in young adult fiction?
Problem solving	*Which of the triangles on the board are congruent with one another, and why?*
	Why is the equation on the board incorrect, and how would you fix it?
	Read this thesis statement and think about how you expect the rest of the essay to be organized.

Give enough time for thinking. Make sure students have time to take out any readings, resources, or tools that may help them think. Offer time for them to jot down ideas in a notebook or on a sticky note. Let them know how much time they will have to think. Is it 30 seconds? Three minutes? Or, let students decide when they are ready to pair up by giving you a thumbs-up.

Pair:

Set students up to discuss with a partner. After students have had enough time to think, make sure they are ready to discuss. What follows are some common challenges and some strategies to help support students.

COMMON CHALLENGES	STRATEGY
Students sit staring at one another, and no one begins talking.	Make one partner even and one odd, and on even days that person goes first and on odd days the other person goes first.
Students each say one idea and then stare at each other awkwardly.	Bring out sentence stems and model how to use them to respond to what their partner just said.
One student dominates, and the other does not have time to say anything.	See the previous strategy on rotating who goes first, and teach students to kindly interrupt a person who is taking up too much space by saying, "I'd like a turn now please." Of course, also teach the person who dominates to recognize how long they have been talking.
After the first person shares the other person just agrees with no elaboration.	See the previous strategy on rotating who goes first, and teach students to bring up alternative ideas even if they do not agree by saying something like "Some people might think . . . because . . ." You can also teach them to add on their own evidence for why they agree.

Listen as students talk. Use the pairing time to walk around and listen as a form of formative assessment. Notice patterns in what students say. Jot down next steps or misconceptions you might want to address later on. Don't feel the need to correct during this time, but do notice future teaching that might be needed. You can also notice who would be a great pair to share first with the whole class because their ideas are compelling. Use the pair talk to plan for who you will ask to share with the whole group.

Share:

Invite pairs to share with the whole group. Purposefully choose how you want pairs to share with the whole group and also in what order. If you hear a group that is way off in their thinking, it is kind to all to have them listen first because they may change their thinking by listening to their peers. Here are a few engaging ways for more of the class to share:

- Have each pair add to a shared Google Doc or Jamboard.

- Use a jigsaw approach and form new pairs where the partners share with one another (see page 117).

- Have students get out of their seats, walk around, and share with multiple partners (the speed-dating approach).

- Conduct a student-led whole-class conversation while you, the teacher, scribe the big ideas they are saying on the board for all to see.

KEY IDEA

Think-pair-share is a quick method that can be used to support student understanding and engage students in collaborative learning.

Invite conversation using stems as needed. Bring out tools and scaffolds such as sentence stems and use them during the sharing conversations. The more students practice using them, the more authentic they will become. This also leads to a greater chance of transfer.

HEADS UP

Teacher wait time. Practice giving instructions for thinking and then forcing yourself to remain silent for an appropriate time. Research suggests, for instance, that most teachers wait less than one second before prompting responses to a simple question, while three seconds or more improves student processing (Rowe, 1986).

Skipping one or more steps. Often we simply skip to the "share" portion, expecting a rich class discussion or brainstorming session without giving students time to enter this thinking space safely and independently.

Pairing partners purposefully. Avoid pairing students who will serve as tutors and tutees, and instead pair up students who will work well together and also collaborate. Sometimes triads work best because they allow for more perspectives and opportunities for more ideas.

Lines of Positionality

WHY?

Imagine what would happen if you simply threw the following statements out to a class of students and asked them to discuss each one:

- It should be legal and accepted for scientists and companies to genetically engineer plants for food crops. (science)

- Statistics are always misleading and can't be trusted. (math)

- There are no real standards for judging the quality of art; beauty lies in the eye of the beholder. (arts)

These statements have the makings for thoughtful student discussion—or a chaotic chorus of students talking past each other. To bring about the former, teachers can rely on line discussions and other techniques, which serve as guardrails toward civil discourse. During a very polarizing time in the United States, the ability to see a spectrum of ideas and truly listen is a valuable citizenship skill as well as a collaboration tool.

A line discussion lends structure and promotes the use of evidence, listening skills, and the respectful consideration of counterarguments. In the simplest form, a line is what it sounds like. Students line up (or perhaps post sticky notes on the board to mark their positions) according to how they feel about a topic. Then they discuss.

Line discussions do all of the following:

- Show that there is a spectrum of opinions in the class.

- Make explicit that it's not enough to hold a belief or opinion; we each have a responsibility to also share why we think as we do so others can evaluate the quality of this evidence and respond to it with countering evidence if they wish.

- Allow the teacher to balance discussion by choosing those with different opinions to speak.

- Encourage the use of evidence rather than agreement with the majority.

- Encourage listening skills and awareness of different perspectives.

Combined with discussion stems and norms for talk in your classroom, a line discussion is a simple but powerful means for accountability and comfort, two important factors for conversations that promote listening and learning (Gilmore, 2006).

QUICK TIPS

- Allow about 5 to 10 minutes of class time for a line discussion focused on a single question or statement.

- The teacher can become a note-taker (on the board or on paper) to track ideas.

- Choose discussion topics that you know will provoke a variety of student responses. But remember that not every topic has another side to it. Be mindful to choose issues that are research-based and relevant in the curriculum and ones that do not trigger traumatic responses in students. Avoid topics about identity and politics for this sort of activity.

GETTING STARTED

Almost any classroom could potentially result in a line that encourages students to talk and explain themselves with evidence. This is true despite the complexity of the question. A few types of lines of thinking questions are described in the table that follows.

TYPE OF QUESTION	EXAMPLES	LANGUAGE STEMS
Yes/no or agree/disagree questions	*I think we will prove our hypothesis in this experiment.* *I think Juliet should have been more distrusting of Romeo when they met.*	*I agree/disagree because . . .* *The conclusion is correct/incorrect because . . .*
Multiple-choice questions	*I think the word that best describes this character is misunderstood because . . .* *Of the presidents on Mount Rushmore, I think Lincoln was most effective.*	*Of the choices, ____ is best because . . .* *The most accurate is ____ because . . .*
Spectrums	*To what extent should we hold companies financially responsible for their carbon footprint?* *How much do I agree/disagree with the idea that . . . ?*	*Some people think . . .* *Others believe . . .* *One the one hand . . .* *The perspectives include . . .*

In any of these cases, it would be simple to have students show their thinking using a variety of methods; they could:

- Raise their hands.
- Draw a line on their individual papers and mark their own position on it.
- Put a sticky note on a line on the board to show where they stand.
- Literally stand in a line according to their opinions.

As you try out line discussions, we recommend paying attention to the following:

- *Be clear about instructions.* Setting up a line discussion is relatively straightforward, but it's important to be clear. Students like to know the rules: Do they have to choose a side? Can they stand anywhere

Variations on the Line Discussion

VARIATION	DESCRIPTION
Surveys	A survey is made of a group of discussion statements that focus on an overall idea, as in this example: • A comedy must have a happy ending. • A comedy must have an element of romance. • A comedy should not deliver a moral lesson. • A comedy must employ poetic justice. Students agree or disagree with each statement on a 3- or 5-point scale (e.g., *strongly agree, agree, not sure, disagree, strongly disagree*). Then they add up their total points and line up accordingly.
Four Corners	Instead of a straight line, four corners discussions allow students to move to one of four sides of the room. The four areas might represent responses to a single statement: *strongly agree, agree, disagree, strongly disagree*. They could also represent four choices in response to a question. For instance, in response to the question "What's the most important quality of an effective leader?" students might choose to move to corners labeled *strong communication, honesty and integrity, decisiveness*, and *ability to inspire*.
Get Off the Fence	This variation, rather than presenting discussion as a spectrum, intentionally polarizes: Students go to one side of the room if they agree with a statement, and to the other side if they disagree. Students who are uncommitted may remain in the center of the room, but they may not speak. After a discussion in which you call alternately on students from either side of the room, anyone in the middle must choose a side and explain the choice (thus generally validating the argument of someone else in the room).
Step In, Step Out	This activity also uses a simple agree/disagree format for discussion. Students stand in a circle. You read a statement or question, and those who agree or answer "yes" take a step forward, into the circle. They then turn around and face the outer circle and discuss the statement or question with one or more people who did not step forward. After a short time, the class re-forms a single circle and begins again with a new statement or question.
Opposing Lines	In this activity, students form two lines that face one another so that each student is facing one other student. Lines can be formed randomly for initial discussion, or you can use a spectrum line, taking the students on each side of the center point and having them form the two lines. Once the lines are formed, students discuss a topic or statement with the partner across from them. After a short time, one line shifts sideways so that each student faces a new partner (the person on the end comes back to the start of the line). Students can then discuss the same statement or question with the new partner or can address a new subject.

along the line? You may find it helpful to draw the line on the board and label the sides of the room. Try to remain consistent throughout a course—if one side of the room represents "yes," it should always represent "yes."

- *Allow processing time.* If you simply instruct students to move to a position in the room, more than likely they'll watch where their friends move first. Writing down a position or even just thinking about it can make it safer to take a stance and can also help solidify students' thinking.

- *Support outliers and dissenters.* It's tough to be the only person standing to one side of a line, or even part of a minority. At moments where students have obviously set themselves apart, offer subtle reminders of discussion norms. If no one stands to one side, that's a good time to ask if anyone would like to play devil's advocate and try to argue the position for the sake of argument.

- *Balance discussion:* Once a group has staked out positions on a line, make sure to balance the discussion by calling on students from different parts of the line and inviting them to respond to one another. Remember to encourage the use of evidence and references to class content. This part of the discussion process is where the teacher as facilitator becomes vital—how you validate student answers or ask for responses can easily send messages to students. Your goal should be to show approval of robust discussion without taking sides in the actual conversation. If you need to clarify the facts, make it clear that you're doing so and why.

- *Allow opportunities to change opinions:* Sometimes students change their minds about where they're standing, either because of what another student argues or just because they've had more time to think. You can invite this type of movement and ask students to explain why they've moved (more than likely, they'll validate the argument a classmate has made). You can also make it clear that such movement is allowed at any time, but that you may call on someone who moves to offer an explanation to the class. This reinforces an important life skill of being open to information and willing to change one's mind when deeper understanding occurs.

- *Follow up:* Thinking doesn't end just because the discussion ends. It's good practice to reinforce the ideas that come up in conversation quickly. Consider these possibilities:
  - Ask students to write down and respond to a point of view they heard during the discussion that challenged them or changed their thinking.

- Ask students to find evidence to support an idea from the discussion.
- Have students write down both an argument and a counterargument as an answer to the prompt—possibly in the form of a thesis statement.
- Have students compose questions that could extend the discussion.

HEADS UP

Some topics are just too controversial. Good classroom discussions are rooted in the curriculum. It's not wise to introduce a discussion on a topic where no students really want to change their minds, or that isn't rooted in what you're teaching, and you should be especially careful about political or religious topics. It's one thing to discuss how government should function generally because you're teaching dystopian fiction; it's entirely more precarious to ask if the current administration's policy is positive or negative. Some districts choose to send a letter home to families with the topics and inquiries students will engage in for full transparency.

It's hard to overcome group bias. It's not a bad idea to have a student or group play devil's advocate, but if you find yourself teaching a group that is almost entirely homogeneous in ideology, that approach may get old. Help students recognize the bias of the group early on and plan ways to counteract that bias if necessary—then avoid discussions that will just be so one-sided that they're not profitable.

It's hard to overcome your own bias. Students can make outlandish comments, or comments that *you* think are outlandish but that others might support heartily. It's tempting to correct, ask questions, or outright disagree with students, and on occasion this might be warranted. While you don't want to let egregious comments (such as hate speech or language that makes any student feel unsafe) into your classroom, it's also not helpful to seem too biased yourself.

KEY IDEA

Line discussions add energy and structure to classroom conversations about nuanced topics. Use line discussions to create more balanced discussions that lead to further investigation.

QUICK TIPS

Fishbowls

WHY?

A fishbowl discussion includes an outer circle of students who listen actively as a smaller, inner circle talks about an issue, topic, or text. The inner circle holds a student-run conversation while the rest of the class sits around them with the purpose of learning from and with them. It positions the students as models for their peers. It is engaging for both groups—the inner and outer circles—because they each have an important role. The teacher's job is to set up the fishbowl and listen and learn alongside their students.

According to a 2017 study by Effendi, fishbowl experiences had a positive impact on students' self-efficacy in speaking. Self-efficacy is a key element needed in learning according to Bandura (1997) and is the belief in one's ability. The beauty of the fishbowl discussion is that it promotes whole-class engagement with structure and purpose.

- Some students speak while others listen.

- Everyone gets a turn to talk.

- The teacher listens as well.

- Students learn from each other and serve as models.

- To make this work most effectively, students sit in a circle.

GETTING STARTED

Arrange your classroom. The fishbowl requires two circles—an inner circle and an outer circle—arranged as shown in this image. The number of chairs in the center circle may vary depending on the size of your class, but we would suggest that the inner circle contain at least three and no more than five chairs.

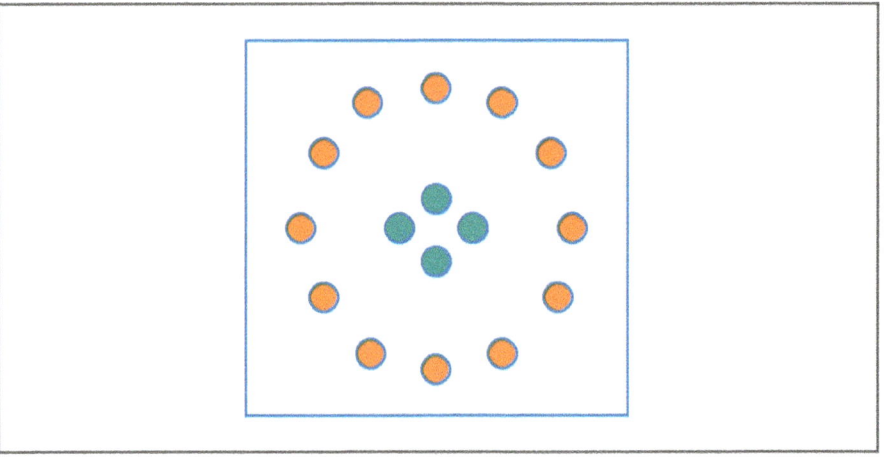

Explain the routines. Some examples include:

- Only students in the inner circle may speak.

- No student can be made to leave the inner circle until they have the chance to speak at least once (and have finished speaking).

- After a student speaks at least once, anyone may tap them on the shoulder. A tapped student returns to the outer circle, and the tapper takes their place.

- A student may not reenter the inner circle until two minutes have passed.

- These rules apply to the teacher as well.

Pose a question or claim worth discussing. As with a line discussion, both extremely worded statements and nuanced questions will work in a fishbowl scenario. You can even add questions to clarify parts of an existing question. With some classes, the overarching question is enough. Generally, though, you want to be ready to pose clarifying questions for students as the discussion unfolds. You can also stop the discussion partway through and allow students to compose their own questions, then use those to continue the conversation. Listen for the types of thinking students are doing and, if needed, pause and ask a different question that sparks a new type of thinking. For example, if students are stuck retelling a historical event's facts, redirect the conversation by asking "What might have happened if . . . ?" to encourage more creative thinking.

Support the discussion. The primary role of the teacher in a fishbowl discussion is to keep the talk productive. The role you should *avoid* is the typical role of teacher in front of a classroom in which you might respond to each individual student comment. The role you *should* play could involve a number of tactics:

- Change the question or statement when discussion starts to lag.

- Remind students of the norms or of the need to take notes as they listen to others talk.

- Insert your voice from the *outer* circle only to correct nonfactual information or to remind students of the discussion norms.

- Tag into the discussion yourself, make a point or ask a question, and then make it clear you should be tagged out.

- Pause the discussion so students can research, compose questions, write down thoughts, or catch up on note-taking, then restart the conversation or discuss whether everyone is expressing similar ideas and why. Be cautious not to pause more than one or two times per fishbowl group.

KEY IDEA

Use the fishbowl approach to structure conversations in which students listen to and learn from one another.

- Give time warnings before you conclude so that the discussion ends after all of the students have had a final chance to speak, being sure to wrap up with writing, reflection, or final thoughts.

- Take the last minute or two for everyone to jot down their thinking so they have the final word of the day. This allows for students to stay engaged until the end and also creates a written artifact to come back to and revisit later on.

Pivot if you need. When the fishbowl format flounders, it's often because the topic isn't engaging or complex enough for students to feel energized by. Sometimes students also struggle if the question is phrased in a way that all students are in agreement. Conversation fizzles quickly when there are no alternate points of view to explore! When that happens, consider these alternative moves:

- Rephrase the question to see if that jump-starts talk.

- Allow those in the inner circle to tap *out* and force someone to take that seat who might enliven things again.

- Require that everyone participate at least once (but be careful not to create anxiety and undermine the quality of the discussion—know your students and what works for them).

- Just stop using the fishbowl entirely if the conversation is floundering, and try a different method.

HEADS UP

Don't let the discussion continue too long. Any discussion that fosters repetition of the same ideas instead of new points of view will lead students to disengage. It's important to get the timing of a fishbowl discussion right so that all ideas get expressed without going on too long.

Don't let some comments go unchecked. Given this level of autonomy, students may make statements that others find offensive, that are unfounded, or that lack support. If this happens, step in, don't let it continue, and reflect on how to learn from the experience.

Promote participation. Assign all students to be individual question leaders (with preparation time) so that everyone knows they will start a fishbowl discussion at some point during class.

Jigsaw

WHY?

Just like jigsaw pieces fit together to help you see the whole of the picture, the jigsaw collaboration structure helps students make connections between aspects of a topic and form larger ideas and interpretations. Jigsaw is a research-based cooperative learning technique developed in the early 1970s by Elliot Aronson and his graduate students. Aronson claimed his comparison studies between classrooms that used the jigsaw method and those that did not were powerful. Students in the jigsaw classes did all of the following:

- Expressed less prejudice and negative stereotyping

- Were more self-confident

- Reported liking school better

- Were absent less often

- Showed academic improvement

- Scored significantly higher on objective exams (Jigsaw Classroom, n.d.)

There are several steps in a jigsaw that can be broken down into a few main parts. First, students develop a level of understanding in one part of the topic. Then, students meet with others who studied the same topic to share what they learned, clarify, and fill in any gaps. Next, students are grouped with others who studied a different part, and they teach one another. The group discusses connections, ideas, and interpretations from across the different parts.

During the discussion phase at the end, listen for the types of thinking students are doing. Use the discussion to highlight the types of thinking you would like all groups to develop by using students as models for one another. Pause the class and ask a group to share their example out loud. Jot down thinking you hear that would be helpful for students to add to their notes. This builds confidence in the group that is modeling and serves as teaching for the others.

GETTING STARTED

1. **Teachers Prepare for the Jigsaw**

Frame the jigsaw with an overarching question. Start with an inquiry question that the class will all be studying. Make sure students understand and are interested in the topic. This can be the same essential question that you began the unit sharing with students. See page 26 in Section 1 for essential question ideas.

QUICK TIPS

- Use a variety of reading materials that are engaging and accessible to students. Look for videos, podcasts, articles, and infographics for students to read in order to develop expertise with an aspect of a topic.

- Students can be paired up and work together on a jigsaw part. This may be helpful for students who are not yet independent, who are in the early stages of language acquisition, or who are hesitant to teach their peers. Each pair takes on one part of the topic instead of individuals.

- Tie the jigsaw texts and topics back to the unit goals and essential questions so students see a clear connection between their part and the whole picture of the class study.

Break down the question into parts. Some questions are much easier than others to break down and see the parts. The following chart can help you think through the parts based on the type of question the class is studying.

IF THE ESSENTIAL QUESTION TOPIC IS FOCUSED ON:	YOU MIGHT BREAK IT DOWN BY:
People	• Background • Traits • Key accomplishments • Conflicts • Time period • Perspectives
Places	• Location • Norms • Climate • Time period • Customs • Conflicts
Events	• Time period • Key figures • Choices • Causes • Effects
Cycles	• First step • Second step • Third step • Fourth step
Relationships	• Power/hierarchies • Connections • Pressures • Tensions

Gather texts for students to study. These texts can be articles, infographics, videos, podcasts, picture books, photographs, news, and so on. This is often called a text set. Incorporating different types of texts makes students more engaged and helps students who are not reading on grade level still have access. Many teachers use Padlet to curate and share the texts by topic with students. A screenshot of a Padlet collection follows.

2. Students Begin Developing Expertise in One Area

Form home groups of students. The home group is who the students will eventually be working with. Each student in the home group should select a part of the topic to study. In the Padlet example, that means one student will study a short story, one will study music/poetry, one will study nonfiction articles, and so on until each student has a category to focus on.

Students study texts and take notes on key information. Students have time in class (and possibly also at home) to read, view, and listen to the texts that match their part of the study. They can take notes so they are developing a deeper understanding and also to be prepared for a discussion with their groups. This is a good time to reteach or model some of the graphic organizers that are explained in detail in Section 3 on page 78. When students select their own graphic organizers to take notes, they develop more ownership and understanding and are more engaged in the process.

Students meet with peers who studied the same information as they did. Before meeting back with the home group, students can gather with others who studied the same texts and topic and share what they learned. This is a helpful scaffold for students to clarify confusions, confirm key information and ideas, and fill in any gaps they might have missed. Encourage students to add to their notes during this meeting.

3. **Students Collaborate With Their Home Groups to Understand the Whole Picture**

Students meet with their home group to share and teach each other what they learned. Make sure to remind students of the essential question they are studying so they don't lose their focus. Each student is now bringing their "puzzle piece" to the group and helping all of the members understand their part. Teachers can support students during this time by reviewing some structures and tools that are already in place. For example:

- Using sentence stems to help teach your peers (see page 101)

- Showing their graphic organizer or another visual (see page 78)

- Using the moves of the share-out (see page 126)

Students create an artifact that shows all of the pieces together. After each person shares and teaches about their part of the essential question, students in the home group can look for connections, big ideas, and claims they can make that go across the texts and topics. Large chart paper, Google Docs, or Jamboard can be used so students can visually document their understanding and show their thinking about the essential question.

An optional final step is for all students to gather from across the home groups for a whole-class conversation. This is a time for students to hear the claims each group made, to follow up with questions and connections, and to ask for clarification on claims that are different from their own. Any of the collaboration structures already mentioned in this section can be used during the final conversation. Of course, you can also keep tension in the class steady by keeping the Jamboard or whole-class conversation going across days, rather than wrapping it up right away. One way to engage students is to maintain tension so that students look forward to coming back to class tomorrow.

HEADS UP

Make sure text sets show a variety of perspectives on a topic. This will help students develop critical thinking and empathy skills and encourage them to consider whose perspective they are learning about.

Involve students in adding to text sets. In many cases, students can work to add a text to the collection of texts. This can be tied to research standards and offer an opportunity to teach about reliability of information (especially on the internet).

Keep a good thing going. When making home groups for the jigsaw, consider keeping groups together for more than one experience. It can take time to develop the relationship and collaboration to jigsaw well, and having multiple opportunities to learn together across a unit can help.

KEY IDEA

Using a jigsaw method of collaboration helps students learn the value of each member's contribution as well as how a team can work together. It is a helpful structure to use when there is a lot of content and not enough time to dive deep into it all.

QUICK TIPS

- Take time to explicitly state the reasons why you are doing a silent conversation instead of more typical out-loud conversations so students are clear on the purpose.

- Use silent conversations as written artifacts that you can refer back to as formative assessment. Look for ideas, interpretations, and misunderstandings you may want to teach more into.

- When introducing silent conversations, connect the learning to social media or text messages so students understand they already are quite proficient in this medium.

Silent Conversations

WHY?

Consider how many conversations we have online that exist entirely in written form: the comments we make under social media posts, the thumbs-up or -down, the emojis. Conversations in classrooms can also take on a silent, written form.

Carving out time and space for conversations to happen more slowly in writing slows down thinking and makes it more likely that students will really consider what is worth saying. Because writing takes more effort and more time, it makes participants really decide what is most important. Having a silent written conversation also helps students who are more visual learners who struggle to keep up with fast-paced oral conversations.

During a silent conversation students come prepared with an idea they want to explore. Each person in the conversation has a corner of the big paper to jot it down without talking. After a minute or so the teacher says "Rotate" and the paper gets rotated so that each student can read and respond to a peer's idea (Gilmore, 2006; Goldberg & Houser, 2017). The teacher keeps asking students to rotate until the paper comes back to the original writer, who gets to have the final word in their corner. An image of students participating in a silent conversation follows.

Silent conversations are helpful at key points in a unit to reinforce different kinds of thinking. These moments include:

- When conflict arises

- Where there are multiple interpretations

- When inquiry has led to students making initial claims

- When students are getting ready for debates or formalized claim-based writing

- When a new perspective is included

GETTING STARTED

Like any form of collaboration, silent conversations work best when there is time to prepare, participate, and reflect.

Prepare

- Prepare for silent conversations by getting clear on your idea before the conversation begins. Give students a few minutes to prepare by reviewing the question, looking back at notes and previous work, and thinking about what they want to say.

- Make resources from other forms of conversation available such as sentence stems that students are already familiar with. Tools can be taken out and reviewed before beginning.

- Connect the purpose of the conversation to the larger unit goals. Remind students how this conversation connects to the larger context of what you are studying and exploring.

Participate

- Set a timer, and every minute students jot down an idea or read and respond to what others have written in their corner.

- Encourage students to use different-colored pens or markers so each person's response can be distinguished.

- Let students know they can use arrows, emojis, and intentional font choices to show emotion that can usually be communicated more easily with our voices.

- Remind students to refer back to evidence and use sentence stems to clarify their points.

- End with each person getting to read all of the responses to their original idea and having a final word. They may change their mind or take a firmer stance.

- While students participate, you can be the timekeeper and also notice student moves such as who is using the stems chart and who is looking back at a text to get a quote. This gives you insight into a student's process.

Discuss and Reflect

- After a few minutes of the silent conversation, it ends with a discussion out loud. Students can talk about any of the following:
  - How did your thinking change?
  - What ideas were you exposed to that you were not thinking about before the silent conversation?
  - What are you left thinking more about?
  - What ideas do you want to talk about now?

- If time allows, students can choose one thread from a corner to talk about at length. Then they can reflect upon why that idea brought up the most thinking.

- Wrap up with a final whole-class conversation or have each group add to a class Jamboard with their big ideas.

Variations to Silent Conversations

VARIATION	DESCRIPTION
Digital silent conversation	Each group can have a page of a Jamboard and use a similar structure. Students each add a sticky note idea and then rotate through responding with their own colored sticky note.
Extend the conversation across days	Students can keep the conversation going by responding to each other on a regular basis. Students who prefer written communication with the ability to think and respond at their own pace have time to really think before having to immediately respond.
Jigsaw silent conversation	Adapt the original conversation by having a person at each corner who has an idea about something different. For example, each corner idea may be about a different character or historical event. This form of conversation is less about consensus and claim formation and more about teaching one another key ideas.

HEADS UP

Start with low tech. While it is tempting to move everything to digital tools, there is something about physically writing and moving the page that sets a different tone and is highly engaging for students. Start with large paper and only move to digital tools if and when students seem ready.

Tie the conversation to unit essential questions. Silent conversations are great ways to bring back the unit essential questions on a regular basis.

Make the silent conversations available for ongoing reference. Since the conversations are written down, the ideas can be referenced in more formalized debates and writing assignments and be used as a tool to look back at details and ideas. Make sure all students have a copy (even if it is just a photograph) of the paper so they can use it as a resource.

KEY IDEA

Creating space for silent, written conversations allows students to slow down and prioritize thinking, collaborate and respond intentionally, and develop resources to refer back to.

QUICK TIPS

- *Consider space:* It is helpful to have a dedicated space for students to share with the whole class. It may be the space you model from. If you have access to a document camera or SMART Board where students can project their work, it makes it easier for all the listening students to see the example.

- *Make everyone the model at something:* Try to make sure all students get the chance to share out across a unit or every few months. This means that everyone in the classroom is positioned as a model at something. If a student is struggling with content, they can still share out a learning habit or mindset that others could benefit from hearing about.

- *Build in quick rehearsal:* When students are new to sharing out or not yet comfortable with it, add in a quick rehearsal with them so they know what they will say and show. You can even offer a sentence stem or two to help them get started.

Share-Outs

WHY?

While there is so much benefit to teacher modeling, sometimes seeing a peer model something or show an example has a bigger impact. Research, especially in science classrooms, has shown that peer instruction improves learners' conceptual understanding (Mazur, 1997). Students sharing their process and work samples with one another makes the learning seem less daunting and more attainable. Because students who are just learning something are not yet fluent, they are slower and more aware of their steps. This makes it easier for them to describe to others not just what they did but how they did it. Finally, students are often more engaged when listening to a classmate explain something because the way they speak is more directly relatable to many students.

Share-outs tend to happen in the last few minutes of a class. It is a time to gather students together after they have been working on their own. The share-out can happen in small groups or within the entire class. Teachers select who will share either by using observations during class or by asking for volunteers who want to share something they tried and learned. Generally, you want to choose students to share out who can positively model a type of thinking the other students would benefit from hearing and seeing.

Share-outs tend to have a predictable structure so students feel safe and clear on their roles.

TEACHER'S ROLES	SHARING STUDENT'S ROLES	LISTENING STUDENTS' ROLES
• Select or facilitate deciding who will share.	• Show something they tried or learned.	• Listen actively.
• Set up the class for what to look and listen for as the student shares.	• Explain their process for what they did and how they did it.	• Think about how the process of the student who shared is similar to and different from their own.
• Model active listening and learning.	• Reflect on what worked and what they might suggest others try out.	• Reflect on a next step they might try after learning from their peer.
• After the student shares, ask them to reflect on what they may try to do next.		

GETTING STARTED

Take time to model how to share out in a way that helps teach others. You might even create a chart that students can refer to as they prepare.

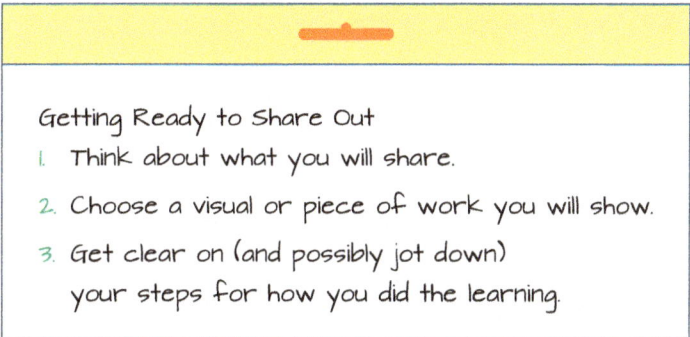

Getting Ready to Share Out
1. Think about what you will share.
2. Choose a visual or piece of work you will show.
3. Get clear on (and possibly jot down) your steps for how you did the learning.

Once students are up in front of their peers, it can be helpful to have a very basic chart of the moves they might take. What follows is one example.

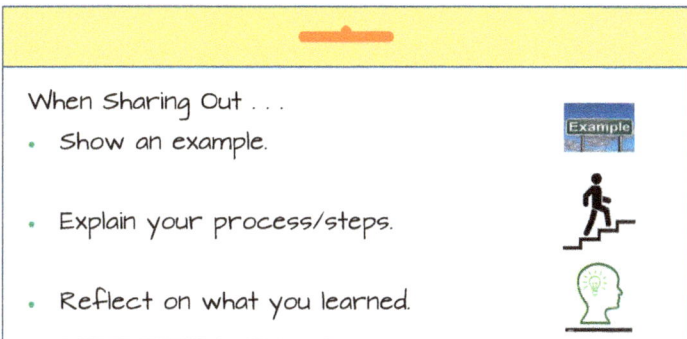

When Sharing Out . . .
- Show an example.
- Explain your process/steps.
- Reflect on what you learned.

So that share-outs don't become too repetitive, it can be helpful to consider the many different types of share-outs. While each content area might have their own variations based on unit goals, the following list can apply across curricular areas. Try to mix up the types of share-outs and think of them as either reinforcing past teaching, preteaching something that will be coming up soon, or adding depth to a class study. Share-outs should be engaging opportunities for students to learn from one another.

Different types of share-outs include the following examples.

TYPE	EXAMPLE
An idea and how it was formed	"After reading about gravity and then doing the falling experiment, I realized that the objects speed up as they fall. I am thinking that . . ."
A strategy and its steps	"Here are my steps for organizing the data in this chart: First, I created categories for the data. [*Points to screen example on the board.*] Then, I sorted the data by category. [*Points to the example again.*] Next, I . . ."
An example that aligns with unit or personal goals	"Since one of my goals for this unit was to finish reading the entire book, I made a calendar for myself and mapped out how much I could realistically read each day. [*Shows the calendar.*] I also found a quiet spot and put my phone away. Some days I easily read, and other days I was just too tired."
A challenge and how it was solved	"I know we were supposed to work together on planning the evidence for our arguments, but I don't like working with others. Usually I just do it all myself, or I do nothing at all. Since I was paired up with my friend, I wanted to at least try to work together. We took some time to meet and just talk about how we wanted the work to go . . ."
A question to add to a class inquiry	"Based on the video my group watched and the conversation we had after, we were wondering about how we could impact our parents' generation to actually stop using so much fossil fuel. Can we add that to the class list of questions?"
A resource or tool and how it was helpful	"I made this sticky note to help me keep track of who all the different characters are in this book. I jotted their name and a few traits under it. I keep the sticky note inside the front book cover so when I get confused I can quickly look at it. This might help some of you too. [*Shows note.*]"
A misstep or failure and what was learned as a result	"I tried to eat healthy all week like we discussed in class. We made that meal plan, and I was going to try to cut back on eating so much sugar. I totally failed the first day. I didn't eat breakfast, and then I got to school and ate some candy my friend had and got a headache. I need to eat breakfast, so I am going to try . . ."
Feedback given and how it was helpful	"I was stuck and had no idea how to end my writing. Then my partner suggested I go back and read some of the endings to short stories that I liked. I was still stuck, and then I thought about some songs I like and that helped. I noticed a lot of them end with a line that repeats, so I tried that. It totally worked."

HEADS UP

Look for strengths. One of the most important benefits of share-outs is they provide opportunities for you to notice the strengths in all students. It can be so habitual to identify what students are not yet doing or need help with, but taking the time to notice a strength builds strong teacher–student relationships and helps you identify who to call upon to share. Keep a clipboard handy with a class grid so you can jot down student strengths as you notice them. This can serve as future planning for who you will ask to share and what you suggest they share. When meeting with students one-on-one, you can comment on what you were enthused to see.

Celebrate learning, curiosity, and risk-taking. When we always ask students to share who got the right answer (often without too much effort), we are reinforcing being right and could be setting students up to have a fixed mindset. Make sure you are also looking for students who tried and persevered, who displayed curiosity, who attempted something that didn't quite work out but learned along the way, and who reflected on what to do differently next time.

Mix up small-group and whole-group share-outs. For some students, sharing in front of the entire class would be so painful. Small-group share-outs allow others to learn from them in a more intimate way. Also, you can differentiate the share-outs by grouping students who would benefit from hearing from certain peers.

KEY IDEA

When students have the chance to share and teach one another, it leads to more engagement and confidence. Adding in a few minutes per class period across the week makes this a powerful structure for building trustful relationships.

Reading Routines

5

Reading closely is essential in every subject area, yet many secondary students need more explicit instruction on how to read carefully. By developing some core reading routines that can be used across the day and curriculum, students are more likely to develop independence, ownership, and deeper understanding. The following table shows how reading routines support student thinking. No matter what content areas you teach, taking time to teach all students various ways to engage with text is time well spent.

READING ROUTINE	HOW STUDENTS MIGHT USE THE TOOL TO DEVELOP INDEPENDENT THINKING	HOW STUDENTS MIGHT USE THE TOOL TO DEVELOP CREATIVE THINKING	HOW STUDENTS MIGHT USE THE TOOL TO DEVELOP PROBLEM-SOLVING THINKING	HOW STUDENTS MIGHT USE THE TOOL TO DEVELOP EMPATHETIC THINKING
Close Reading Page 133	Interpret passages and support your thinking with textual evidence	Develop your own interpretations and theories based on the text	Use the text to gain insight into a problem or challenge	Make connections to people, places, ideas, and events
Identifying Central Ideas Page 137	Form your own ideas about the author's central ideas and whether they were supported by evidence	Choose a purpose for reading that pushes you to consider new central ideas	Use central ideas across texts to answer open-ended questions and challenges	Understand the author's perspective through their main ideas

(Continued)

(Continued)

READING ROUTINE	HOW STUDENTS MIGHT USE THE TOOL TO DEVELOP INDEPENDENT THINKING	HOW STUDENTS MIGHT USE THE TOOL TO DEVELOP CREATIVE THINKING	HOW STUDENTS MIGHT USE THE TOOL TO DEVELOP PROBLEM-SOLVING THINKING	HOW STUDENTS MIGHT USE THE TOOL TO DEVELOP EMPATHETIC THINKING
Using the Elements of Nonfiction Page 142	Use the elements of nonfiction to form your own ideas about a topic	Put elements of nonfiction together in new ways as you research a topic	Use different elements of nonfiction to understand the parts of a problem	Use the elements of nonfiction to understand different perspectives
Independent Reading Page 147	Choose texts and topics that are important to you to explore	Develop your own interpretations and theories based on the text	Use what you learned from reading texts you chose to develop new ideas to address current problems	Put yourself in someone else's shoes and understand the other person's experiences
Reading Clubs Page 151	Share and compare your thinking with others	Work together to develop new ideas and revise past ideas	Work together to offer solutions based on the text	Listen to and respect alternative thinking that is different from your own
Learning New Vocabulary Page 157	Consider the impact of word choice	Use words with intention to explain and explore thinking	Find precise language to reexamine challenges in a new way	Understand the meaning and feeling behind others' word choices

Close Reading

WHY?

In a classroom with honors chemistry students, Gravity asked them to show and explain how they read to prepare for class. She explained she wanted honest answers and they would not be penalized for being frank. Students looked around the room and smirked with a "How honest should we be?" expression. Gravity was not their teacher, and as a result, they did begin opening up.

At first one student at a time shared, and then it was an explosion of conversation with students laughing and talking over one another. They explained that they went first to the questions at the end of the chapter or the worksheet and then they went back into the text to find the answers. They shared strategies such as looking chronologically in the text because most questions are written in the order of the book. Not one student in an *honors* chemistry class actually read the text.

Gravity followed up by asking how well this method worked. They all said they were getting good grades. She then asked how well they understood the material and was met with downcast eyes. It turns out they didn't really understand and relied heavily on their teacher's notes and lectures to make any sense of the material.

The next day she asked students how they read their text messages from friends or potential love interests. They rolled their eyes, a few blushed, and then they shared the many ways they read these messages over and over again looking for clues about the intent, the tone, and what was implied in the message. For example, what emojis were used? Were any capital letters used and, if so, in what way? How long did it take the person to respond to the previous message? Were there photos? Of what? What did they mean? The students often shared messages with friends and discussed what they thought each message meant. They sought out alternative perspectives and considered what the evidence showed. The list went on. They certainly paid very close attention to the ways they read these text messages.

When we say that students need to be taught how to read closely, we are assuming they don't already have the skill set. What this series of conversations, and many experiences after, showed is that students do know how to read closely when they are invested—when they see the value of taking the time to do so. Instead of teaching students how to read closely, we can begin by naming for them what they already know how to do, as well as why and how they can apply those same skills to academic content, and then give them the space and discussion time to practice.

GETTING STARTED

It is helpful for students to get the hang of close reading in three phases. The first phase is building confidence and clarity with reading everyday messages and naming what they already know how to do. The second phase

- *Let students in on what "close" reading means.* Beers and Probst (2012) explain, "Close reading should suggest close attention to the text; close attention to the relevant experience, thought, and memory of the reader; close attention to the responses and interpretations of other readers; and close attention to the interactions among those elements" (pp. 36–37). They go on to explain that close reading should bring the reader and the text close together.

- *Keep it student-centered and interactive in its vibe.* According to Lehman and Roberts (2014), powerful close reading instruction must:
  - Raise engagement and joy, not diminish it . . .
  - Lead to student independence, not dependence on teacher's prompting . . .
  - [Be] designed in response to the strengths and needs of your students (p. 5)

- *Encourage reading with more than one lens.* As students become more proficient at reading closely, they can read with two lenses or reread with a different lens in mind. This helps them analyze and interpret a text with more depth.

is applying that same skill set to a text you read together as a class. The third phase is to practice the same skill set independently in a class text.

Building Confidence in Everyday Close Reading

Since most students are proficient close readers of text messages, body language, video games, and social media posts, you might want to begin by showing students what they already know how to do.

1. Begin by projecting a sample text message thread (or photograph, or social media post, etc., that is school appropriate).

2. Then, ask students to read the text/image with a lens in mind. Choose a lens that will support the type of thinking you want students to try out.

Some Lenses for Closely Reading Across Disciplines

ENGLISH	SCIENCE	SOCIAL STUDIES	MATH
Author's purpose	Author's purpose	Author's purpose	Author's purpose
Tone	Theory	Perspective	Problem variables
Character relationships	Method	Time period	Relationships
Themes	Phenomenon	Power	Procedure
Craft	Implications	Historical significance	

For example, a teacher may ask students to read this thread through the lens of the author's purpose—why did the author write this?

3. Students can pair up and discuss what they notice with the lens in mind. Ideally, they reference the text as they talk. You might want to offer some feedback when you hear students going back to the text with examples.

4. Next, ask students to notice how they formed their thinking (in this case around the author's purpose).

5. Create a class chart of what students noticed. Make sure the chart is not text specific so it can be referred back to with other close reading texts. Here is one example.

We noticed the author's purpose through:

- Word choice
- Punctuation choice
- Font choice
- Image choice
- Sequencing of information
- Thinking about who has power
- The feeling it created
- What was said
- What was not said

---

6. Wrap up by explaining that this sort of close reading is something they are doing all the time and it will also be an important part of how you read texts in your classroom.

Apply Close Reading Skills to a Content-Area Close Reading Experience

Taking the experience of closely reading an everyday text, do the same series of steps using a class content-area text that you read together.

1. Project a text (or part of a text) on the board.

2. Give a lens to read the text through.

3. Pair up students to talk about what they notice.

4. Ask students to reread thinking about *how* they formed their thinking.

5. Discuss and chart what you found together.

You can reread the same text through a different lens and see how it changes what students notice and think about. Later on, when students have more experience, they can choose their own lenses for reading too.

KEY IDEA

Make sure students have a clear purpose for why they are reading with a lens in mind. Modeling this process and making sure there are multiple opportunities for high-success and playful practice sets students up to be much more engaged in more dense and challenging texts later on.

Plan Time for Students to Practice Close Reading on Their Own

Once students have some success reading closely as a class, offer regular opportunities for students to practice close reading on their own, using the same process. As students develop proficiency, make sure to offer more and more choices. Students can choose the text, or the part of a larger text, to read closely or the lenses to analyze through. Richer class discussions happen when a variety of perspectives are brought into the conversation in this way.

1. The student chooses a text (or part of a text) to read closely.

2. The student selects a lens to read through.

3. The student reads and jots down what they notice.

4. The student rereads considering how they formed that thinking.

5. Students come together in small-group or whole-class discussions to share their thinking.

HEADS UP

Create joyful engagement. Asking students to closely read a text over and over again can take away the joy and engagement. Rereading a few times with different purposes and lenses and participating in discussions can create engagement. Ask students for feedback and adjust the texts you are using, the focus areas, and the format.

Make it a flexible exploration of thinking. Allow for flexibility—it's okay that the steps may change as students add a step in, take one out, or change the order. This means they are matching the way they are closely reading the text and task. We want this to develop so students can take more ownership of the process. If you find that you are overly focused on making sure students only follow the steps exactly how you first taught them, you may need to model how to flexibly adapt to the current reading context.

Teach what to notice. Students often need a lot of modeling and collaborative practice to know *what* to notice and where to look. For example, in trying to infer a character's emotional state or agenda in a scene, a reader might zero in on a character's diction in dialogue. Is it open? Guarded? Who is speaking in short sentences? Why? What might a longer soliloquy suggest? What has the author added in terms of speaker tags as further clues? Have fun helping students become like forensic geologists of texts. Help them notice what *isn't* there, too—for example, in a nonfiction article, how thorough was the author in quoting experts from multiple and diverging viewpoints on the topic?

Identifying Central Ideas

WHY?

We have all asked students what they think the central idea is in the nonfiction text they are reading only to be met by blank stares, wild guesses, or rereading of a fact directly from the page. So many students struggle to figure out central ideas even though we teachers have been teaching it year after year since at least the first grade. When students summarize a text or pick a fact directly from the text, it reveals some misunderstanding about what *central* means and often what we mean by *idea*. Sometimes the best way to figure out that students struggle with identifying central ideas is by simply looking at their notes. If they list everything as equally important down a page (or write nothing at all), it often indicates they are not yet synthesizing small facts to figure out central ideas. All of our disciplinary standards emphasize this skill, so in theory students should be able to transfer their learning from English to social studies to science, and yet that is often not the case.

Proficient readers in any discipline know what to focus on as they read. They recognize what is important and less so. In the book *Mosaic of Thought*, Keene and Zimmermann (2007) explain, "There are at least three levels at which proficient readers make decisions about what is important in any text: the whole-text or idea level, the sentence level, and the word level" (p. 210). Of course, what is important depends on the purpose for reading. Students need to have a clear purpose for reading a text, ideally not just to get a good grade in a class, but an authentic purpose that stems from curiosity and inquiry.

Many students struggle to determine importance because they are unclear of the purpose of the reading. It is essential to have that clear purpose because it focuses the reader as they read and helps them note key words (word level), connections and explanations (sentence level), and bigger ideas and themes (whole-text level). At first you, the teacher, may set a purpose for reading, but over time you can also invite students or groups of students to collaborate to generate their own purpose and/or inquiry questions to pursue.

GETTING STARTED

Every time we ask students to read a text, whether it is a whole-class text or a text they chose, the first step is to make sure they have a clear purpose. The chart that follows gives a few examples. You can refer to your own standards and curriculum maps to make a chart like this for your students. Either students can select a purpose from a chart, or you can assign them one. No one can read a text for all of these purposes at once. A chart like this might

QUICK TIPS

- *Make it intentional.* Every reading needs to have a clear purpose that all students understand.

- *Invite students to set the agenda.* Create opportunities for students to create their own purpose for reading based on their curiosities to increase engagement.

- *Define the terms.* Explain what *central* means and what *idea* means so students recognize the difference between a summary or tiny fact and a central idea.

- *Take it easy.* You can practice this skill with accessible texts such as visuals, videos, or even pop culture examples before asking students to try it with challenging academic texts to develop student confidence.

grow across the year, and you can add the bullets one at a time until you have a collection students can choose from. Underscore for students that readers in so-called real life often go into a piece paying attention to a few facets (purposes) and then may reread to examine additional aspects. They then "roll up" all they have noticed to form a nuanced, comprehensive take on the text. Lessons on determining central ideas are all part of learning to read closely; when we select a purpose for reading, we often then look through a few distinct lenses to discover what we want to discover.

Some Purposes for Reading True Stories

- Understand the human experience.
- Learn more about character relationships.
- Interpret themes that can be used in our own lives.
- Examine how settings impact characters and how characters impact settings.
- Connect past events to current events.

Some Purposes for Reading News

- Understand the *what*, *why*, *when*, and *how* of an important event.
- Make connections between key events.
- Interpret motivations.
- Identify perspectives and bias.
- Recognize who has power and how they use it.
- Form our own nuanced ideas about controversial issues.

Once students know their purpose for reading, it is helpful to model a lesson like the one that follows. Through this modeling, you can actually show them the thinking that happens in order to determine central ideas across a section of a text.

A central idea tends to have three parts to it, and most of us have only ever taught students two of the parts. Here are the three parts that help students understand what a main idea consists of:

Part 1: The general topic

Part 2: The specific category (or part of the topic)

Part 3: The idea

Yes! A central idea has to have an idea in it. Many students think the central idea is a word or phrase such as "causes of the war," but a central idea is a sentence that contains all three parts. Let's take a look at this example. Say we are reading a section from *Top Dog: The Science of Winning and Losing* by Bronson and Merryman (2013):

> For decades, social science theory has professed that, in competition against others, our motivation is extrinsic, while when we perform an activity on our own, motivation is *intrinsic*. Thus the concern is that competition skews people to be extrinsically motivated, and they'll lose touch with their natural intrinsic love for an activity. But it's not really that simple: some people *love* to compete. For them, competing makes an activity *more fun*. A study of distance runners, for instance, reveals that those who compete at the national level (for money, medals, and glory) have the greatest intrinsic motivation. It's only the intermediate runners who are externally focused. Similarly, ROTC cadets learning to shoot rifles develop more love of it—and more respect for their opponents—when they are part of a team-based competition than when they are taught to master and excel at rifle shooting without competition. (pp. 18–19)

Part 1: The general topic: Motivation

Part 2: The specific category or part: Competition

These first two parts are right in the text. The tricky part comes with part 3—the idea. This is because the reader has to read the facts and synthesize an idea about this topic and category. In other words, they have to consider, "What idea can I form about this topic and category based on the information given?"

Part 3: The idea: Some people are intrinsically motivated by competition, and it allows them to both love what they do and excel at the highest levels.

The confusion lies in the common misconception that the central idea is the specific category. Students tend to stop at part 2 and think the category is the central idea. A typical student response could be "Motivation and competition is a central idea," but this is missing the idea part. When you model the process, it helps to create a visual of what your notes might look like as you read.

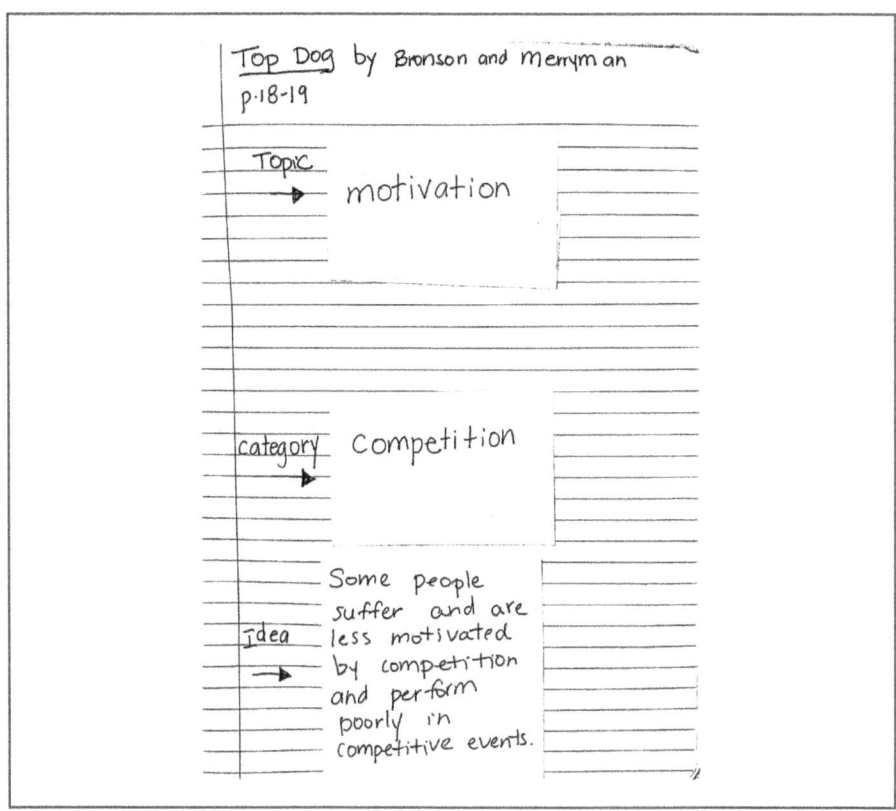

After modeling how you figured out central ideas of a section, you can look across sections and form a larger central idea across an entire chapter or text. Place each section's central ideas side by side and show how you connect them to form an even bigger idea.

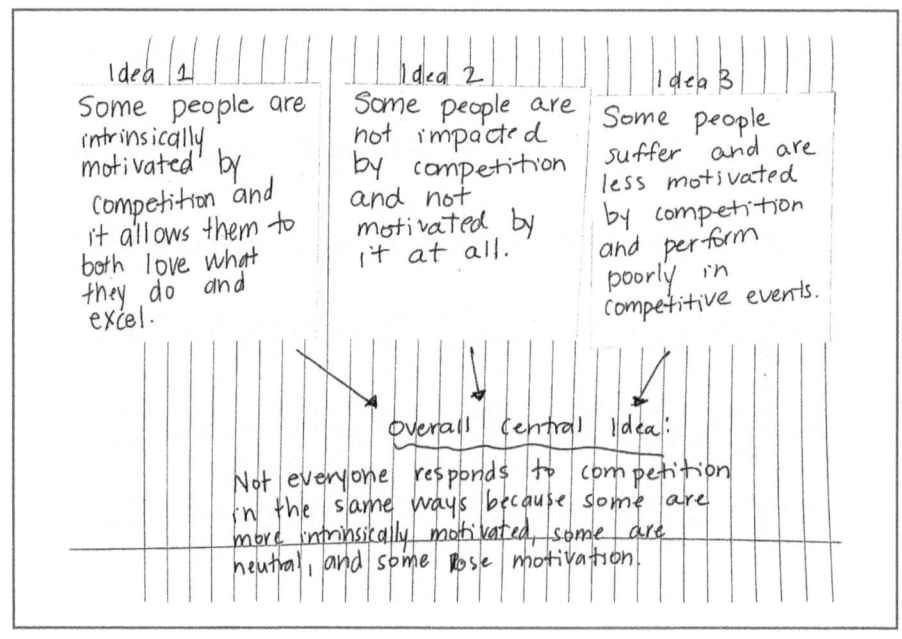

HEADS UP

Keep it open-ended. Be aware of turning central idea development into a multiple-choice experience. While every state's tests do ask a multiple-choice question about a central idea, teaching students first how to generate their own will lead to deeper understanding of the content and the strategy itself. Once they can create their own central idea, you can teach them how to do similar work on a state test question.

Acknowledge there are multiple central ideas. Students will form their own language and ideas based on the details of the text. As long as the central idea is supported by the information in the text, there can be more than one idea. Comparing students' ideas and talking about why they formed the ideas yields rich conversations and deeper content knowledge than trying to get everyone to agree to one idea (which is often our own). Students often come up with compelling ideas that we can all learn from (even us teachers).

Lead with curiosity. Encourage students to bring their own authentic curiosity to texts when deciding on a purpose for reading. This is especially helpful when conducting research and inquiries. Two or three students may be reading about the same topic with the same texts but have different purposes, thus leading to different ideas.

KEY IDEA

When teaching students to identify central ideas, make sure they have a clear purpose for why they are reading. Model the three parts: general topic, specific category, and idea.

- *Talk through and
  walk through each
  type.* Introduce
  each type of
  nonfiction and
  model how to
  identify the way it
  is organized.

- *Challenge students.*
  Offer opportunities
  for students to
  preview a text and
  determine what
  type it is and why.

- *Include real-world
  examples.* Bring
  in social media
  examples for
  access and also
  to help students
  be more critical
  consumers of what
  they read on the
  internet.

- *Tap into the power
  of text sets.* Offer
  as much choice
  as possible and
  consider using
  text sets when
  asking students
  to learn about a
  topic. A text set
  is a collection
  of texts that are
  often presented in
  different formats
  all around the same
  topic.

Using the Elements of Nonfiction

WHY?

Most of what we read is nonfiction. We read the news, sports scores, weather reports, recipes, directions, and maybe even a beloved blog. By middle and high school, students have been immersed in reading nonfiction for years, and this can lead to skillful reading but often also leads to misconceptions about what nonfiction is and how to read it (Stewart & Correia, 2021). First, nonfiction is not just "not fiction" as the name implies. There are many subcategories and types of nonfiction just like there are in fiction. Let's break it down into a few organizational categories.

Narrative Nonfiction

Narrative nonfiction covers true stories. They often sound like fiction in voice and tone and include popular genres like memoir, biography, historical accounts, and true crime stories. They also include travel blogs and first-person-narrated investigative reporting. It is helpful for students to know that some nonfiction is actually written like a story and to use the strategies they already know for reading fiction here as well.

- Get to know the characters who happen to be real people.

- Follow the events and pay attention to sequence.

- Look for conflicts and resolution.

- Think about themes you can take with you from reading these true stories.

Expository Nonfiction

This is typically what students picture when they hear the word *nonfiction*. Expository texts are not written like stories and instead are organized by categories and subcategories of information. Most standards call these informational texts. Popular forms of expository nonfiction include manuals, textbooks, news articles, infographics, wikis, and informational articles. If students try to read expository nonfiction the same way they read narratives, they are often confused.

First, students need to preview a text and recognize that it is an expository piece. They can look for text features such as subheadings and the table of contents for clues. Once they establish it is written in expository format, they should read looking for the categories and details instead of characters and conflicts like in narratives.

Persuasive Nonfiction

Many texts students read are persuasive in nature. Persuasive texts are based on claims an author is making and on reasoning to support them. These texts include essays, document-based questions, debates, op-eds, letters, speeches like TED Talks, advertisements, commercials, and some TikTok videos and Instagram posts. Students need to be fully aware that any text may be trying to persuade them to take action or think differently, but with persuasive nonfiction, the writer's primary purpose is to get the reader to agree with their point of view. Instead of reading for events (narrative) or categories (expository), students must read for claims and reasoning supported by evidence.

Mash-Up Nonfiction

Much of what is written does not fall neatly into one category of nonfiction and is actually a mash-up of a few different types. For example, most textbooks start with a true story (narrative), then switch to headings and details (expository), and may have an open-ended question or controversy box (persuasive). Once students have skill in identifying each type of nonfiction and reading them in ways that match the type, they can identify mash-ups and shift the ways they read each section of a text based on how the type changes throughout. Other mash-ups may include blogs, podcasts, YouTube videos, nonfiction books, and documentaries.

NARRATIVE	EXPOSITORY	PERSUASIVE
• Recounts a story (true or fictional)	• Presents information or explains ideas and concepts	• Presents a side stance or claim • Provides evidence to support that claim or refute the counterargument
• Organized by a series of events	• Organized by category	• Organized by supports and reasoning
• Goal is to engage the reader in the journey of the characters	• Goal is to be a teacher to others	• Goal is to prove a side

NARRATIVE	EXPOSITORY	PERSUASIVE

☐☐☐☐☐
↑↑↑↑↑
──────
↓↓↓↓
☐☐☐☐
	Topic
	  Category
	   • detail
	   • detail
	   • detail
	   • detail
	  Category
	   • detail
	   • detail
	   • detail
	   • detail
		Claim
		  Support A
		  Support B
		  Support C

GETTING STARTED

Once students know there are different types of nonfiction and how to identify the type, conduct a class inquiry into what they notice about the features of each type. Later you can go back and show them how to use each feature to understand the text. Here is one example that is partially filled in. It is more engaging to create a chart like this with students rather than simply lecture and hand it to them; plus, students may notice features you have not preplanned.

SOME NARRATIVE NONFICTION FEATURES	SOME EXPOSITORY NONFICTION FEATURES	SOME PERSUASIVE NONFICTION FEATURES
• Timelines • Photographs • Story-sounding language • Descriptions • Dialogue • Historical figures presented as nuanced individuals	• Table of contents • Headings and subheadings • Images with captions • Word boxes • Diagrams • Procedures • Tables and charts • Maps • Data/statistics	• Speaking directly to the audience/readers • Call to action • Claims and counterclaims • Expert quotes • Data/statistics • Adjectives and adverbs that show perspective or bias

After learning the types of nonfiction and conducting an inquiry into the features of each, students often benefit from learning how each feature helps them as readers and learners. Some are obvious and can simply be stated, while others are more nuanced and may need modeling and guided practice to be understood. Here is one example of taking a feature (subheadings) from a chart and modeling how to use it as a reader.

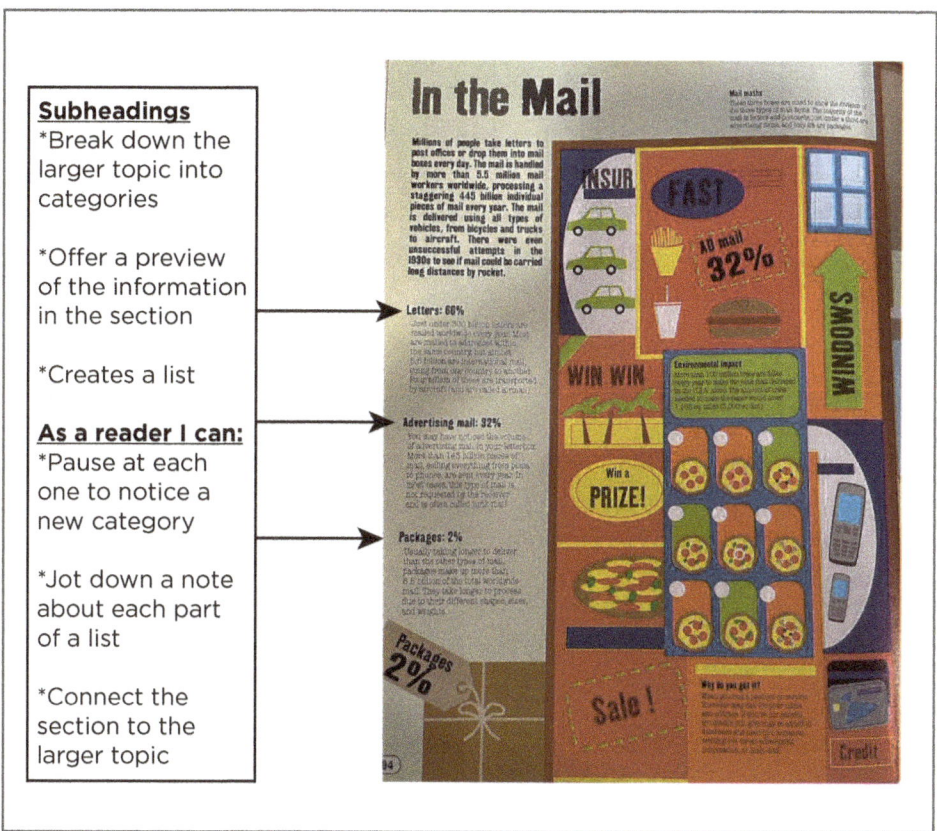

Subheadings

*Break down the larger topic into categories

*Offer a preview of the information in the section

*Creates a list

As a reader I can:

*Pause at each one to notice a new category

*Jot down a note about each part of a list

*Connect the section to the larger topic

Source: Esposito (2014).

When we model what a feature does (top of callout) and how we use it as a reader (bottom of callout), we make our process clear so students can access complex texts on their own, applying what we've modeled. It can look like magic to less proficient readers if we do not explicitly show them both parts.

As students read, they use the features of the text to preview what the text is likely about and how it is structured. This helps them choose a note-taking structure that will align with the text. For example, if students only ever list when taking notes but the text is really set up in a cause and effect structure, a list won't be that helpful. Instead, using a T-chart will be helpful because they can see the relationship between the parts. The following table could be helpful to create with students so that they match the way they read and take notes to the way the text is set up.

IF THE TEXT IS SET UP AS . . .	YOU MIGHT TAKE NOTES WITH . . .
A series of events (narrative)	• A timeline • A story mountain • A storyboard
Categories of information with headings (expository)	• A box and bullets (box the category and bullet the details) • A web (center the category in the circle and connect the arms to details) • Sticky note details sorted by category and given a heading
A claim with evidence (persuasive)	• Reverse box and bullets (bullet the evidence and then box the claim) • A three-column chart (claim/evidence/counterclaim) • Four quadrants (claim in box 1, evidence listed by reasoning in each of the other three boxes)

KEY IDEA

The goal is for students to recognize the type of nonfiction text they are reading by previewing it first, then to have them understand how to use the features to read deeply and closely.

HEADS UP

Use high-interest texts. If we only use textbooks and worksheets for nonfiction reading, students tend to zone out or skip the reading altogether. Reach out to colleagues and library media specialists to locate places that have a variety of high-interest texts. Some popular sites include:

- www.newsela.com
- www.nationalgeographic.com
- www.history.com/news

Avert boredom by spicing it up. We are hardwired to enjoy an element of controversy, and adolescents will enjoy reading nonfiction more if we spice up the text engagements with variety and revelation. So ahead of any unit, search for current scientists and historians who are unearthing truths suppressed from earlier textbooks. Podcasts are a terrific source for this material. Documentaries too.

Check for understanding. Even when using highly engaging texts, whether print, visual, or auditory, you need to check to ensure all students are feeling steady in terms of comprehending the information. If students are confused and can't comprehend, they won't be able to think deeply. Widen the ways students can demonstrate understanding by making sure they can talk, write, or visually represent the information.

Independent Reading

WHY?

According to the Pew Research Center (Gelles-Watnick & Perrin, 2021), 23 percent of adults surveyed in early 2021 had not read a book in part or whole in any format—print, digital, or audio—in the past year. These adults are the products of our schools; it's imperative that we cultivate students' reading skills and habits so that it's no longer the case that reading declines as children move up the grades. The publisher Scholastic has decades of research showing that around age nine students begin reading less. This means by the time students enter your secondary classrooms many do not read regularly and have not for years.

While there is no single cause for this lack of reading, and no simple answer to helping students read more often, one place to start is with book access. "Giving kids access to books may be one of the most overlooked solutions to helping ensure kids attend school with the tools they need to succeed" (Wong, 2016). Book deserts are locations, often underresourced neighborhoods, where children lack access to books when they are outside of school. Many studies have shown what happens over the summer when students do not read, often due to lack of high-quality book access, and refer to this as the summer reading "slide" (Allington & McGill-Franzen, 2018).

While book deserts are typically thought of as a lack of access to books outside of school, more and more schools themselves are finding they lack adequate books to engage students. The National Center for Education Statistics (2011–2012) has reported that 17,000 schools in the United States do not have a certified full- or part-time librarian on staff. When visiting schools and speaking with students, we often find that the school library has gotten rid of hundreds or even thousands of print books and used the space for more computers and technology. Schools themselves are not often providing a rich environment for students to browse for and select books they can and want to read.

By creating collections of books that are housed in their classrooms, students have access to and support from their teachers to read. English classrooms may choose to organize books by author, genre, topic, or theme and build in time for students to recommend books to one another. Teachers become reading mentors who help students find something they care about and are interested in reading. Social studies and science classrooms might have books and other texts organized by topic. Teachers and students can collaborate on creating text sets around a research question and help students find something to read that connects to the class theme. Smaller collections in a math classroom that highlight math figures in biographies or real-life math applications in architecture, home design, and sports

can pique students' interest and engage them in reading more. If we want students to read, we need to provide both easy access and some mentorship in finding texts they are interested in. Classroom libraries provide one concrete pathway in helping students read more, engage more with the content of your classroom, and see the value of reading in their lives.

Classroom libraries:

- Show students that books and reading matter.

- Create a place to build community around reading.

- Offer immediate access to books and other reading materials.

- Include opportunities for book recommendations from student to student.

- Provide mentoring by the teacher for how to find a text you want to read.

- Create student choice in what is read to meet curricular goals.

- Make differentiation possible for students to find the text that most appeals to them.

GETTING STARTED

What you need to start a classroom library is included in the following table:

WHAT YOU NEED	WHY YOU NEED IT
Print books with varying genres, styles, and lengths (novels, graphic novels, biographies, realistic fiction, historical fiction, romance, horror, dystopian fiction, narrative nonfiction, memoir, short stories, poetry, spoken-word videos, etc.)	Many students still like to pick up a hard copy of a book to preview it and read it. By offering different genres, teachers invite students to explore interests and challenge themselves to read in new ways.
Various **functional texts** (recipes, magazines, directions, gamer manuals, sports pages, etc.)	To get hooked on reading, some students need to begin with shorter and often more recognizable texts with immediate applicability to their lives. Sometimes even experienced and engaged readers need a shorter text they can read in one session and go do something with what they learned.

WHAT YOU NEED	WHY YOU NEED IT
Bins with student-created labels	When books are organized in bins with the covers facing out, it often piques students' interest in reading more. With the books organized in bins, students can take out a whole bin and browse the bin to help them make a choice. For example, if they know they want a memoir, they can go to that bin, or if they know they like humor, they can go to a bin that is labeled "Funny Books." When students create the labels, they are often more interesting and engaging to their peers. Instead of a bin labeled "Horror," they may choose to call it "Books That Will Keep You Up All Night," or a memoir bin about social justice warriors might be labeled "Role Models" or "Upstanders."
QR codes with links to **digital texts**	Within a book bin you might have a card with a QR (quick response) code that links to digital texts such as blogs, videos, podcasts, or articles that connect to the theme or topic (see suggested websites in the next section on reading clubs). Many students find it more accessible to watch a video or read a blog before attempting to read an entire book on a topic. Teaching students how to read a video or listen to a podcast can transfer over to reading a book or article.
Shelving	You will need some place to store and display the books. Some schools invest in shelving on wheels if a classroom is used for multiple subject areas, and the shelving can move with the teacher/class.

KEY IDEA

By investing in classroom libraries, we build community spaces that offer students choice and support. Students are more likely to apply learning standards on their own because they are engaged with the text in their hands.

HEADS UP

Turn "I don't have time" to a can-do "make the time" attitude. Without time in school to read and support from adults, many students become aliterate—they can read but choose not to. Independent reading is a regular practice, not a once-in-a-while event where students choose the texts they want to read. Students read for extended periods of time and meet with other students and teachers to share their reading identities, preferences, opinions, and ideas. It is where the joy and appreciation for reading comes to life each day, and how students develop important reading stamina.

Connect what students are choosing to read and the standards we are required to teach. For example, the Common Core State Standards for science and other technical subjects include "cite specific textual evidence to support analysis . . . summarize complex concepts, processes, or information presented in a text . . . and analyze how the text structures information or ideas" (Council of Chief State School Officers & National Governors Association, 2010). These standards can and often need to be practiced in a text that a student reads on their own in order for ownership and transfer to occur.

Tighten the loop between reading skill development and independent reading. Offer students time to apply what they learned in a whole-class text in a text they chose and read on their own. This also sets students up to perform better on standardized tests where they will be asked to read a new text you have not read to or with them and apply the standard on their own.

Reading Clubs

WHY?

In her best-selling professional book *Cultivating Genius*, Gholdy Muhammad (2020) explains the importance of literacy being a social and community-benefiting experience. She researched Black literary societies and claimed, "Literacy was to be developed in a socially constructed environment so that new ideas and information learned from texts could be shared and spread among one another and those in the community" (Muhammad, 2020, p. 26). This research is relevant today as entire social movements have been created and spread by teens who are using literacy to literally change their worlds. Rather than lean into apathy and complacency, many teens are energized to solve local, national, and global challenges through collective questions, research, and sharing. For just a few examples of teens who are leading social movements, check out the following articles:

- "Youth Activist Movements of the 2010s: A Timeline and Brief History of a Decade of Change" by Jameelah Nasheed (2019)

- "6 Youth-Led Political Movements to Inspire You to Vote" by Claire Trageser (2020)

In many ways, social media has helped students form communities around common issues and topics in the same ways we would like them to work together within the walls of our classrooms. Online social communities that create safe and productive spaces tend to:

- Encourage participation.

- Have a common vision and clear goals.

- Create norms that help everyone feel welcome.

- Invite discussion and civil discourse.

- Support co-creation of ideas and artifacts.

- Be open to learning and changing one's mind.

We can create similar safe and productive spaces within our classrooms where students want to show up having done the reading, ready to share, by learning ways to bring students outside of school literacy experiences more explicitly into the school in clubs (Cherry-Paul & Johansen, 2019).

Research on adolescent development and engagement also points to the need for students to feel connected to both the content and community when learning about a topic. By forming small groups of students into

QUICK TIPS

- Take student input when forming the clubs so students work with peers with a common interest. But, help build bridges between students by also putting students together who may not choose one another, yet will likely work well together.

- Begin each day's lesson by modeling a reading or discussion strategy for how to do things such as take notes as you read, list topics you want to discuss with your club, listen with an open mind, and challenge ideas without making it personal.

- Try to offer choice of what students read with their clubs as long as it connects to a larger class essential question, topic, or theme. This will help with engagement and lead to more interesting whole-class conversations as well.

- Let students know ahead of time how many days/weeks they will have to read the texts they choose so they can make a schedule for how to finish in time (see template on page 152).

reading clubs, they can develop safe spaces to come together to discuss content and build community. A reading club:

- Is a group of three to six students.
- Centers on peer-led discussion.
- Focuses on a common text or essential question or issue.
- Meets consistently and regularly across several days or weeks.
- Is mentored by a teacher who offers modeling and coaching.

Teachers might choose to use reading clubs when they are beginning a research unit, studying social issues, or about to begin a complex text in any subject area that takes more than a week to read and understand. While there are many variations, one common way for reading clubs to work follows.

1. The teacher introduces the essential questions, topics, or themes the class will be studying.
2. Students are placed into a reading club.
3. Each reading club meets to make a plan.
4. Students have some class time to read independently and some class time to meet to discuss their reading with the clubs.
5. The teacher rotates who they meet with. They spend time listening to each club to offer coaching of what they may want to do more or less of as a group.
6. A few times across the reading clubs unit or at least at the end, the entire class comes together to have a larger discussion about what they found.

A template like this can be helpful for students who are just getting started. They agree on how many pages they will read by each date ahead of time to pace out the text. Each time they meet, they can end by adding in what they will focus on talking about in the next session.

DATE	PAGES	DISCUSSION FOCUS

GETTING STARTED

In the table that follows we'll look at each part of the reading club process as well as what the teacher may be doing and what the students may be doing. Depending on your group of students, each step in the process may take a single period or a few weeks to complete. A suggested time range is listed here, but use your curriculum and your students to map out your timeline.

STEPS IN THE PROCESS	STUDENTS' ROLES	TEACHER'S ROLES	KEY LESSONS
Introduce the focus 1–2 days	Add their own questions, discuss their interest in the focus area, jot down some curiosities they want to explore	Introduce the essential questions, topics, or themes on a class chart	How to find your own curiosities on a larger topic
Reading clubs are formed 1–2 days	Consider who they may work well with and list some peers they may want in their club	Take student feedback and form clubs around those who have common interests and who you think will work well together	How to create club norms for how we will work together, include everyone, and show up ready to learn
Reading clubs make plans 1–2 days	Create a plan together that includes the goal(s), a schedule of when they will meet, and a list of what they will read if they are given some choice	Model how to create plans and then meet with each club to go over their plan before they get started	How to set goals together How to pace out reading a text on a calendar How to choose texts you can and want to read to reach a goal
Students read independently 5–15 days	Follow the reading plan and use some class time and some out-of-class time to complete readings (Students might alternate between a reading day and a discussion day.) Take notes as they read to bring ideas to discuss to the club	Offer time in class for students to read While students read, have conferences with students to support them and get to know them better	How to take notes in ways that match your goal and help prepare you for club discussions

(Continued)

STEPS IN THE PROCESS	STUDENTS' ROLES	TEACHER'S ROLES	KEY LESSONS
Reading clubs meet to discuss **5–10 days**	Meet having done the reading and prepared some notes to discuss Usually clubs meet every other day and alternate between a reading day and a discussing day Listen to club members and add on and challenge ideas	While students discuss, listen and take notes on what you find Reinforce strengths by naming what you hear students doing well Model strategies they may not be using yet Coach students to try a discussion strategy	How to share information that goes with the focus How to synthesize common ideas across the texts How to interpret information to form central ideas How to provide support and evidence to explain an idea
Reading clubs come together in whole-class discussion **1–2 days**	Move into a large class circle and share out what each group learned from their clubs—central ideas, claims, and lingering questions Ask for support or thinking from other clubs to add to their own club's ideas	Set up the conversation but spend time scribing what students say to create a written record in class chart form instead of leading the conversation yourself	How to ask for ideas from others How to synthesize ideas across multiple texts How to revisit essential questions and use information from many texts to answer them

Popular Sources for Engaging Reading Club Texts

Reading clubs do not have to be focused on full-length books. Many students thrive with shorter texts and visual or auditory texts. The following lists provide resource ideas when curating texts for clubs.

- **Poetry:** Educator Brett Vogelsinger in his 2023 book *Poetry Pauses* makes the following suggestions for finding excellent poems:
  - **Sign up for daily poetry emails.** The *Writer's Almanac*, Poets.org, and the *Slowdown* podcast emails provide a wealth of student favorites.

○ **Follow #TeachLivingPoets on Twitter.** A devoted group of teachers will introduce you to an ever-expanding online library from living poets with an emphasis on social justice.

○ **Explore *Poetry 180*.** Though it is almost 20 years old, this compendium is still available for free on the Library of Congress website and provides a poem a day for the whole school year.

○ **Get involved in National Poetry Month projects.** The Geraldine R. Dodge Poetry Program, National Council of Teachers of English, and Poetry Foundation each have their own.

• **Podcasts:** There are podcasts for almost any topic. Check the rating to be sure it is appropriate for your students' age group. Some popular listens include:

○ **Storytelling:** TheMoth.org is a curated collection of true stories told live. Note that some are focused on adult content, so preview the ones you will use first.

○ **Psychology and the human condition:** HiddenBrain.org takes complex ideas and breaks them down into actionable ideas and steps.

○ **Understanding phenomena:** Radiolab.org takes a topic and explores it from multiple perspectives and angles, with firsthand interviews and research.

○ **Informative talks:** NPR, via www.npr.org/programs/ted-radio-hour/, offers short TED Talks that are thematically connected with extra interviews and commentary to offer more context.

○ Of course, there are also true crime and advice columns as well as interview shows. If you crowdsource students, they can likely recommend some of their favorites.

• **Infographics:** Visually representing data is engaging and creates accessibility. Many students enjoy reading and discussing infographics across content areas. You can find entire books of them as well as websites. Just like with any website source, make sure to teach students how to evaluate the credibility of the sources they read. A few examples follow.

○ Subscribe to the website www.slow-journalism.com or find the book *An Answer for Everything: 200 Infographics to Explain the World* (Delayed Gratification, 2022).

○ Read *Talk Nerdy to Me* (Fullman et al., 2014).

○ DailyInfographic.com allows writers to submit infographics on a variety of topics.

○ The website https://history.infowetrust.com is full of historical infographics.

○ Google a topic and the word *infographic*, and you will likely find dozens of examples.

KEY IDEA

By forming reading clubs, students form communities of curiosity to read and discuss with. They also see the value in reading to pursue a question and discussing their thinking with others in order to develop big ideas.

HEADS UP

Turn past challenges into today's teaching. Many teachers may be fearful of "group work" because of their own past experiences as students that were less than ideal. Make a list of those pitfalls and then teach students how to avoid them. For example, if you found yourself doing most of the work and resented your peers not "pulling their weight," you can teach students how to make sure everyone does the reading and note-taking. Discuss what happens when someone doesn't do the reading to come prepared. In most cases the student who did not come prepared can read on their own while the rest of the club members discuss until they catch back up. Use those negative past experiences as possible teaching points to help your students fare better than you.

Set up clubs of collaborators, not tutors and tutees. Avoid the tutor–tutee dynamic as it leads to frustrations for all. Instead, group students by interest and/or differentiate the groups and the readings themselves so that all of the students in the group can read them. Or make audio versions available for students who cannot yet read the text on their own but still are interested in a particular text.

Focus on goals and essential questions. If you are choosing to use reading clubs, lean into the focus on essential questions instead of a single text. Doing so invites more genres in. For example, instead of teaching a unit on *The Giver* (Lowry, 1993), students could be in reading clubs around a variety of student-chosen texts that are all dystopian or are all exploring the question "How do settings impact people, and how do people impact settings?" Your goal as a teacher would be to teach students how to answer this question with whatever text they chose to read instead of teaching each text's plot. Another example would be in science to explore the question "How do technologies impact the ways people live?" Each club could be reading about a different technology, and the teacher could be helping students form central ideas and synthesize information instead of learning the facts about one text and technology.

Learning New Vocabulary

WHY?

In order to read and comprehend texts across the disciplines, students need to develop vocabulary strategies that allow them to not just decode a word but understand what it means in context. Context matters because many words are used differently across subject areas and topics. Teaching words in isolation does not lead to deep learning or transfer to authentic contexts (Dutro & Moran, 2003), but daily practice has also shown how often students memorize words and pass a test and then forget them the next day.

Tiered System for Choosing Vocabulary to Teach

Tier 1 Words	Everyday Words	• learned from everyday use
Tier 2 Words	Academic Words	• learned from reading a lot • across different subject areas • not in everyday speech
Tier 3 Words	Domain-Specific Words	• connected to the subject area or content • mostly in informational texts • help us understand key concepts

State standards across disciplines call on students to have strategies to acquire new vocabulary and use it in speaking and writing. What we focus our teaching on needs to focus on both acquisition and use. The following list highlights key standards for vocabulary:

- Determine or *clarify the meaning* of unknown and multiple-meaning words or phrases, choosing flexibly from a range of *strategies.*

- *Use context* as a clue to the meaning of a word or phrase.

- Consult general and specialized *reference materials*, both print and digital, to find the pronunciation of a word or determine or clarify its precise meaning or its part of speech.

- Demonstrate understanding of figurative language, word relationships, and *nuances in word meanings.*

- Distinguish among the *connotations* (associations) of words with similar *denotations* (definitions).

QUICK TIPS

One of the challenges in teaching vocabulary is knowing which words to choose to teach. Researchers Beck et al. (2002) developed a tiered system that helps teachers make their decisions (see table at left).

- Their research claims there is no need to teach tier 1 words.

- Tier 2 words ideally are taught in every subject area because they are often used frequently. Some examples of tier 2 words are *interpret, analyze,* and *predict.*

- While tier 3 words are often taught in subject areas and highlighted in textbooks, they should not be the only words students focus on. Teachers can teach tier 3 words and also, often more importantly, model strategies for how students can figure out the meaning of tier 3 words as they read and listen to texts on their own.

These standards call on all teachers to help students clarify the meaning of words using strategies, using context, consulting reference materials, recognizing nuance in word meanings, and distinguishing connotation and denotation. While taking the time to teach all of these aspects might seem daunting, you'll find that students are much more likely to learn the content of the subject area when they acquire these skills.

GETTING STARTED

Teach Students to Acquire Vocabulary

Model and chart how readers figure out new vocabulary.
Create a chart like the one that follows and model how you use each strategy in the context of your class reading. You may want to model a few per day, but it may be overwhelming to model them all at once.

Strategies for Figuring Out Unfamiliar Words

- Break up words into parts (prefix, suffix, root).
- Look at etymology.
- Use context clues.
- Try a synonym.
- Use print and digital resources.
- Consider the connotation (feeling).
- Listen for the sound of the word (try pronunciations).
- Where else have you seen/heard this?

Once you model each strategy, provide a copy of the chart for students to reference. They can be encouraged to self-reflect on which ones they tend to use and never use and set goals for themselves.

Model how to use context clues, but not to rely too heavily on them. There are four different kinds of context clues—misdirective, nondirective, general, and directive—and not all of them are helpful when figuring out unfamiliar words. Misdirective contexts direct the reader to an incorrect meaning. Nondirective contexts do not offer any assistance to readers. General contexts provide the reader with enough information to place the word in a general category (the type of word). Directive contexts lead a reader to the specific and correct meaning (Beck et al., 2013). Misdirective and nondirective contexts offer no help to readers, and general contexts offer just enough to help a reader get started or confirm an idea. This means that teaching students to rely too heavily on context is not that helpful. This does not mean that we don't teach context; it just means we teach students to always use another strategy with context clues. What follows is a chart of some general and directive contexts that you may want to model for students.

Use Context Clues to Begin Figuring Out Unfamiliar Words

- Read and think about what would make sense.

- Look for clues within the sentence (*this means, in other words,* etc.).

- Look for clues in the sentences before or after.

- Look for clues in the text features or visuals.

- Confirm the meaning with another strategy or two.

Study roots across disciplines to develop word part knowledge. When teachers across disciplines study roots, students think across content areas and begin to develop both the word part knowledge and the disposition of someone who collects, compares, and studies words. What follows is one process for studying roots. This can be done within one class or across classes and disciplines.

1. Introduce a root.

2. Generate other words with that root.

3. Compare words and look for patterns in meaning.

4. Develop a definition of the root.

5. Locate other words with that root.

Here is one example:

	Rising Temperatures Affecting Humans and Bears
Look at the word malnourished. List other words that have the same prefix. • malnourished • maladaptive • malformed What do you notice about words with this prefix?	Fossil fuels and deforestation have pushed global temperatures up by nearly 2 degrees Fahrenheit since the 1800s, and the Arctic is warming faster than anywhere else. This is driving polar bears onto natives' doorsteps. Sea ice retreats past the shallow continental shelf in the Beaufort Sea off north Alaska into waters that can be too deep for foraging. Increasing numbers of polar bears are then forced to find land on the coast. If they're hungry or curious enough, they roam into Arctic villages. Warmer temperatures have also melted locals' traditional permafrost freezers that they have relied on for more than 100 years to store whale meat, called muktuk, after their hunts, leaving them open to hungry bear raids. While images of malnourished polar bears have become a national symbol of the effects of climate change, they are a front line reality for Alaska Natives, who face them on their own property and do not want them to get hurt. SimsKayotuk would occasionally see a polar bear near her small village of Kaktovik as a child, but never one at her door. This is a sign that they are getting bolder. "Now we have like 40 bears that are hanging around our area," she said. "You always have to look out when you step out of your house."

Source: Adapted from PBS NewsHour and Newsela staff (2016), https://newsela.com/read/polar-bears-alaskan-natives/id/23211/

Teach students how to consult references. Gone are the days where we ask students to take out hefty dictionaries and page through them to copy down definitions. Students often benefit from a few lessons on which references are worthwhile and how to use them. For example, most students simply google a word they don't know. While this strategy can sometimes be helpful, it also has its limitations.

- Show students Vocabulary.com as an alternative to Dictionary.com. It is full of helpful resources that students can use with ease, once shown how to use each part.

- Explain each part of the site.

- Model how you use each part.

- Offer time for students to try it out themselves.

- End with a discussion about which words are worth taking the time to look up. Students may say something like "words that come up often," "words that are in titles and headings," or "words that are important to figuring out the central ideas of the text."

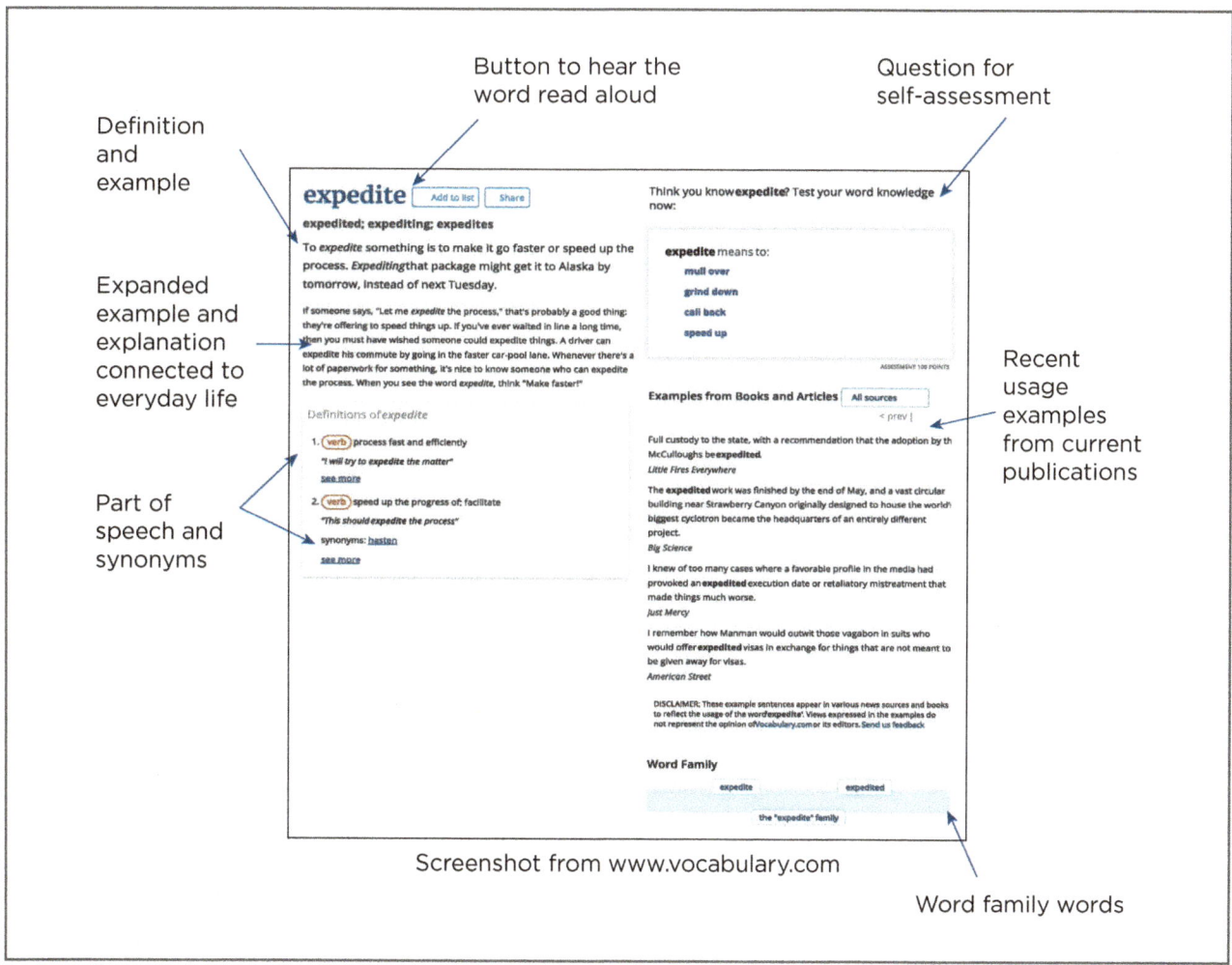

Button to hear the word read aloud

Question for self-assessment

Definition and example

Expanded example and explanation connected to everyday life

Part of speech and synonyms

Recent usage examples from current publications

Word family words

Screenshot from www.vocabulary.com

Teach Students to Use Vocabulary

Create opportunities for students to talk. When teaching students to acquire new vocabulary (both tier 2 and tier 3 words), it is helpful to know what researchers have found is most beneficial. Word learning tends to take place when students engage in *purposeful talk* with others that embeds target words (Corson, 1995). In addition, *meaningful contexts* must be used for functional use of vocabulary (Dutro & Moran, 2003). These findings remind us of the power of student conversations both before and after reading so they have multiple opportunities to use and apply the words they are learning.

Create a class vocabulary wall and student vocabulary digital notebook. Depending on the focus and student needs, you can create class vocabulary walls, and students can create their own vocabulary notebook entries to collect, organize, and then use words. Three types follow—words organized by topic, category, and tone (connotation).

Organize words by topic. One tool is an A–Z chart.

Topic: Solar System

A astronomy	B	C constellations	D
E Earth	F	G	H
I	J	K	L
M Mars Milky Way	N	O	P planets
Q	R	S stars Saturn	T telescope
U	V Venus	W	X
Y	Z		

Organize words by category. The categories could be part of the larger class topic or a personal research topic.

Topic: Rats

SURVIVAL	RELATIONSHIP TO PEOPLE	FOOD	REPUTATION
Collapse	Dependent	Scavengers	Evil
Wriggle		Creative	Dirty
Gnawing			
Senses			
Thigmophilic			
Whiskers			

You can also model how to track words that come up across lots of texts:

WORDS	TEXT A	TEXT B	TEXT C
gnawing	x	x	
dirty	x	x	x

Organize words by tone. When writing an argument piece, choose words that match your tone. List some words you might choose to match the tone. This can begin as a whole-class discussion, then small groups and individuals can continue adding to it.

HOPEFUL	FEARFUL	DISAPPOINTED	URGENT
luckily	cringe	unfortunately	right now
	tremble		last chance

Create concept continuums. Choose a word from the text or topic and ask students to generate other words that have a similar meaning. Then each student places the words on a continuum and explains why they created the sequence they did. For example, the starting word might be *gnaw*. Students add the words *scarf*, *nibble*, *chew*, and *peck*. Each student's continuum might look different, but one example follows.

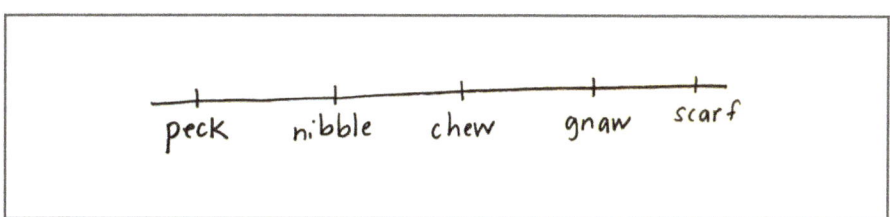

KEY IDEA

Developing a knowledge of the specific words in your curriculum is important, but so is teaching strategies for how to acquire and use words on their own. By modeling lessons and supporting students to develop the dispositions of someone who studies words, you help students begin to deepen understanding of new words and disciplinary content at the same time.

By sharing and explaining why they placed each word on the continuum where they did, students develop a nuanced understanding of how the words are different and what they mean. The goal is not for all to agree on where they placed them, but for all to more deeply understand the concepts.

HEADS UP

Choose words thoughtfully. Keep in mind that you want to focus on the conceptually rich terms of the content yet balance that goal with a more general word curiosity that includes brand-new words and colloquialisms. What words are students generally interested in exploring? Start there.

Honor students' language use. When English is a new language, students may fear using a word incorrectly, or they may shift between their home language and English. Rather than correcting language use, listen for understanding and name the strength the student is bringing with them. Correcting is not teaching and can get in the way of students taking the risk to try out new words.

Personalize. Instead of teaching vocabulary strategies to the entire class the same way, consider the learning needs of different students. Some are already proficient at using context clues, and others rarely use them. Some often try out new words when they participate in discussions, and others are less willing to try them out in front of peers. One way to avoid the one-size-fits-all model is to introduce and model a few strategies and then use small-group instruction to differentiate. Students can self-select the group they think they need, or you can choose for them. Here is one example of a student sign-up sheet for small-group vocabulary strategies.

Please sign up for one or two small-group lessons focused on vocabulary strategies. Reflect on what you struggle with, tend not to use, or want more support with. Thank you.

FOCUS	USING CONTEXT CLUES	USING WORD PARTS	USING REFERENCES	COLLECTING AND ORGANIZING WORDS
Student Names				

Writing Routines

6

Writing well is a communication tool that, like reading well, sets up students for successful lives. In this section, we focus on how to use writing routines to deepen thinking and demonstrate understanding. In the chart that follows we show how core writing routines can support purposeful student thinking across the content areas.

WRITING ROUTINE	HOW STUDENTS MIGHT USE THE ROUTINE TO DEVELOP INDEPENDENT THINKING	HOW STUDENTS MIGHT USE THE ROUTINE TO DEVELOP CREATIVE THINKING	HOW STUDENTS MIGHT USE THE ROUTINE TO DEVELOP PROBLEM-SOLVING THINKING	HOW STUDENTS MIGHT USE THE ROUTINE TO DEVELOP EMPATHETIC THINKING
Planning for Writing Page 166	Plan in ways that work for them	Match the ways they plan for the audience and purpose	Adjust plans as challenges arise	Put themselves in the reader's shoes and plan in ways that will help them get their message across
Considering Audience Page 172	Choose an audience and purpose that matters to them	Match the ways they write to their audience	Use feedback to revise writing choices	Imagine what the audience wants and needs as they write
Studying Mentor Texts Page 177	Choose to use writing moves they found effective in others' writing	Select, combine, and organize writing moves in unique ways	Notice how authors have managed writing challenges with success	Understand others' perspective and process by noticing their writing choices
Developing Central Ideas for Essays Page 183	Develop their own idea about a topic or text	Generate an idea others may not have considered	Develop ideas for how to navigate a challenge	Understand their own perspective on a topic so they can understand others

QUICK TIPS

- *Begin with an I-go structure.* Model how you plan for writing so students get to see the process of planning and not just the end product.

- *Show various approaches.* Offer choices so students can find ways to plan that work for their audience and purpose.

- *Set aside ample time.* Make some class time available for planning so students see its value and so that you can meet with students and offer feedback early in their writing process.

Planning for Writing

WHY?

When students, or really writers of any age, sit down to write without first planning how it will go, they often end up staring at a blank screen with an apparent writer's block, or they create meandering writing. Taking time to get clear on the audience, purpose, and message of the text that is being written leads to more engagement and much more clarity. However, planning does not mean the same thing to every teacher or every student.

Think about the ways we may plan for a party. Some of us focus on the music, creating fantastic playlists. Some of us get out cookbooks and begin preparing a list of the dishes to serve. Some of us are all about the beverages while others attend to beautiful table settings and accessories. What we focus on as well as how we focus on it depends on our preferences. The same can be said about planning for writing. Some of us prefer to talk our ideas through with a writing buddy, and that oral rehearsal alone helps us feel ready to get started. Some of us need to create elaborate outlines with bullets and sub-bullets. Some of us just freewrite and give ourselves permission to throw out half of what we wrote to get at the heart of our real message. While all of us have ways to plan, not all of our ways have been sanctioned and taught in schools.

The first step to get students in the habit of planning is to fully reckon with why they resist it or don't do it all. According to researchers Lassonde and Richards (2013), there are four main reasons why students report they do not plan for writing:

- They do not know how to plan.

- They do not recognize what they do is planning because it was not taught to them in school.

- They do not find it helpful because the ways they were taught to plan in school do not work for them.

- They find it too time consuming to be worth it.

We contend that there is a fifth reason students skip the planning phase, and Gravity's action research supported our experience. Teachers often assign planning as homework, and students assume that if it's not valuable enough to take up class time, it's not worth the effort. They can skip it and still get a good grade on the final paper they hand in.

Judson (2001) of the Minnesota Writing Project explains that planning is important because it "encourages experimentation while giving the first draft organization and purpose" (p. 1). Students who choose to plan their writing are more conscious of their thinking and create opportunities to compose with more independence, purpose, and confidence

(Lassonde & Richards, 2013). Research also finds that more experienced writers plan more than less experienced writers (McCutchen, 2006).

In our teaching experiences we have found a huge impact on student engagement, clarity, and elaboration when students spend time planning for their writing. In addition, students are often more willing to revise their writing once they have a clear plan and vision for what they are trying to create. We have seen firsthand that test scores on standardized writing tests go up once students learn how to plan before they begin writing, and they make better use of the time given to them on the test. Finally, going back to our party planning metaphor, if you don't plan for the party and just have people show up, it can still be a great time, but it can also be a huge flop. It is a big gamble to take and will waste a lot of people's valuable time if the party does not go well. To plan for writing is a sign of respect and care for your audience, just like it is a sign of care for your friends and family to put effort into creating a fun and inviting party experience.

GETTING STARTED

Incorporate the following three moves into your classroom so that students understand the purpose of planning and actually choose to plan for their writing.

Model how you plan. We all know the expression "practice what you preach." The best way to engage students in understanding planning is to show them how you do it yourself. The next time you assign a piece of writing, think about how you would plan for this piece if you were writing it. Open up a blank page and show students the ways you think, jot, and organize your ideas on the page. Even if you are not a confident writer, that is totally okay. In fact, the more you show your own struggles and think aloud about your process, the less intimidating it will be for students. You might try using language like the examples that follow to show not only what you plan but *how* you plan.

- "I always have trouble getting my ideas down on the page, so I am just going to give myself permission to write down what I do know . . ."

- "Before I start drafting I jot down my thoughts like this . . ."

- "In my head I am thinking about . . . and then I begin to sketch it out like this . . ."

- "Since my purpose is to . . . I am going to choose to plan like this . . ."

In the beginning, you can't overdo thinking aloud about your choices so students fully take hold of the idea that the types of planning reflect the genre. For example, if you plan to write a brief persuasive letter to the editor of a newspaper, disagreeing with an article they published, chances are you'll plan in some kind of linear form, listing points and supporting evidence. If you are writing a story, however, you might lean on more visual/spatial approaches, such as sketching and filling in ovals for character similarities and differences or drawing an arc to plan plot development.

So, in short, form follows function—there are no set rules, and playfulness and planning go hand in hand.

Offer students choices for how they will plan for their writing.
You might have one go-to way of planning that works for you. Great! But that often will not work for every one of your students. Let students know there are many ways to plan and that you will show them a few such as daydreaming, sketching, and storyboarding. They can choose which way they plan, but choosing not to plan at all is not one of the choices.

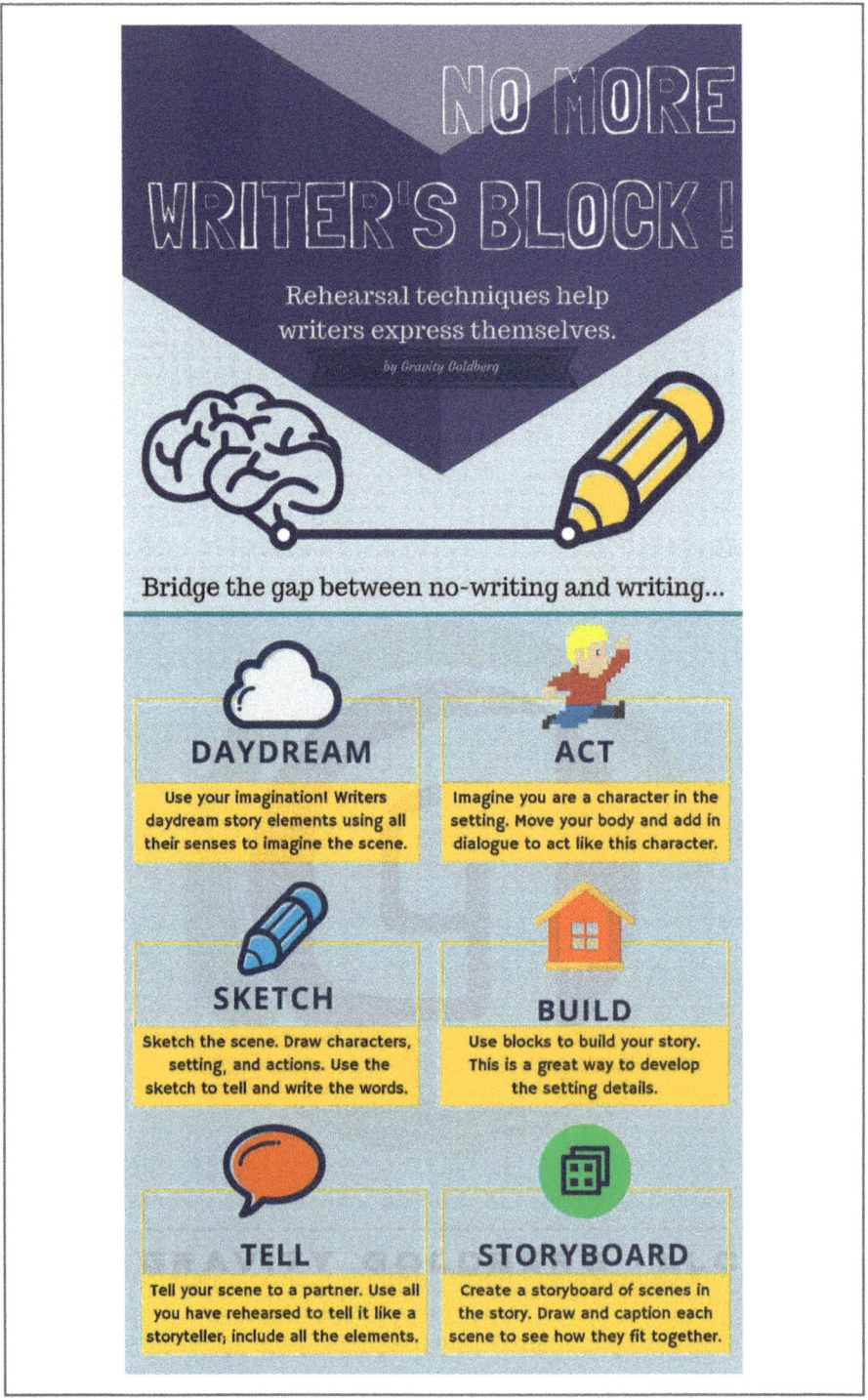

Let students try out different ways of planning and then give them time to reflect upon how it helped them. They can make different choices across the year and explore a variety of ways to plan. The goal is for them to find the ways that do work for them so they are more likely to plan for writing in the future as well as in your class today because they have experienced its positive impact.

Build planning time into class time. Whether it is one period toward the beginning of the writing project or a few 10-minute writing sessions across the week, make time in class for students to plan. This sends the message that planning is valuable and also offers time for feedback from peers and teachers. It is so much better to get feedback at the early stages of the writing process so you can revise your plans instead of getting feedback at the end once you hand it in. You might have class time that looks something like this.

> Teacher Shares a Variety of Ways to Plan: 10 minutes
>
> Students Try Out Ways to Plan: 20 minutes
>
> Writing Partners Engage in Feedback and Reflection: 10 minutes

Match Planning to Purpose

Many students plan the same way no matter the class or writing task. Whether writing a lab report or a short story, they might dash off a list of bullets. The results of their efforts won't be as strong as if they'd matched the type of planning to the text type. Further, these are the students who wind up concluding planning isn't a worthwhile step. Here we share three examples of planning that are well aligned to three main text types.

Narrative Writing

Narrative is the fancy word for story. Whether students are writing a true story like a memoir or a fictionalized story like a fantasy picture book or recounting a historic battle, all narratives are a sequence of events. Teach students how to make a basic timeline and to list the events so the sequence is clear and logical. For visual learners they can add a sketch to each event on the timeline so it is more of a storyboard.

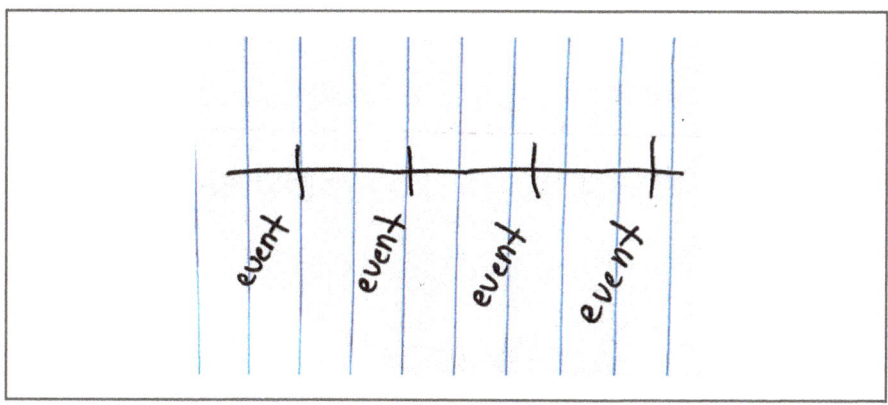

Informational Writing

Informational writing is all about taking a topic and breaking it into categories and teaching about one category at a time. You can teach students how to plan by using boxes and bullets. The box becomes the category, and the bullets are the supporting details that go with that part.

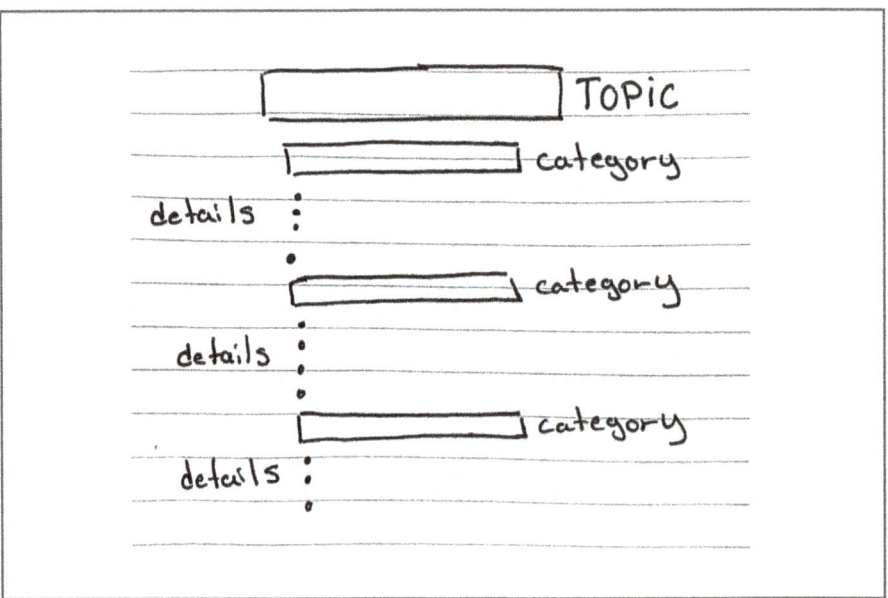

Argument Writing

Argument writing is focused on a claim and then supporting that claim with relevant and compelling evidence and examples. Teach students how to make a chart that shows how the claim is supported by the evidence.

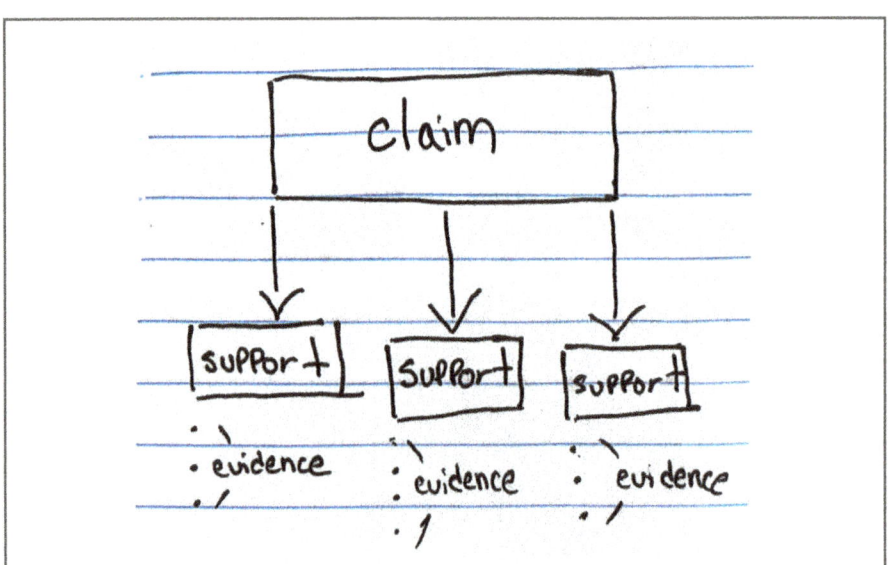

HEADS UP

Keep it simple. Avoid assigning lengthy outlines as planning as it can actually turn students off to planning in the future. Instead, show some basic templates such as lists, boxes and bullets, webs, and timelines that can all be completed in less than one period.

Start with free. Offer some time for freewriting as a form of planning for those who are not even sure where to start. This could also be reframed as "free talking" for those who really don't feel confident writing. Offer students three to five minutes to simply "free talk" to a partner about what they may write about. Then give them a few minutes to jot down anything they said that they want to remember.

Use tech. For those who are immediately turned off by having to write, encourage the use of tech tools instead of making everything written in words. This could mean voice-to-text apps, Screencastify, or simply using voice memo on a smartphone to record ideas. The goal is to create a way to plan that works for each student, and that doesn't always mean it needs to be written down or typed up.

KEY IDEA

When students are aware of their audience and purpose, they can choose a way to plan that will work for them. Giving them models and class time to work on their plans and get feedback helps the rest of the writing process go smoother and helps students experience more writing success.

QUICK TIPS

- *Encourage careful consideration.* Before beginning the writing process, offer students time to choose the audience they are writing for.

- *Do a trust fall to include more informal writing.* Allow students true choice by creating projects that are not always formal writing pieces. Remember most state standards actually require students to write for different audiences and purposes and to be able to choose the level of formality that matches.

- *Guide constructive use of feedback.* Help students receive feedback from their intended audience and then use it to revise their pieces.

- *Tap the power of technology and social media.* Support students in publishing their pieces in a medium that will reach their intended audience. This often means we take our cues from students, who show us new vistas of information sharing.

Considering Audience

WHY?

When students write for the sole purpose of getting a grade from the teacher, they almost always do the minimal amount needed, and engagement tends to be lackluster. On the other hand, when students write for real audiences and purposes beyond the teacher and their gradebook, they will often put in more effort and take much more ownership of the writing process. For the most part, we don't blame them because it feels like human nature to care much more about anything when it is created for someone else as a gift, an offering, or a gesture.

Think of it this way: In our own adult lives, why is it that most of us will clean our homes with extra care and detail when we know we are having guests over? Isn't it because we care about the people who are coming over and our relationship with them? We want them to feel special, cared for, and comfortable. Tidying up is about our guests as much as it is about how we want them to view us. We don't want to be viewed as messy or unconcerned with others.

All of this applies when writing. When students have a real audience they are writing for, they show much more care and attention to the details; they "tidy it up" and consider how their audience will feel when they read it. By adding in steps before, during, and after the writing project, you can help students take much more ownership of the writing by teaching them how to choose an audience, get feedback, and revise with the audience in mind.

GETTING STARTED

It may take up a little more class time to teach students how to consider the audience in their writing, but the payoff is totally worth it. It also can be incorporated in just a few minutes a period across a writing project.

Brainstorm lists of possible audiences.

Spend class time brainstorming possible audiences for each writing project you are taking on. One way you might do this is to make a T-chart and ask students to discuss and contribute ideas to it. On one side of the chart you can list purposes for writing and on the other side possible audiences who you think would enjoy or need to read it. What follows is one example of this sort of chart for argument writing. You can make a new chart for each type of text you are studying.

Purpose	Audience
Convince others to care about our planet	Other teens around the country
Persuade people to use historical lessons when making choices for today	Local politicians and voters

Help students choose an audience before beginning to write.

It is essential to know the intended audience before writing begins so that every choice in the writing process can consider them. For example, when working with a student who was doing informational writing about lacrosse, Gravity as the teacher suggested he add in more background information about some of the well-known players he was listing. He looked at her and said, "But you are not my audience. My audience is other people who play and love lacrosse, and they would all know who these players are." Gravity loved his pushback, because it meant he had been asking himself, "What does my audience already know? What do they need to know? How will I use my writing to teach them?" Considering the audience in this way pushes student writers to analyze their content and contour it for their audience, in terms of background information, tone, and length. Having students decide upon, write down, and establish their audience before beginning helps them stay focused and allows you as the teacher to know who they are writing for.

Teach students how to get feedback from their intended audience after they create a first draft.

So many students and adult writers resist revising their work. While there are many reasons for this, one main one is a lack of authentic feedback that could help them know what to revise for. Revision is not just changing a word here and there, but being so focused on your audience and purpose that you can adjust what you say and how you say it to be as clear and engaging as possible.

By adding in a few days of homework where students find a member of their intended audience and then ask for feedback from them, you will help them get much clearer on the kinds of possible revisions they might make. For example, going back to the previous brainstorming chart of audiences, a student who chose to write for other teens would have a teen read their work and offer feedback. Or if a student was writing for local politicians and voters, they would find someone who is a politician and/or voter and ask them to read and respond to their work.

The goal is not to have the audience correct their work or even write on it, but instead to have them answer a few questions by writing back or participating in a conversation with the student writer. A few sample questions follow.

- What part of this writing piece was most engaging?

- What part of this writing piece was unclear? What may have made it more clear?

- What were you wanting more of?

- What were you wanting less of?

- How did my words and details match you, my audience?

- Is there anything you would like to offer me to help me revise this piece?

Teach students how to receive feedback from their audience.

It can be painful if student writers take feedback personally and think it means they are doing it "wrong." We know from Carol Dweck's (2006) research on mindset that when someone has a fixed mindset, they are less open to feedback. We also know that having a growth mindset and being open to feedback can be taught. A few ways to teach students how to receive feedback include the following:

- Don't defend. Even if you don't agree, still listen to what they have to say.

- You don't need to take all of the feedback you are given. Ask yourself if this was helpful feedback, and if not, you can choose not to use it.

- Ask for clarification if needed. If you don't understand the feedback, kindly ask the audience who gave it to explain more or give you an example.

- Try not to take feedback personally. When someone gives it to you, it is because they care enough about you and your work and want to help you.

- Everyone can grow as a writer. Even published and highly successful writers get feedback. It is not a sign of weakness to receive feedback. It is an essential step in the process.

Show students how to turn audience feedback into a revision action plan.

After receiving feedback, model how to turn it into a revision action plan. For example, student writers can make a plan that looks something like this.

REVISION ACTION PLAN
They wanted to know why the topic mattered to me, so I can add in a mini personal story.
They liked how I began with song lyrics, so I could weave them in more throughout the piece and end with them too.
They suggested I use a different word instead of crisis over and over again, so I will look up other words I could also use.

Students use technology to publish their work for their intended audience.

One of the main reasons why a paper does not need to end up only on the teacher's desk is that students can reach a much wider audience with a few clicks. Think about how teens who are tired of school gun violence may use their voices to reach a national audience, getting others not only to care and listen but also to march and take action. Or consider the thousands of teens every day who write fan fiction and upload it to sites for other superfans. In reality no one writes for a teacher once they graduate and leave school, so we should be teaching students how to write for a real audience now. If they are writing to a politician, they should email or mail their piece to them. If they are writing for teens around the country, they may want to create a social media page, blog, or website to spread the word.

Grade based on clear criteria and attention to the audience.

Even though you are not necessarily the audience a student is writing for, you can still read, assess, and grade the piece. You will need to know students' intended audience when assessing and when grading and include this in part of their grade. For example, if you are grading on the following criteria—accurate content, organization, and elaboration of ideas—also include a category for attention to the audience. Have students turn in their work with a summary of the audience along with their feedback and revision action plan so all of this can be part of the final evaluation of the work.

KEY IDEA

When student writers consider their audiences throughout the writing process, it helps them to choose the content they need to include and to consider the style and word choice, as well as the medium in which it will be published. This leads to deeper student thinking and engagement, and much more interesting writing for us teachers to read, because of the variety and authenticity.

HEADS UP

Not all writing has to be formal and academic. Of course, students need to spend time learning how to write in formal academic ways, but also provide opportunities for students to write in ways that are more connected to life outside of school so they see the value of writing beyond the grade.

Brainstorm real genres to try out. List all the possible kinds of writing for each main text type. Then offer choice or mix it up so that students have experiences with as many kinds of writing as possible. One example is to think about argument writing and list all the kinds that exist such as documentaries, TED Talks, debates, ad campaigns, public relations campaigns, op-eds, and so on. Consider replacing an essay unit with one of these other kinds of writing, and watch engagement rise and transfer occur.

Seek authentic publication outlets. Educators have been advocating for authentic writing publication for decades. You can find out much more about how to help students publish for a real audience in the following resources.

- *Who Owns the Learning?* by Alan November (2012)

- "Publishers, Participants All" by Will Richardson (2011)

- "Writing for an Audience Beyond the Teacher: 10 Reasons to Send Student Work Out Into the World" by Katherine Schulten (2018)

Studying Mentor Texts

WHY?

There is a reason YouTube videos are so popular with teens and really almost everybody. If you want to learn how to do something, chances are someone online has created lots of video tutorials to show you how. For example, one middle school boy Gravity met taught himself to do yo-yo tricks by watching videos and ended up winning international yo-yo competitions! A friend's daughter learned to do fancy updo hairstyles and professional-quality makeup by subscribing to channels. She now gets paid to do her mother's friends' hair and makeup. Before Gravity wrote her first Amazon book review, she read dozens of them. She got to know the qualities and characteristics, the length, tone, and craft. This helped her make choices about how she would write her own reviews. No matter what is being learned, it helps to see examples of what it looks like and sounds like from those who are already quite proficient. It is so much easier to learn something when you have examples of what success looks like. This is why mentor texts are essential for writers.

A mentor text is a high-quality text that can be read, studied, and admired so that writers can use some of the same moves the author used in their own writing. As Lynne Dorfman and Rose Cappelli (2007) state, "Mentor texts help writers notice things about an author's work that is not like anything they might have done before, and empower them to try something new" (p. 3). Katie Wood Ray (1999) explains the importance of all students reading like writers. That means they notice the author's craft, talk about why a writer might use this craft, and envision a time they might use it in their own writing. Kelly Gallagher (2011) says, "It is essential that my students move beyond simply telling me what a text says; I want them to tell me *how* the text was constructed" (p. 20). Mentor texts become the examples writers can come back to over and over again for ideas and inspiration.

GETTING STARTED

As a student, Gravity recalls learning rules about writing such as never use the word *I* and always write in complete sentences. Now as an adult writer she realizes there is really no such thing as a writing rule. Each type of writing has its own conventions and norms. It is the writer's job to read examples of the type of text they are creating and to know the conventions and use them. It is totally fine and essential to use the word *I* when writing a memoir. And writers of fiction often use fragments and run-ons to create a mood or develop realistic dialogue. Instead of teaching rules, we can teach students how to study the conventions in a mentor text and then apply them in their own writing. The use of mentor texts also ensures we are not just telling students what to do or handing out assignments without instruction,

QUICK TIPS

- *Rivet attention.* Choose mentor texts that are engaging and accessible. Make sure students can read and understand them.

- *Lean on current wealth.* Look for contemporary examples of texts that students are likely to create outside of school too. Choose fan fiction, advertisements, blogs, podcasts, and TED Talks, to name a few.

- *Start with shared reading.* By reading the mentor texts together first, you give all students a running start on interacting with and understanding the text. Then send students off to continue their analysis on their own.

- *Come at it again.* Return to a mentor text a few times with a different writing focus to study in mind.

and instead showing them some possibilities of what they might create. So, as you try the following ideas, let the concept of hard-and-fast rules recede, and consider the idea that developing avid, strong writers with voice is best done by exposing them to many text types and genres.

Choosing Mentor Texts

Typically, we use mentor texts at the start of a new writing process and then return to them across time. You will first want to choose the text, then teach students how to analyze it and finally use it to make a plan for drafting and revising their own writing.

When choosing mentor texts, you can divide them into two categories—ones you will choose for students and ones they will find themselves. When choosing for students, you might consider the following:

- What real-life writing examples exist that match this type of writing?

- Will my students be able to read and understand this text?

- Will my students engage with and care about the topic of this text?

- Are there specific craft moves the author made that I want my students to try?

You can also enlist students in the work of finding mentor texts. Often students surprise us with examples that are not so obvious but still powerful examples of good writing. These may include song lyrics, poems, videos, speeches, and graphic novels. Any piece of writing can be analyzed for craft, and we don't want to limit what students choose to only academic papers.

> Here are some great online resources to help you find mentor texts:
>
> - *Two Writing Teachers* Blog: https://twowritingteachers.org
> - *The Classroom Bookshelf* Blog: https://classroombookshelf.wordpress.com
> - International Literacy Association's Young Adult Book Awards: www.literacyworldwide.org/get-involved/awards-recognition/awards-grants/ila-children's-and-young-adults'-book-awards
> - Goodreads: www.goodreads.com

Learning Craft From Mentor Texts

Once texts have been selected, it is important to model how to study them. One way to begin is to show students three questions they can ask about any text and to create a simple chart to record what they find.

WHAT DID YOU NOTICE IN THE TEXT?	EXAMPLE	WHY DID THE AUTHOR DO THIS?	WHAT IS IT CALLED?

The following is an example of one mentor text chart based on the opening pages of the memoir *Yes, Please!* by Amy Poehler (2014). Even if students are not writing memoirs, you can study an author's craft and use it in a variety of texts. In this case the students were about to write memoirs when they created this chart.

WHAT DID I NOTICE IN THE TEXT?	EXAMPLE	WHY DID THE AUTHOR DO THIS?	WHAT IS IT CALLED?
I was laughing at parts	"Annie taught me that orphanages were a blast and that being rich is the only thing that matters."	To point out shallow ideals with sarcasm Engaging to readers	Humor
Pop culture references	Annie Grease The Wizard of Oz	Relatable to everyone and we all know them—"me too"	Relatable examples
Not all the information was given, and she left out a big part in the first sentence	"I was in fourth grade and in trouble." I wondered, "Why was she in trouble?"	To hook me in and I wanted my question answered	Building curiosity with omissions

(Continued)

(Continued)

WHAT DID I NOTICE IN THE TEXT?	EXAMPLE	WHY DID THE AUTHOR DO THIS?	WHAT IS IT CALLED?
The first sentence was in all capitals	"I WAS IN FOURTH GRADE AND IN TROUBLE."	To grab attention and emphasize the importance of this time and event	All caps
Short and long sentences—some sounded serious and some rambling	Short: "But the Wizard of Oz was the ultimate." Long: "Grease taught me that being in a gang..."	She wanted to move between being serious and funny and used sentences to show that	Varying sentences and tone
Narrator's voice sounded like the age of character	"It dealt with friendship and fear and death and rainbows and sparkly red shoes."	To put the readers in the mind of the character and the time period—stay in the moment	Realistic narrator voice

The goal is not the mentor text chart. The goal is for students to use what they learned from making the chart to study texts with intentionality so they can then incorporate techniques into their own writing pieces. Make this very clear to students so they don't think this is just a worksheet activity. Through discussion and minilessons over time, students' awareness of all the aspects of craft to notice and borrow expands. Celebrate when you see use of conventions showing up in students' writing. For example, you may see sentence fragments to convey a character's shock; a poem written in second-person voice; humorous asides that talk directly to the reader set in italics; dialogue in odd numbers of lines to convey tension—these are all telltale signs of students using mentor texts to find their way as writers.

After modeling how you make a mentor text chart and how you decide what to write down, do this with students as a shared writing experience and ultimately have them try it on their own. Take it all the way through the gradual release of responsibility model; mining mentor texts is both simple and complex, so the collaborative practice is important.

Using Mentor Texts When Drafting

Often students think about *what* they will write but not always *how* they will write it. Part of being ready to draft is thinking about both the what and the how. Ideally, students have at least a few mentor texts they have studied and a few charts to refer back to when they begin to draft their own pieces.

After they have planned and developed their ideas for what to write about, they can use the mentor text chart to think about how they will write. One way is for them to reread their mentor text charts and highlight and make notes next to craft moves they noticed other authors make that they might want to try. They can even jot down where in the text they might try it in their drafts. For example, if a student wanted to use humor the way Poehler (2014) did, they might highlight that row on the chart and add the note "Try humor using sarcasm in the intro." They might also want to try building curiosity with omissions and could note that in the chart. The idea is to refer back to the ideas and examples before drafting and also while drafting so the craft that was studied ends up being applied in one's own writing. Of course, not everything the student notes in the mentor text will end up in the draft, and that is not only fine but preferable. It could lead to confusing drafts and overwriting if the student thinks they need to do it all in one piece.

Using Mentor Texts When Revising

Mentor texts are *very* useful at the revision stage. Looking back at a revered mentor text or two can help a young writer improve sentence-level craft and take on "bigger" considerations like beginnings, setting, and core conflict. For example, if a student read four mentor texts and realized that each one has a different type of ending, during revision the student might try out a few of these endings before deciding which one works best.

Revision can seem daunting and vague for students. They may know their piece isn't where they want it to be, but they may not know what to focus on. By going back to their mentor texts, they can be reminded how the author approached all sorts of things, and be inspired to then try a few more sophisticated writing moves during the revision process. It is also helpful to have students reread the mentor texts throughout the writing process because they always notice new elements each time they read, and this gives them more ideas for what they might try during later stages of the process.

KEY IDEA

Mentor texts demystify writing by showing students examples of what they might try out when they plan, draft, and revise. These texts also allow students opportunities to think about how they write and not just what they will write about. When we open up the classroom to mentor texts that are contemporary and engaging, it helps students see that there are multiple types of writing and not just academic rule-based writing.

HEADS UP

Use audio, visual, and video texts as mentors. If we only focus on written texts, we are marginalizing some cultural displays of literacy as well as the very passions that could motivate students to study texts even more. You may want to invite students to bring in audio, visual, and video mentor texts because they can be studied just like written mentor texts and also to show them how to read them a bit more critically then they currently do.

Focus on transfer. Sometimes our focus on "fixing" a student's writing actually helps the writer's current piece of writing but doesn't necessarily help them transfer the skill to future writing pieces. It can be helpful to find one or two key teaching points and to let a few other aspects of the writing go for now so that you can teach for depth instead of surface-level fixes. Ask yourself, "Which focus in the mentor text can the student carry with them again and again?" Choose these areas over very specific moves an author made that don't really transfer.

Multitask across content areas. Collaborate with colleagues in different departments and see if some mentor texts might be useful across classes. This helps students see the connections between courses and also shows them how to use writing skills across contexts. For example, maybe the op-ed you use to show how to form a claim and support it with evidence can be used in science, social studies, and English.

Developing Central Ideas for Essays

WHY?

A large amount of time in school is spent on academic writing, which is often synonymous with essays. While this cannot be the only type of writing students experience, it is one type that is traditionally valued and tested. All of the state standards include some form of argument essay writing where students create a central idea and turn it into a claim statement (historically referred to as a thesis statement but called a claim in most state standards). No amount of writing instruction or flashy writing technique will help an essay that is developed around a weak or confusing central idea. The central idea is the foundation the rest of the essay is built upon.

Many teachers have seen students struggle to develop clear and powerful central ideas on their own, so they resort to telling students the idea and then simply asking them to write an essay that proves it. While this sort of adaptation is understandable, it is required that students develop their own central ideas in the standards. In terms of a lifelong writing skill, it is essential that students learn how to develop ideas on their own. When they write in history, science, economics, feminist studies, law, or any other number of courses they may pursue, it will serve them to know how to form their own ideas as they will not be able to pass college-level courses without this skill.

Beyond college, the life skill of forming your own idea is key to being an informed, free-thinking member of our democratic society. If we want students to be able to recognize bias and be able to read others' arguments critically, it always helps them to be able to use what they know about forming their own opinions as writers to analyze the logic and thinking of others. For this reason, teaching students to develop central ideas is a skill that is necessary to fulfill their roles as citizens in the free world.

Because it is such an important skill, but also a challenging one, making time in school across subject areas to teach idea development is often a necessity. It is also an opportunity to explore complex ideas across content areas so that every teacher and every class becomes a place where high levels of thinking develop. If we want students to write well about central ideas, we first need to teach them to be *thinking* about ideas across the curriculum and across the day.

GETTING STARTED

Many students are confused about what a central idea is, and some textbooks only contribute to the misunderstanding. Create a chart like the one that follows and explicitly discuss what ideas are and are not. Make sure all students know what they are working toward before trying to form them.

- *Define it and check for understanding.* Teach students what central ideas are. Central ideas are not facts that can be right or wrong. There is not one central idea of a topic or text. Show students that there are many possible central ideas, which can all be valid as long as they are supported with evidence and explanation.

- *Model how to form central ideas.* Showing students a clear process they can try out themselves is so valuable. Knowing how to select and develop a central idea is something we all keep getting better at for a lifetime, so it stands to reason that it's a skill that takes a lot of modeling and discussion.

- *Walk the talk of exploring ideas.* Give students time to play with and refine their ideas while they read and learn about a topic. Waiting until the end to form a central idea is often daunting. Students can be forming ideas as they read and study.

CENTRAL IDEAS ARE . . .	CENTRAL IDEAS ARE *NOT* . . .
• Ideas	• Facts
• Based on thinking across text or time	• Based on one piece of evidence or one part of a text
• Open-ended, and there are always more than one	• One right answer
• Able to be supported with logic, reasoning, and explanation	• Opinions with no evidence or support
• Authentically developed by the thinker	• Formulaic and developed by the teacher or textbook

Model a Process for Forming Central Ideas

Depending on the topic or subject area, the process for forming central ideas might be a bit different. What is common across domains is the need for an idea based on multiple pieces of evidence that can be supported and explained. In order to form a central idea, students need to pay attention to the smaller details, notice patterns, and then turn those patterns into an overarching idea. This requires them to synthesize information from across text and to make inferences about what they are learning. Here is a thinking strategy that teachers can model with examples from different subject areas.

Pattern strategy: As you read, notice patterns and jot them down. Then ask yourself, "What does this pattern reveal about the topic?"

CONTENT AREA	EXAMPLE
English	When I was reading, I noticed a pattern in the way the character responded to pressure from other characters. He always seemed to get angry and sometimes even violent. This pattern makes me think a central idea is that too much pressure can be dangerous.
Social Studies	A pattern I am noticing is that every time European explorers found a new place, they exploited it and took whatever they wanted by force. This pattern makes me think that a central idea is that explorers should really be called thieves or conquerors.
Science	A pattern I am noticing is that with each technological advancement some scientists are excited about the possibility, and many nonscientists are fearful about change. This pattern makes me think a central idea is that fear can get in the way of progress.

List strategy: As you read, view, and discuss the topic, jot down what you learned as a bulleted list. Then reread your list and ask, "What ideas emerge from this list of information?" Make a new list of ideas. Then reread that idea list and circle the ones that you can say the most about.

Create a visual map: Once you have a possible central idea, jot it in a box. Then visually show the supports for that idea, followed by the evidence. An example, similar to the chart for planning argument writing provided on page 170, follows.

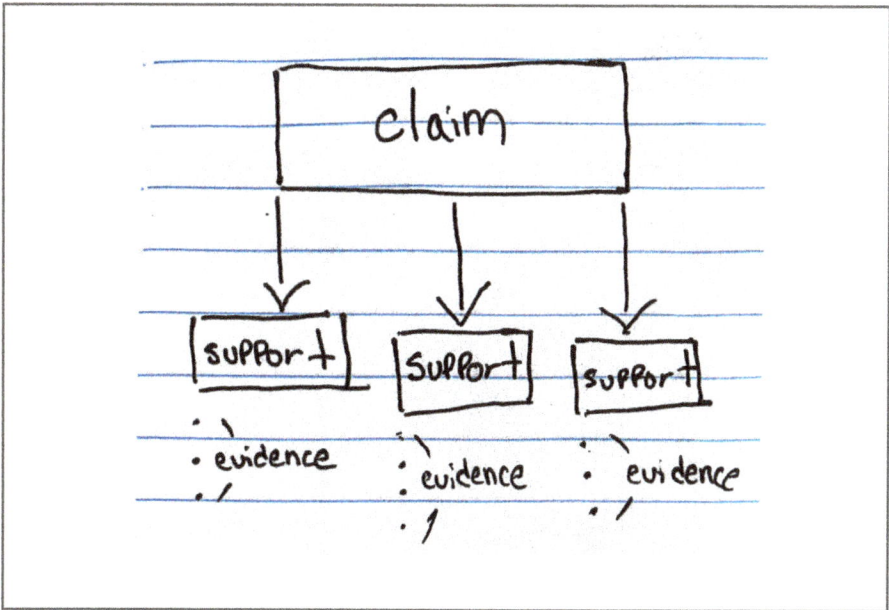

Test out the visual by making sure every part is connected. Talk it out with a partner and revise any parts that don't seem to fit.

Form Ideas Throughout the Study. If students wait until the end of a book or topic to form ideas, it is often too late. Let them know you want them to explore ideas all along the way. Then give them time for idea exploration. This might look like:

- Ending the period with five minutes of freewriting ideas students currently are thinking about

- Giving students five minutes to talk about their ideas with a thinking partner and then jot down what they discussed

- Creating a Google Doc or chat page that students contribute to across the unit with their ideas and current thinking

- Having homework assignments that are time to jot down thinking and revisit past thinking before coming to class with ideas to share

KEY IDEA

Taking the time to teach students how to form central ideas will pay off because the rest of their essays will be clearer and better able to be developed. It also pays off because student understanding of the content and topic is often much deeper when this level of thinking is happening to form the central ideas.

HEADS UP

Model the process. When we only show mentor texts or completed writing examples, students miss the chance to see how the piece came together. Take time to show students your process and how you form a central idea.

Make sure examples are focused on a different topic. When you are showing examples and modeling, make sure you don't model with the same topic or text students are writing about. This leads to copying, and students will think your example is the right way. Instead, use previously taught topics or examples or make your own example about a slightly different topic. Also take time to show and discuss published examples of pieces in which the author fails to provide a strong central idea. It takes time for students—and anyone—to spot when a piece *seems* to put forth a central idea that one can "stress test" the validity of with evidence, but is actually just an opinion.

Think beyond written essays. All of the strategies for forming central ideas can be used beyond essays. Encourage the use of speeches, op-eds, presentations, and even TikTok videos so students see the value of forming central ideas and explaining them beyond formal essays in school. And as always, make the point that as readers, we don't always have to agree with the central idea being put forth, but we do need to recognize it so we can reckon with it and think through our response.

Assessment Opportunities

7

We can think of assessment as an opportunity to uncover students' thinking. We have opportunities to get to know what they think and how they think. This information helps us plan our next steps and moves as teachers. The following table shows how assessments support student thinking.

ASSESSMENT OPPORTUNITIES	WHY?	WHEN?
Formative Assessment Page 188	Understand what students already know and how they currently think	Before a unit, ongoing as the unit unfolds, and when shifting to a new goal
Feedback Page 193	Reinforce student strengths and use them to identify next steps	When students move from one goal to another and as they work through challenges in a learning experience
Conferring Page 198	Get to know students as thinkers and people, tailor instruction to their unique strengths and needs	Regular meetings throughout a unit so students see you every week or two
Learning Progressions Page 203	Map out the steps a learner tends to go through when learning a new skill or concept to identify next steps in learning	When you offer feedback and confer with students
Portfolios Page 208	Support curation and reflection on learning so students can show all they learned	At the end of a unit, semester, and/or year
Performance Assessments Page 212	Identify how a student transfers, applies, and consolidates learning in an authentic experience	At the midpoint and/or end of a unit

QUICK TIPS

- **Be intentional.** Create a formative assessment plan for each unit as part of the preparation process. Decide on which types of formative assessment you will use and when.

- **Be at ease.** Make formative assessments low-stakes events so students feel safe to show you what and how they think. Consider how you talk about formative assessment to students and how you might include them in the process. You put students at ease when your words and tone are full-on supportive mentor, as opposed to authoritative grader.

- **Be organized.** Develop a system for tracking all of the information you glean from formative assessments so you don't end up spending hours or days trying to write it all down. Keep it simple and, again, include students in the process as much as possible.

Formative Assessment

WHY?

The word *assess* comes from the Latin root *assessus*, which means sitting by. We can think of formative assessment as the information we get sitting by students as they work on, grapple with, and demonstrate learning. While the term *assessment* has often become a synonym for *grade* or *test*, the two are not the same.

When we formatively assess, our goal is to gather information about learners to make instructional decisions about what students are ready to learn next. The "form" part of the word *formative* helps us remember that it informs instruction. Formative assessments may include observations of students, student feedback, conversations and conferences with students, looking at student work samples, and student self-reflection, to name a few. Formative assessments can be ongoing, may be low stakes, and do not get graded. Every interaction with a student is an opportunity for formative assessment because we get to know them and their thinking better.

By contrast, summative assessment is a time at the end of a unit when students show what they have learned. It can be an end-of-unit test, but it does not have to be. It can include a piece of writing, a presentation, a concluding conversation, and so on, and it's often graded.

In this section we dive into types of formative assessment and how you might organize and use the information you gather. If you take on the stance that your job is to sit beside students—literally and metaphorically to get to know them—you can bring joy to assessment opportunities because they help you build relationships and make more informed decisions. Oftentimes when we take the time to look and listen to students, they tell us exactly what they are ready for next.

GETTING STARTED

Make a plan. Before beginning a unit, create a formative assessment plan. Consider the goals of the unit and your students' preferences when making the plan. The following list is by no means exhaustive but can help you think beyond the first few types you may tend to use now. What might you try?

TYPE	EXAMPLE
Observation	Use a class grid to watch students' writing process. Have some categories on the grid to guide the observations. | STUDENT	PLANS BEFORE WRITING	REFERENCES CLASS CHARTS AND RESOURCES	GOES BACK TO THE TEXT TO CITE EXAMPLES
---	---	---	---
Listening	Use a listening tool while students participate in collaborative conversations. Notice what they say, how they say it, and what misconceptions and understandings they seem to have. Jot down what you hear.
Conversation	Wondering what students are struggling with in the unit? Ask them. Take a few minutes one-on-one or in small groups to ask students to share their process and what challenges they are facing.
Mental Model	Invite students to create a mental model by sketching, based on the information they have learned so far. Use labels, arrows, and captions as needed. This could be a model of a cycle, a relationship, or a process.
Reflection	Ask students to think and create a T-chart about what they know and are still wondering about. The wondering column could be a confusion or something they have not learned yet. 	WHAT I KNOW	WHAT I AM WONDERING ABOUT
---	---
		  This could also be done with a Google Form so you can see all the student reflections in one digital place.
Student-Created Goal	Students jot down a goal and explain why this goal is important for them right now.
Collaborative Document	Use a Jamboard or Google Doc with a few prompts that students respond to. You can keep it anonymous or ask students to add their names. Students can add their name to someone else's idea so teachers can see a pattern in the class. A few sample prompts might be: • I learned . . . • I am confused about . . . • I would like support with . . .
Preassessment Experience	Students are asked to try a part of the end-of-unit performance assessment at the start before any instruction has occurred. This helps teachers understand what students already know how to do before the unit instruction begins. Students can label what they are confused about if they don't know how to do a part yet.

Collaborative Conversations Checklist

GROUP	BEFORE THE CONVERSATION	DURING THE CONVERSATION	AFTER THE CONVERSATION
A	☐ Jots down ideas to talk about ☐ Notes a specific part of the text or experience to share	☐ Active listening ☐ Adding on ideas ☐ Challenging ideas ☐ Referring to the text ☐ Sharing the "air time" ☐ Staying on topic	☐ Jots down new thinking from the conversation ☐ Makes a plan for what to do next
B	☐ Jots down ideas to talk about ☐ Notes a specific part of the text or experience to share	☐ Active listening ☐ Adding on ideas ☐ Challenging ideas ☐ Referring to the text ☐ Sharing the "air time" ☐ Staying on topic	☐ Jots down new thinking from the conversation ☐ Makes a plan for what to do next
C	☐ Jots down ideas to talk about ☐ Notes a specific part of the text or experience to share	☐ Active listening ☐ Adding on ideas ☐ Challenging ideas ☐ Referring to the text ☐ Sharing the "air time" ☐ Staying on topic	☐ Jots down new thinking from the conversation ☐ Makes a plan for what to do next
D	☐ Jots down ideas to talk about ☐ Notes a specific part of the text or experience to share	☐ Active listening ☐ Adding on ideas ☐ Challenging ideas ☐ Referring to the text ☐ Sharing the "air time" ☐ Staying on topic	☐ Jots down new thinking from the conversation ☐ Makes a plan for what to do next

Create a system. Once you have decided on the types of formative assessment you will use, create a system for collecting, tracking, and using the information you are gathering about students' thinking. Some teachers prefer a three-ring binder for each class and carry note-catcher forms with them. Others like digital tools such as Google Forms. It doesn't matter what system you use as long as you have one so the information does not get lost along the way.

Take a look at the Collaborative Conversations Checklist above (a full-size version can be found in Appendix E and on the companion website). This simple formative assessment tool can be used across content areas to support student collaboration. Simply photocopy the form and jot notes. You can also share it with students so they know what you are looking for. What gets checked off is a strength you may not need to teach students how to do. In fact, a group that already is able to do something can be a model for the other groups. What is not yet checked off becomes an outline of what you might teach next over the next couple of weeks.

If you prefer digital tools, you can create a Google Form and collect the same sort of information. A screenshot of a Google Form follows. The information from the Google Form can be viewed in a spreadsheet automatically and sorted by student or question, which can help you see patterns and form small groups.

Student Name

Your Answer _____ 🅜

Before Writing

☐ Rereads the prompt or task description

☐ Reads documents (articles, infographics, maps, etc.)

☐ Makes a plan (outline, list, box and bullets, etc.)

During Draft

☐ Uses the plan to draft

☐ References class charts and resources as needed

☐ Looks back at documents to site as examples

☐ Does their best with spelling and grammar but does not get bogged down by it

Revising and Editing

☐ Rereads writing and deletes parts that don't fit

☐ Rereads writing and adds in examples and explanations

☐ Rereads writing and moves information that belongs in another spot

☐ Checks spelling and grammar with digital tools

Submit   Clear form

KEY IDEA

Formative assessment can offer you information that makes instructional decisions more aligned to your specific students. By planning how, when, and in what ways you will use formative assessment information, you can integrate it into unit plans.

HEADS UP

Think feedback, not grades. Grading formative assessment can actually undermine the information and also turns it into something else. When we grade, it shifts us from a learner about students to an evaluator of students. Instead of grading student performance during formative assessment, you can give feedback about what you learn. (The next section will dive deeper into feedback.)

Be transparent. We want students to feel safe to share their thinking with us during formative assessments and not hide their confusions or misunderstandings. In order to make the context safe, explain to students what you are doing and why you're doing it. This way, students will know the purpose of the observation or conversation is to get to know them and their thinking, so they can't actually do it wrong.

Feedback has a short shelf life. Schedule time to look at formative assessment information each week. The purpose of the information is to use it right away and not let it pile up. Will you look back at your notes each day? At the end of the week? During professional learning community or team time? Make it a routine so it doesn't feel like one more thing to do.

Feedback

WHY?

In their book *Thanks for the Feedback*, Douglas Stone and Sheila Heen (2014) explain that "feedback is not simply a thing the giver hands you and you receive. The two of you are building a puzzle—together" (p. 241). Feedback has the power to bring two people closer together on a learning journey. The puzzle metaphor helps remind us that we want feedback to connect—connect us as teacher and student and connect the student to the content we are studying.

Feedback ideally feels useful, timely, and specific to the receiver (Hattie, 2012). We are not ready to give feedback until we know the learner well enough to name their process, ways of thinking, and strengths, not just their needs. By gathering information from a variety of formative assessment opportunities, we can give this targeted and impactful feedback.

Jan Burkins and Kim Yaris (2016) use the term *next generation* in their book *Who's Doing the Work?* to help us rethink past practices in a new way. Based on their concept of the next generation, the following chart can help us think about what feedback tended to be like in the past and what it might look like today.

Conventional Feedback:	Next-Generation Feedback:
— Teacher directed	— Student directed
— In the form of grades and numbers	— In the form of discussion with student work at the center
— Often summative	— Formative (as you go) and summative
— Often about what is wrong and not wrong	— Focuses on strengths to build from
— Can feel scary to students	— Students look forward to it

GETTING STARTED

Be a Mirror

In Gravity's book *Mindsets and Moves* (Goldberg, 2015) she researched ways feedback could help students' mindsets and strategies. She calls the feedback stance being a mirror for students. A mirror reflects back what they see but doesn't add in their judgments and evaluations. Effective mirroring includes four qualities.

QUICK TIPS

- *Walk the talk.* Many students don't yet know how to ask for feedback or how to receive it. Model lessons on this. Show them how you ask for feedback and how you use it. This is an important life skill as well as academic skill they can use across time and content areas.

- *Be asset-based.* Focus on what the learner is doing, not what is missing. Feedback is more easily received when the learner feels seen, heard, and valued. This does not mean we ignore things learners are not yet doing, but feedback is not the time to address it. Give feedback on a strength. Use teaching (like modeling or guided practice) to support a student trying something out that they do not yet do.

- *Emphasize interactivity quality.* When students are new to feedback, let them know they have an important role and are not supposed to just sit and listen. They can ask for feedback in a given area, ask for follow-up examples, ask questions, and make an action plan with next steps.

FEEDBACK MOVE	DESCRIPTION
Be specific.	Use the formative assessment information to name something specific the learner is doing. Make sure you identify a strength the learner can build from.
Focus on the process.	Name what the learner is doing as a series of steps, a process, and not simply an end product. Make sure to include *how* they did something.
Make sure it can transfer.	When choosing what to focus on in your feedback, choose something that can transfer to other learning experiences. Name the thinking and process the student took in a way that the student can choose to do it again in another context.
Take yourself out of it.	Rather than focus on what you think and on your judgments as the teacher, focus on how it impacted the learner. Avoid saying "I like . . ." and instead try "When you . . . it helped you to . . ."

Engage Students With Reflective Questions

According to Michael Bungay Stanier (2016), author of *The Coaching Habit*, the questions we ask can lead to autonomy and ownership so learners end up having the aha moments themselves, rather than waiting for you to tell them what to do. Imagine how we can help set up more independent and engaged learners with the questions we ask! Stanier's list of questions includes some of the following:

- What's on your mind?

- And what else?

- What's the real challenge here for you?

- How can I help?

These questions position students as active participants who can help lead the feedback session. It is also much more likely our feedback will have an impact when students are asking us for it. If students are new to answering these sorts of questions, chart them and model how to answer them before asking the class to try it.

Use Goals to Focus Feedback

Sometimes it can be challenging to decide what to offer feedback on. There is the obvious area—did they get a correct answer?—but so much of what students do in the learning process is about not only the answer but also the thinking and learning process that got them there.

The following list gives you some ideas for how you can use unit goals and students' personal goals to help you focus your feedback. In focusing it, the feedback becomes more actionable for the learner, more replicable. Once you have a focus, consider what it might sound like in that given area. You still want to try to be a mirror for students—reflecting back what you see them doing without layering in evaluation—and yet you are offering specifics of actions, thinking, and behaviors that are admirable, and that you want the students to keep building on.

FEEDBACK FOCUS	WHAT IT MIGHT SOUND LIKE	EXAMPLE
Learning habit	"When you did . . . it led to . . ."	"When you took the time to reread your notes before the conversation, it led to some new ideas you were able to bring to the group."
Taking a risk	"Even though it was a challenge and something new, you tried . . . and it helped you to learn . . ."	"Even though it was a challenge, you tried to have the whole conversation about food in French, and it helped you to learn you do know key food vocabulary and also adjectives for how to describe the food."
Building stamina	"It helped you stay focused and keep going by . . ."	"It helped you stay focused and keep going with the challenge problems by focusing on one at a time and taking a long exhale between problems."
Using a strategy	"First you . . . Then you . . . Next you . . . This helped you to . . ."	"First you read the source. Then you jotted down the main idea. Next you bulleted out the supporting details. This helped you to organize your thinking and remember the main ideas."
Synthesizing information	"By putting this [idea/text/part] together with this [idea/text/part], you were able to come up with a bigger idea that . . ."	"By putting this idea about free speech together with this idea about academic freedom from the two different articles you read, you were able to come up with a bigger idea about the importance of citizens being able to form their own ideas and beliefs."
Inferring cause and effect	"As you were [reading/viewing/listening], you thought about the relationship between these two parts, and it helped you to understand . . ."	"As you were viewing the water cycle video, you thought about the relationship between the heat of the sun and the impact on the plants. It helped you to understand how transpiration allows plants to use water more efficiently to survive the heat."
Contributing to a conversation	"When you . . . it helped your group by . . ."	"When you paused and asked Bella to share her thoughts, it helped your group by making space for her to share a new idea you had not yet discussed."

How to Receive and Use Feedback

So many students are regularly given feedback, but they are not sure what to do with it. This can be extremely frustrating for teachers who take the time to offer comments on student work when it seems like the students do not even look at it. If we teach students how to receive and then how to use feedback, it leads to much less frustration for teachers and more transfer and application for students. The following are examples of charts made with students when explicitly discussing how to give and receive feedback, whether it be from peer to peer or between student and teacher (or anywhere in life really).

When Offering Feedback . . .	When Receiving Feedback . . .
— Avoid judgment	— Avoid arguing why the person is wrong to have their perspective
— Be specific	— Try to be open-minded
— Ask questions that prompt thinking	— Remember you can choose not to take the feedback
— Choose words that show support	— Ask for clarification if needed
— Ask for clarification as needed	— Ask for an example or a model as needed
— Stick to focus	— Bring feedback you are not sure about to another person for their perspective
	— Say "thank you"

After discussing and charting how to receive feedback, you can model how to use feedback. This often includes jotting down some notes and making an action plan. The following chart was used in English classrooms to help students learn how to take peer feedback on writing and then actually use it to revise. The purple columns were completed by the writer who was asking for feedback and then using it. The green columns were completed by the reader of the piece who was offering feedback. The reader could be a peer or a teacher, and the chart could be adapted for other subject areas as well.

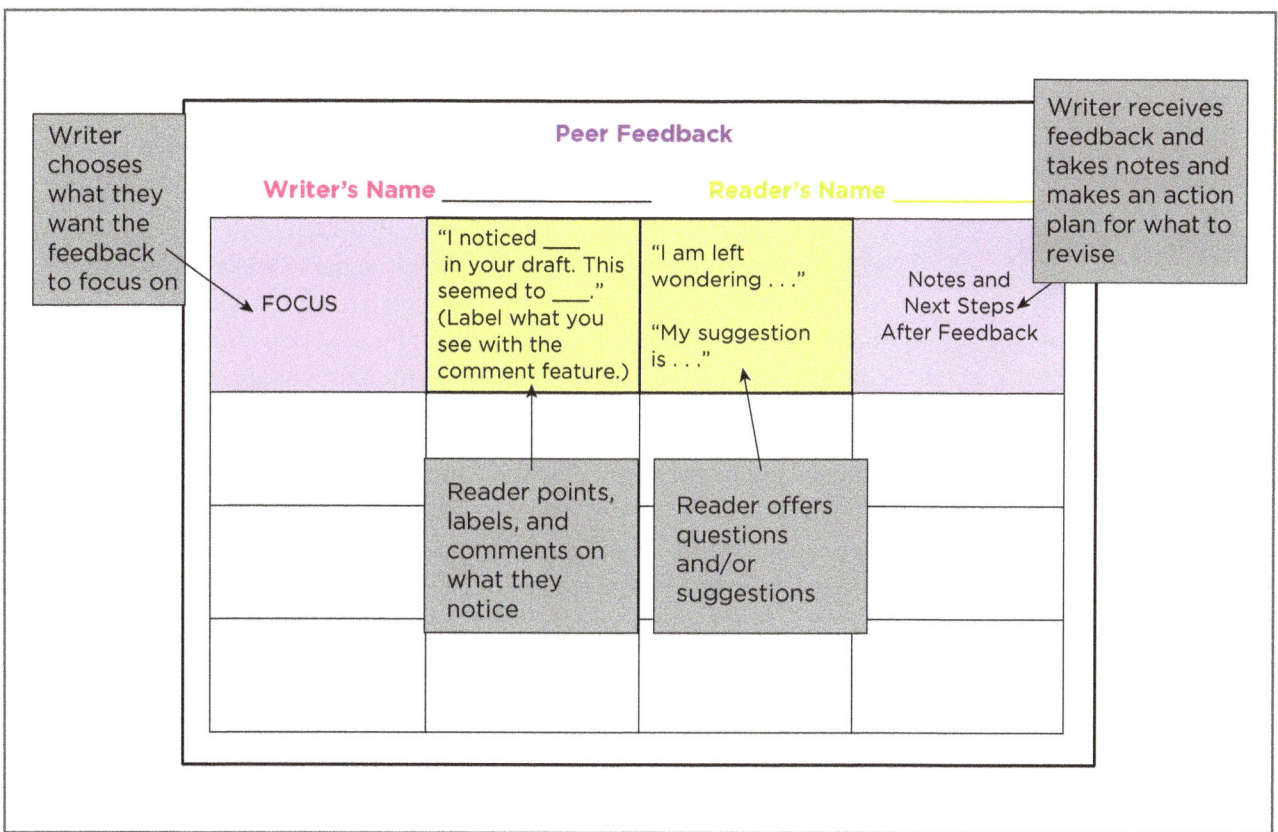

Peer Feedback

Writer chooses what they want the feedback to focus on

Writer's Name _____   Reader's Name _____

FOCUS	"I noticed ___ in your draft. This seemed to ___." (Label what you see with the comment feature.)	"I am left wondering . . ." "My suggestion is . . ."	Notes and Next Steps After Feedback

Writer receives feedback and takes notes and makes an action plan for what to revise

Reader points, labels, and comments on what they notice

Reader offers questions and/or suggestions

HEADS UP

Get feedback from students. One of the most effective ways to model receiving and using feedback and also creating a classroom culture of respect is to ask for feedback from students. Consider how you might get feedback from students and then model how you carefully consider it and use it to make an action plan.

Include conversation. Students tend to actually use feedback when it is done in conversation and not just as comments on written work. (In the next section we will look at how conferring with students is a highly effective way to give feedback and help students start using it right away.)

Keep track of feedback. Some students may end up getting lots of feedback while others get far less. This could be because students are proactively asking for feedback or because we gravitate toward them. Keep a class list handy so you can keep track of who you give feedback to so that students don't end up overwhelmed by too much or accidentally slipping between the cracks with none at all.

KEY IDEA

All learners benefit from feedback when it is timely, supportive, and specific. Taking the time to give students feedback and support peer feedback, and then showing them how to use feedback, can lead to more engagement and learning growth.

QUICK TIPS

- *Make it a special time.* In our busy lives, everyone benefits from moments fully dedicated to us. While you confer with students one-on-one, the rest of the class can be focused on independent or small-group work. Set behavior guidelines and practice them so the power of the conferring isn't eroded by interruptions. Conferring often happens during the independent portion of a workshop but can also happen anytime the rest of the class is engaged in meaningful work.

- *Make a calendar.* Literally map out who you will confer with each day so no one gets skipped. Each conference takes about five minutes, so plan on doing three to five a day at most. It will take a few days to two weeks to get to all students, and that is okay.

- *Mine it for data.* Take notes after a conference to add to your formative assessment information. This could be on a class grid, a goal-based chart, or an individual student form. (See Appendix F for examples.)

Conferring

WHY?

Conferences are intentional conversations that stem from curiosity and support. In a conference the teacher's job is to get to know students as people and thinkers by unearthing how and what they think. This allows them to name strengths and offer support for next steps. These conferring conversations are not just teaching opportunities, but also offer a powerful structure for making assessment a relationship-building experience.

Zaretta Hammond's (2015) book *Culturally Responsive Teaching and The Brain* explains the importance of an educator's ability to recognize students' cultural displays of learning and to respond positively and constructively with teaching moves that create a social-emotional connection. Conferences allow teachers to slow down for a few minutes to really understand how a student thinks—what strategies they use and what challenges they are facing.

Rather than assuming the written work students submit tells the whole story of learning, talking to students with genuine curiosity about their process helps make assessment a much more humanizing event. Knowing that Steven loves photography helps the teacher make a connection and opens a doorway into the kinds of knowledge Steven can leverage because of his expertise. Knowing that Tanya is an avid reader helps the teacher know she can count on this student to be a mentor to others who do not have this quality yet. When we know our students well, we are not just more accurate in our teaching decisions, but also more able to create a thriving classroom community.

The idea that it takes about 10,000 hours of practice to become an expert was popularized by Malcolm Gladwell (2008) in his book *Outliers*, but it took just one part of Anders Ericsson's research on deliberate practice when making this point (Ericsson & Pool, 2016). Dr. Ericsson's research found that, yes, lots of practice is important for learning, but there are other qualities involved in the practice that make it deliberate. Some of those qualities include the following:

- There need to be clear goals.

- The practice should get increasingly more difficult.

- Learners need immediate feedback and reflection.

- Learners need a coach for individualized practice.

Conferring regularly with students is a way to support all of these elements of deliberate practice. When we confer, we can help students with the unit and personal goals. We can help students by giving them feedback and asking reflection questions. We can offer support that makes the level of difficulty more or less challenging. When conferring, we serve as coaches who can offer suggestions and tips so the learner can make adjustments.

Finally, when teachers reflect about their experiences with conferring, they always smile and talk about the gratitude they have for the moments they shared with students. They lean in and talk about a student with such nuanced knowledge of who they are. They tell stories about what they learned from and with the student. They say it is the most impactful part of the day. Teachers also follow up with a lot of questions about how to make it go smoother and quicker and how to fit it into their schedule more often. This section will offer ideas for many of these questions.

GETTING STARTED

When conferring is new, it is helpful to clarify roles and goals. Take time to explain what the teacher takes on and what students take on. Without this explicit introduction, we've found students often hang back during conferences, presuming they are there to merely receive feedback. The following chart can be used as a visual when explaining conferences to students.

A Conference Is . . .

- A conversation
- A time to share goals, strategies, and challenges
- An opportunity to ask for and get feedback
- A time to name strengths and celebrate growth
- A time for coaching to try something new

If students are not new to conferring, you can make a chart together with them on the teacher and student roles. If they are new to it, you might show a chart like the one that follows and discuss it with them. It is also helpful to ask for a volunteer to model a conference so students can see and hear it in action too.

TEACHER ROLES IN A CONFERENCE	STUDENT ROLES IN A CONFERENCE
<ul><li>Ask reflective and open-ended questions.</li><li>Give feedback.</li><li>Model a strategy.</li><li>Coach the learner to try a strategy.</li></ul>	<ul><li>Help set the focus.</li><li>Explain your process with examples.</li><li>Ask for and receive feedback.</li><li>Be open to new ideas.</li><li>Try a strategy with support.</li></ul>

Prepare Questions

Conferring usually starts with the teacher asking some questions that set the student up to reflect and share. These questions ideally are genuine and open-ended about the process and invite students to explain what and how they are thinking. The following question stems can be helpful when you are starting out. Some teachers even share a list of questions with students as examples of the types of questions they may discuss so students can practice thinking about them before they meet.

Questions That Invite Student Reflection

- What goal are you working toward? How is it going?

- What are you thinking about _____?

- How did you form that idea?

- What strategies are helping you to _____?

- What is your process for _____?

- Show me an example of _____. Take me through your steps.

- What challenges are you facing as you _____?

- How might I serve as a thinking partner with you today?

Prepare Feedback Stems

After students share their process and thinking with you, choose one area to focus on in feedback. Pick something that is new or really impactful or that seems important to reinforce. While you should absolutely use language that feels comfortable and authentic to you when giving feedback, it can also be helpful to have a list of supportive language and phrases handy to glance at. When we don't intentionally choose our feedback language, it can lead to habitual language use that may not support student independence. For example, sometimes we end up doing too much of the work in feedback for students, or sometimes we forget to focus on a strength and get right into teaching. The following stems are examples that teachers use when first figuring out what language works best for them and their students.

Feedback Stems That Focus on Strengths

- Since your goal was to _____, it helped you to _____.

- First you _____. Then you _____, and it helped you to _____.

- Because you _____, you were able to _____.

- Whenever you are _____, you can continue to do _____.

- A strength you can build from is _____.

Prepare Modeling Tools

Not every conference includes teacher modeling, but in many cases, taking an extra minute to show a student how you do something can make it much more likely to stick. It also helps us use more visuals and not just expect students to learn from our words alone.

A challenge is that if we model with a student's work, we have just done the thinking for them. Instead of modeling using the student's work, prepare a few texts, problems, or examples you can model with. For example, if the class is studying the effects of one former president's policies in a U.S. history class, you can have a text about a different U.S. president to model with. The following are some ideas for what you might curate and take with you into conferences so you can choose to model when needed. The key is to model very quickly so students can see an example and then try it.

Modeling Tools to Carry With You

- Texts that are connected to, but not the same as, the ones the students are using

- Sticky notes to jot down steps

- Blank paper or a whiteboard to make a visual

- A copy of a class chart you already created to refer back to

- A previously created example from class you can show again

Use a Coaching Mindset

After modeling quickly, invite students to try what they just learned with some support. You shift from being a model to a coach as the students take over the thinking. Lead them through the steps using guided practice.

A challenge when coaching students is to decide how much heavy lifting you will do as the teacher and how much they will do as the student. You might think of a soccer coach who is on the sideline calling plays and being encouraging, but not on the field actually running with the ball. If you think of this metaphor in coaching students, try to give a prompt, direction, or smile, but also enough wait time for students to try and maybe even struggle a bit on their own before giving more support. The following list helps you use a coaching mindset.

KEY IDEA

Conferring is a structure that includes both formative assessment and feedback that happens in real time. It personalizes the classroom experience and helps build strong teacher and student relationships.

Coaching Moves

- Prompt with steps of a process.

- Wait and watch.

- Smile and nod.

- Point back to a chart, example, or resource.

- Remind the students of previous models.

- Allow struggle to happen before stepping in.

- Point out success and normalize challenges.

- State a next step for students to try on their own.

HEADS UP

See it as a time-saver. While it takes time to sit with each student one-on-one, it can save time to be targeted and intentional with this personalized teaching. Save time by being organized. Prepare ahead of time, set up routines with students, and make a plan.

Be a pattern finder. Conferring can yield data that help inform not only individual teaching choices but whole-group lessons. Take time to look across your notes on conferences to find patterns. These patterns can help you create whole-class and small-group targeted lessons that follow up on what you found in the conferences.

Create a ripple effect. Look at the Section 4 discussion of share-outs on page 140 and invite students who you had a conference with to share something they learned with their peers. This makes the teaching you did one-on-one spread to other students in the class.

Learning Progressions

WHY?

Since we know that learning happens in small increments, it is helpful to have assessment tools that help both teachers and students see the growth along the way. If we only assess with right and wrong answers or some version of "This student 'got it,' and this one 'didn't get it,'" we are missing all the nuanced learning in between.

Learning progressions are tools that can be used by students and teachers that map out how learning develops in a given area. The progression can be pictured as a staircase, where everyone is moving toward the same doorway but might not all be on the same step. Progressions are based on research about what learners can do at different stages of learning (Duncan & Hmelo-Silver, 2009).

Learning progressions can be focused around unit goals and standards and help teachers identify specific next steps for students, as well as support the formation of small groups. The following learning progression is an example of a very specific goal tied to using context clues to figure out unfamiliar vocabulary.

Notice how the learning gets more proficient and developed as it moves from left to right. Consider how you could ask students to show you how they tried to figure out an unfamiliar word, and then identify where they are on this continuum. You would then reinforce what they are doing and teach them one new strategy in the column to its right. Of course, students can be exposed to learning progressions in whole-class discussions and then self-assess and make an action plan on their own as well.

Using Context Clues to Figure Out Unfamiliar Vocabulary

Learning Progression

Rereads the sentence the unfamiliar word is in	Rereads the sentence it is in and the sentences before and after	Rereads the sentence it is in, the sentences before and after, and any visuals on the page	Rereads the sentence it is in, the sentences before and after, and any visuals on the page
		Thinks about the type of word and part of speech	Thinks about the type of word and part of speech
			Rereads the sentence, inserting a synonym, and thinks about if it makes sense

- *Frame as can-do actions.* Learning progressions are verb focused and should not be adjective focused. As you practice making them, look at each characteristic and think of the actions (verbs) a learner uses. Make that the focus of each column.

- *Promote growth first, grades second.* While you can turn progressions into grading tools, it is also helpful to make them formative assessment tools first. If you do need to assign a grade, you can consider if it will be based on growth—moving two steps to the right—or based on outcome—getting to the final column.

- *Stretch, challenge, engage.* Make sure progressions have a next step for all learners in your class. If you find out that students are already all the way on the right and experts on the progression at the start of a unit, add a step so they can be stretched to learn too. Or help the students select a different goal to work toward. It is a waste of time and sends a fixed mindset message if students who are already experts don't have opportunities to grow too.

While rubrics and checklists are quite common assessment tools in secondary classrooms, they don't show you what students need to learn next. Rubrics often have adjectives and adverbs that mark the difference between a 2 and 3, but that is almost entirely subjective and hard to make actionable. Take, for example, a rubric version of the context clues progression. It would have options like *rarely uses context clues, sometimes uses context clues, often uses context clues*, and so on. When frequency is used to define the difference on a rubric, it misses the whole learning opportunity of what the learner is and is not yet doing. It also makes more challenging skills less overwhelming by breaking them down into actionable moves a learner can develop over time. Think about the kind of feedback a student gets if a 2 is circled on a rubric and they need to move from *rarely* to *often*. How do they do that? If instead they see a progression that expects them to "think about the type of word and part of speech," they have something they can learn to do.

GETTING STARTED

When planning a unit, you can look back at the unit's standards, essential questions, and goals to decide what learning progressions might be most useful. You do not need a learning progression for every skill in a unit but do want to consider which skills are high impact and will come up again and again in your department or course. Some departments make learning progressions together so there is continuity of expectations and supports. Some examples follow.

- A social studies department met and made some progressions they would all use for document-based writing and research.

- An English department collaborated and made learning progressions for each type of writing—narrative, informational, and argument.

- A math department created problem-solving progressions and aligned them with each course.

- A language department created conversation progressions they could use whether it was a Spanish, Italian, French, or German class.

Steps for Creating a Learning Progression

1. *Select a focus skill tied to unit goals.* This should be a thinking skill and not simply content knowledge. For example, you would not have a progression for "What is the chemical reaction of ___ and ___?" because that has one right answer. Instead, you might have a focus like "Describe the cause and effect of chemical reactions," because the learner's ability to think about causes, effects, and the relationships between them develops over time. A progression could help the teacher and students see where they are and a clear next step.

2. *Start with proficiency in mind.* Think about what someone who is proficient in the skill does. Make it actionable. Try doing it yourself and naming what you do. By trying it with others in your department, it can help you put words to steps you "just do" without really thinking about it. This proficient set of actions will become your second-to-last column. That way, you can move backward by taking away some of the actions to the left and adding an action to make it more developed to the right. An example of the beginning of a progression from a social studies department follows.

Supporting Claims With Evidence: Social Studies Learning Progression

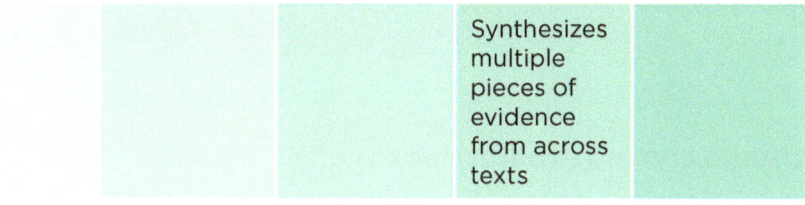

| | | | Synthesizes multiple pieces of evidence from across texts | |

3. *Think backward.* Once you have the actions a proficient learner takes with a given skill, start to consider the actions that led to this. Sometimes you can take something away or think of a first step into that skill to create the columns to the left. An example of the supporting claims with evidence progression follows. Notice how the actions grow from *identify*, to *contextualize*, to *explain*, to *synthesize.*

Supporting Claims With Evidence: Social Studies Learning Progression

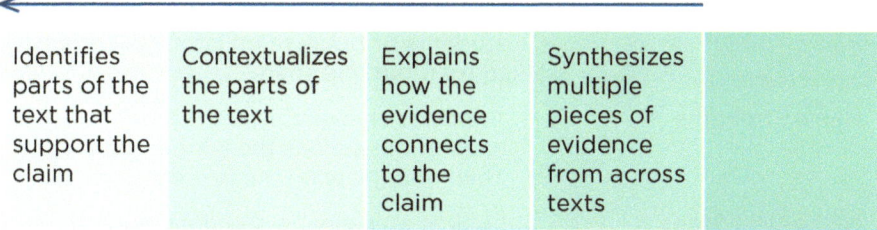

| Identifies parts of the text that support the claim | Contextualizes the parts of the text | Explains how the evidence connects to the claim | Synthesizes multiple pieces of evidence from across texts | |

4. *Think beyond.* Since everyone in the class should have a next step to grow toward, you will want to go back and add a step up from the proficient column. Consider what the next-grade-level learning might look like or what someone who excels in this area might think and do. Add the final column to the right, again making sure to focus on the actions that build across the entire continuum. This final column is not an expectation for all students, but does give some students something to think about and a place to continue to learn.

Supporting Claims With Evidence: Social Studies Learning Progression

Identifies parts of the text that support the claim	Contextualizes the parts of the text	Explains how the evidence connects to the claim	Synthesizes multiple pieces of evidence from across texts	All of the previous columns and . . . Explains information that is missing from the argument (voices, perspectives, etc.)

Using Learning Progressions With Students

Once you develop learning progressions, you can begin to introduce them to students. They are learning and assessment tools, not meant to be high stakes or fear inducing. Try not to show them with numbers at first so students focus more on the content in the columns than the score they would get for each one. What follows is a list of engaging ways to introduce and use the learning progressions with students so they become learning and feedback tools.

ACTIVITY	DESCRIPTION
Example Sort	Show examples you collected and work with students to sort and match them to the columns.
Create Examples	Create examples for each column with students or break them into small groups to try it out and share.
Name Strengths	Annotate an example with students naming the actions the learner did take. Then find those on the progression.
Name Next Steps	Look at an example and then study the column to the right. Discuss what next steps the learner could take.
Revise Together	Revise an example together based on taking an action from the column to the right.
Self-Reflection and Goal Setting	Students self-reflect by identifying where their thinking is on the progression and then set an actionable goal for what they will learn and do next.
Peer Feedback	Partners work together to identify where their thinking currently is on the progression and then make an action plan for what to try next. Then they check back in with each other for accountability and continued collaboration.

HEADS UP

It can be hard to name your own actions. Sometimes it helps to have someone who is not an expert in your subject help you name your steps because they are less fluent in that area. They can often slow down enough to name the actions you are taking because they have to think much harder about how to do them. If you have grade-level professional learning community time with those in another subject area, you can work together across departments.

Add learning progressions to other structures. If you look back at many of the structures already mentioned in this book such as thinking routines and reflection (Section 3), share-outs (Section 4), and feedback, learning progressions can help support that work. Consider where students seem stuck and add in a learning progression to those parts.

Collaborate with students. Once students have experience using learning progressions, they can also help you develop them. Including students in the process gives them much more ownership and understanding. It can be helpful to first include them in developing progressions around habits, conversations, and note-taking because the students have so much experience and these progressions are more concrete than some higher-level thinking progressions around big ideas and concepts.

KEY IDEA

Learning progressions make assessment, goal setting, and instructional decision making clear and actionable. Use them with students throughout the year and across learning experiences.

QUICK TIPS

- *Tether to the unit.* When designing a unit around portfolio assessments, make sure to look back at unit goals and standards to keep focused on the key ideas of your course.

- *Focus.* Offer as much choice as possible with portfolios so students can curate and showcase what they learned. A portfolio is not just a folder with all of the assignments they completed. It is intentionally created with a focus in mind. For example, if a student is creating a portfolio for a music class, they might first select a focus on impacts of women composers and then select work they created around that focus.

- *Curate the contents.* Remind students they can use learning progressions as feedback and include reflection tools they've used as part of the portfolio. Doing so helps learners know they have more than a checklist to use when making choices about what to include and how to revise their work.

Portfolios

WHY?

According to Arter and Spandel (2005), portfolios are purposeful collections of student work that help students showcase their efforts and achievement. Portfolios came into classrooms as a way to push back on the standardization movement. Many educators noted that standardized tests did not adequately or accurately show students' learning. In addition, when the internet became more widely available in classrooms, innovative educators called for more authentic and relevant forms of assessment that matched today's world. If students were able to create a digital portfolio of their work, they could use it for college admissions and when applying for jobs. By *portfolios*, some educators meant blogs, websites, or wikis where they could curate, design, and showcase their learning.

Today many teachers choose to use portfolios because they:

- Document growth over time.

- Support reflection.

- Personalize assessment.

- Create artifacts that can be used beyond school.

- Lead to student ownership.

- Can be multimodal and strength-based.

- Offer information teachers can use to make instructional decisions.

- Give a bigger picture than simply a numerical test score.

While it can seem overwhelming to start using portfolios for the first time, they don't need to be huge projects. You can bring a portfolio lens into any or all of the units across the year. At its essence, a portfolio is a collection of artifacts that allow a student to showcase learning and growth. They can include digital tools and apps, or they can be as simple as a Google Doc with links.

GETTING STARTED

Use the chart that follows to think through the steps of the portfolio process and what the teacher and students are doing during each step.

STEP	TEACHER	STUDENTS
1. Identify the goals of the portfolio.	— Remind students of unit goals. — Show examples of portfolios.	— Select the goal they will focus on.
2. Develop pieces that work toward the goals.	— All unit long, provide modeling and guided practice with unit goals.	— Collect work samples that align with the goal.
3. Reflect on learning and growth for each piece.	— Give feedback and confer with students about their pieces.	— Ask for feedback from peers and teacher. — Self-reflect and jot down reflections for each piece.
4. Design the format for how the pieces will go together.	— Show examples and models of what portfolio pieces might look like, and discuss why you might make each choice. — Revisit the section on multimodal learning to make sure there are a variety of types.	— Make a plan for the format they will use. — Get feedback on the format and try it out.
5. Reflect on learning and growth across the pieces.	— Model how to reflect across the pieces of work on patterns that show growth. — Show how learning progressions could be helpful too.	— Use learning progressions and other learning tools to write up a reflection on what they learned and now know how to do. — Support their reflection with references to specific artifacts in the portfolio.
6. Share the portfolio.	— Create time and space for students to share via a shared document or small-group presentations, etc. — Give feedback on the final piece.	— Share the portfolio and use language that matches their goal and intended audience. — Receive feedback and celebrate growth.

There are many variations on this portfolio process. You could simplify it for a short unit and just focus on the *develop* and *reflect* portions. You could ask students to create mini portfolios all year long that lead to one large one at the end of the year. Or you could work with your department to have students add to a portfolio every year until graduation where they curate their best pieces in a culminating project. Whatever you choose, make sure it is focused on intentionality and purpose so students know why they are doing this and see its value.

Assessing the Portfolio

Use all of your formative assessment tools to assess the portfolio as students create it. That way, they will be getting feedback along the way, and you will know they are making progress. Some ideas to consider include interim due dates that are not graded but allow for formative assessment and feedback. Set up a conferring schedule with students so everyone gets to know strengths and has some actionable next steps to work on.

Create and use learning progressions with students so they know and can name what they are working on. This will also help you manage so many students working on different pieces. When you have a common progression, you can focus on the skills and not solely the content. What follows is a sample learning progression for one aspect of the portfolio: reflection.

Reflecting On Learning and Growth Progression

Names the goal(s) they are working toward	Identifies parts of their work that align with goals	Describes how parts of their work align with goals	Describes the parts of their work that align with goals and shows how they have grown with examples

Of course, reflection is just one part of the portfolio process, so you will also want to use progressions around the specific goals of your unit. These can be the same progressions you created and used throughout the unit with students. See the previous section on learning progressions for more ideas and examples.

What About Grades?

While it is not possible to get into the weeds of how individual content areas and schools grade, it is important to consider the following when grading student portfolios.

- What was the overall purpose of the portfolio, and how did the student demonstrate learning in that area?

- What percentage of the overall grade will it count for?

- Did the portfolio allow the student to show what they truly learned?

- Will I grade this based on growth, outcomes, or both?

- Do I use a standards-based grading system, and if so, what standards am I assessing?

- Do I use mastery-based grading, and if so, what progressions might be useful?

- Will students be involved in the grading process? How so?

- Will students be able to revise and submit?

The list could go on. The important elements here are to remember to humanize the grading experience so students are never framed as numbers or letters and also that we set students up to succeed.

HEADS UP

Structure. Try to find the right balance of structure so that students know what is expected of them and know what success looks like but not so much that the portfolio becomes one long worksheet to fill in.

Make it multidisciplinary. If possible, consider multidisciplinary portfolios so that students can go for depth and make connections across courses. This might mean they create a humanities portfolio instead of one for social studies and one for English, for example.

Make it multimodal. Look back at page 73 in Section 5. Encourage students to use the modalities that work best for them and their focus when curating pieces to include. Perhaps a video would help them show learning more than an essay. Maybe designing an infographic would work better than a report.

KEY IDEA

Incorporating portfolios into assessment opportunities helps students develop ownership of assessment by selecting and reflecting on a body of work they created.

QUICK TIPS

- *Integrate.* Design performance assessments that integrate multiple skills and concepts. This will help students make connections and creates more practice with synthesis. Look back at previous unit goals and how they may be used again in this current unit assessment.

- *Think process.* Consider breaking up performance assessments across days so students have time to work through a process. The first day may be to plan and collect thinking. The second day might be for drafting. The third day might be for revisions. Of course, it might take longer or shorter, but this rough timeline helps students focus on the process and not just the end product.

- *Mirror class experiences.* Performance assessments should mirror the skills that students practiced during the unit and already got feedback on. The assessment will likely be on new content or a new problem to solve, but the skills are ones they have been using.

Performance Assessments

WHY?

Performance assessments are tasks that ask students to integrate and transfer learning from across time. They allow the opportunity for students to show what they can do and not just what they know about a topic of study. The word *performance* does not mean they are up on stage; instead, the root *perform* can help us remember it is about students actively using what they know to do something—to take actions. Performance assessments can happen partway through a unit or at the end of a unit, really anytime students are asked to perform a task or create something that draws upon an accumulation of skills and knowledge. These assessments do tend to be graded but also can be used to inform future instructional choices.

Learning is not just information in our heads but how we can take action and use that information. Performance assessments are opportunities for students to integrate information and apply it to new situations and contexts. They focus on knowing information but also on using it. We can focus on both content and skills in performance assessments.

In many ways, life is a series of performance assessments. For example, someone may be able to read a recipe, but can they actually make something that tastes good from it? Or, someone can pass a written driver's test, but can they safely drive? Knowing what to plant in a vegetable garden is useful information, but can you successfully grow food to feed yourself?

The push for performance assessments came from business leaders who wanted to make sure students graduated with skills that were essential for 21st century jobs. Darling-Hammond and Adamson (2010) explained performance assessments are more aligned to today's context: "Because they allow students to construct or perform an original response rather than just recognizing a potentially right answer out of a list provided, performance assessments can measure students' cognitive thinking and reasoning skills and their ability to apply knowledge to solve realistic, meaningful problems" (p. 7).

From an engagement perspective, performance assessments allow for more creativity and choice making, and students often find them much more interesting than a typical multiple-choice question. Students also tend to find them much more difficult. There is no faking your way through performance assessment like you can with penciling in bubbles. Some research-based benefits of performance assessments are that they:

- Increase students' skill development (Niemi et al., 2007).

- Lead to more student engagement (Foote, 2005).

- Develop complex conceptual understandings (Chung & Baker, 2003).

- Deepen students' critical thinking and problem solving (Faxon-Mills et al., 2013).

You likely already have some forms of performance assessments in the classroom, but you might not call them that. Some examples include:

- Read, take a stance, present an argument, or have a debate.

- Research a topic and present your findings.

- Analyze data and make an informed recommendation.

- Study an author's craft and then try to use similar techniques in your own original piece.

- Create a plan for how to solve a complex problem from your community.

- Critique someone's argument and offer ideas for how they could strengthen it.

GETTING STARTED

When designing performance assessments, consider the goals, the texts, and the products students will create. If we want students to be successful and show what they know and can do, we can design the assessment experience with their strengths in mind.

Consider Goals

Look at standards and goals to ask, "What actionable project might students participate in to demonstrate these skills?" The table that follows gives some ideas for how you might align the type of goal with the type of performance assessment.

IF THE UNIT GOAL IS FOCUSED ON . . .	A PERFORMANCE ASSESSMENT MIGHT INCLUDE . . .
Argumentation	• Debating • Giving a speech • Writing a letter or blog • Creating a marketing campaign • Critiquing someone else's claim
Problem solving	• Solving a new problem • Critiquing how someone else solved a problem • Writing a how-to book • Creating a YouTube-style video tutorial • Developing an interactive journal—what did and did not work and why

(Continued)

(Continued)

IF THE UNIT GOAL IS FOCUSED ON . . .	A PERFORMANCE ASSESSMENT MIGHT INCLUDE . . .
Interpreting perspectives	• Creating a scenario or scene from multiple perspectives • Recording a podcast with each participant representing a different perspective • Rewriting a piece from a different perspective • Making two social media feeds that show a difference in perspective • Annotating a piece with callouts that show the author's perspective
Research	• Making a research-based recommendation or presentation • Creating a memo of what is currently known and unknown about a topic • Conducting firsthand research such as interviews or observations and describing how it relates to previously conducted published research • Explaining research findings for a particular audience, matching modality and language for the audience

Consider Texts

Most performance assessments include some texts. The texts could be anything—poetry, articles, podcasts, infographics, primary sources, videos, statistics, and so on. Make sure the texts you include are accessible enough for all of the students in the class.

You might offer some choice of texts so students are not only performing a skill but also choosing the texts that align with that skill. You might offer choices in:

- The type of text

- The author

- The text

- The perspectives

Look at the example that follows and notice how student choice can enhance engagement and also lead to more critical thinking. Students are offered choices about which musician and song they want to analyze. Think about how assigning everyone the same song to analyze might have very different results because of students' preferences, background knowledge, and experiences with the artist assigned.

Rhetoric Performance Assessment

Choose a musician and one of their songs.

- What is the author's overall message?
- What rhetorical devices did the author make that align with this message?
- How effective were the author's choices?

You can select one of the musicians listed here or link to one of your own choosing.

- Beyoncé
- Billie Eilish
- Ariana Grande
- Taylor Swift
- Drake

Consider Products

Students can demonstrate skills and content knowledge in a variety of ways. It can be helpful to offer choice in the product. Will it be in video, audio, written, visual, or a hybrid format? Looking again at the sample rhetoric performance assessment, choice can be included with how the students share their thinking.

You can explain your analysis in video, audio, written, or a hybrid format.

This might mean some students simply record themselves explaining their analysis in relation to each question. Others might print out the lyrics to a song and mark up the text with comments, reactions, arrows, emojis, and analysis. Others might make a slideshow that presents their analysis. Since this is not a writing assessment, the final product does not need to be in a written format. As long as the goals are clearly addressed and can be assessed with the learning progression, students can focus on the thinking instead of the modality itself.

KEY IDEA

Performance assessments are an opportunity for students to show not just what they know, but also how they can synthesize, apply, and transfer skills to a new situation. It gives teachers a view into the habits of mind, skills, and content students have learned.

HEADS UP

Build confidence with collaborative practice. Some students are used to being told exactly what to do every step of the way, and they freeze when given choices. To boost confidence and offer support, students can practice the elements of the performance assessment earlier in the unit with a partner or small group.

Use feedback to prepare. Instead of going into the performance assessment cold, offer time for students to look back at their previous work, feedback they were given, and big ideas they learned. This can help them feel prepared and also models how to review for an assessment.

Focus on what matters most. Since performance assessments are often lengthy and involved, they can take a lot of time to read and grade. You don't need to focus on every standard or skill in the assessment. Pick a few focuses and stick to those. Just make sure students know the focus too. Perhaps even give them the learning progressions so they know exactly what the goal is.

Conclusion

Teaching From Your Beliefs

The more you seek to create a classroom environment where students are engaged in meaningful experiences, the more they learn to think for themselves. This thinking leads to trusting themselves to be creative, solve problems, and empathize with others.

Author Paul Tough (2012) explains, "What matters most in a child's development . . . is not how much information we can stuff into her brain in the first few years. What matters, instead, is whether we are able to help her develop a very different set of qualities, a list that includes persistence, self-control, curiosity, conscientiousness, grit, and self-confidence" (p. xv). By choosing to teach in ways that engage students' hearts and minds, you are setting them up to develop the character needed to thrive in the classroom and beyond.

We educators have so little control over big aspects of our work like standards and state tests. One thing we do have control over is how we choose to show up for students each day. Yes, you will hone your go-to teaching moves and learning tools, but underneath every choice is the foundation of your beliefs. If you believe your students will be engaged in critical thinking and meaningful learning, you are much more likely to create the context for it to happen.

If we want students to take intellectual risks, we need to be on a similar journey. What new learning are you seeking? How are you stepping out of your comfort zone to try something new? To what extent do you explicitly and implicitly convey to students that you are ever evolving, a curious work in progress? In what ways are you prioritizing depth of thought over covering content? What teaching practice might you let go of to create space for more student thinking to happen?

Teaching for engagement means we are fully invested in turning our beliefs about learning into actions. Our beliefs are built upon research, theory, and experience, of course, but we contend they run deeper than that, tapping into basic but profound faith in human potential. We trust you to design the classroom so that joyful engagement is front and center.

QUICK TIPS

- *Nurture your teacher relationships.* Keep a few teacher colleagues on call for reflection, planning, and connecting. Teachers who have trusted colleagues and friends tend to enjoy their work more and last longer in the profession.

- *Check in with your own learning engagement.* Find professional learning opportunities that allow you to feel engaged as a learner. Your excitement for learning will spread to your students.

- *Let students be your guide.* Believe in your ability to use students' thinking to drive your instructional choices. When you base tomorrow's lesson on today's student thinking, you are much more likely to be successful.

APPENDICES

APPENDIX A

TYPE OF THINKING	DESCRIPTION	WHY IT IS IMPORTANT
Independent thinking	Forming one's own ideas based on experience, beliefs, and knowledge	• Leads to academic and job success • Expands your understanding • Increases ability to navigate the important decisions in learning and in life • Less likely to be manipulated and make shortsighted decisions
Creative thinking	Thinking "outside of the box" by developing innovative ideas	• Develops habits of mind • Encourages intellectual risk-taking • Values seeking alternatives • Opens up endless possibilities • Develops a hopeful outlook
Problem-solving thinking	Addressing challenges by developing possible solutions	• Values the process • Normalizes struggle • Supports a growth mindset • Positions students as contributors • Develops metacognition
Empathetic thinking	Seeking to understand others' experiences, feelings, and beliefs	• Develops compassion • Supports a nuanced view of the world • Humanizes others • Leads to less polarization • Opens up one's mind and heart

online resources

APPENDIX B

PLANNING UNIT GOALS

UNIT	TOPIC/FOCUS	STANDARDS	WHAT STUDENTS WILL KNOW AND BE ABLE TO DO	GOALS
1.				
2.				
3.				
4.				
5.				
6.				

APPENDIX C

Goal: Remember key ideas and details by taking notes as you read/view/listen.

Connect	As a class, one of our goals is to remember key ideas and details as we read articles, watch videos, and listen to talks.
	• Teacher points to class chart of goals.
	We have already noticed that when we don't take notes, we tend to forget some of the most important information. I get it. Many of you don't like to take notes. When you do take notes, I've noticed that some of you always take notes the same way—a long list of details—no matter the purpose or type of text.
	When we choose not to take notes, it is sort of like going grocery shopping without a list and then getting home and realizing we don't have some of the ingredients for the recipe. And when we take notes in only one way, we may be missing out on approaches that suit us better than, say, making a list.
	Today we will learn a strategy for how to take meaningful notes that match the text you are learning from and you, the learner.
Model	Take a look at these charts of a few ways to take notes. The first is an example of taking notes when you want to remember information in sequence, and the second is for when you want to remember the parts or categories of information that go with a bigger topic.
	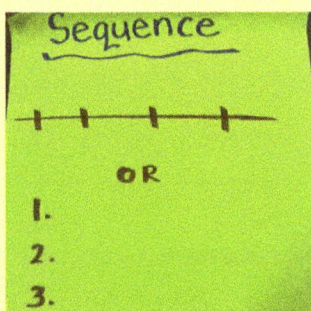 
	Watch how I preview this article and decide how to take notes (in sequence or in parts) based on how the text is set up.
	• Teacher models reading the first few paragraphs and scanning the rest and then thinking aloud about what they notice.

This article seems to be written about the benefits of eating whole grains and how it helps our bodies. But as I skim ahead, I see that the author is going on to address a larger topic of healthy eating. Since this first section on whole grains is a part of a topic and will list benefits of other foods, I am going to look at the second chart and choose either box and bullets or a web to take notes. I like to use a box and bullets, so I will give it a try.

- Teacher reads the first paragraph and models how they take notes.

> **Benefits of eating whole grains**
>
> - High in fiber
> - Reduces risk of heart disease
> - Helps you feel full and satisfied

See how I chose a note-taking format to help me remember the key information (benefits) and then the supporting details bulleted underneath? I'll use this same format to take notes on the next section, on the benefits of eating nuts and seeds.

Using a timeline or numbered list just wouldn't match this text because the information is not set up in a sequence. Using the box and bullets helped. I can remember the boxed idea as a key one and then look back at the details that go with it. If I didn't put the box at the top, I might miss the key category the supporting details go with.

Guided Practice	Now it is your turn to try. Take out the article you are reading today.
	Begin previewing the article and thinking, "How is this text set up? Is it about a sequence of events or the parts of a topic? Or something else?"
	Next, look at the chart of sample note-taking formats.
	• Teacher points back to the chart they modeled.
	Choose one that matches the way you like to take notes and the type of text you are reading.
	• Students set up the note-taking format. Then they begin reading and try it out.
	• Teacher walks around the room for a few minutes as students give it a try. They will not finish the entire article but can begin enough that the teacher can check in and see how it is going.
	• If and when students struggle, the teacher can gently coach and point to the charts as examples.
	Now take a minute to share with a partner how you took your notes and if it is working to help you remember key details.
	• Teacher may ask a student to share their notes with the whole class if there is time.
Link	I will leave these charts up and add them to our class drive as a reminder so you can refer back to them. Remember that whenever you are reading, or viewing a video, or listening to a talk, and you want to hold onto the key ideas and supporting details, you can set up a note-taking format that matches the type of text you are reading.

APPENDIX D

STRATEGY GROUP GRID

Focus:	Focus:
Students:	Students:
Focus: Students:	Focus: Students:
Focus:	Focus:
Students:	Students:

224

APPENDIX E

COLLABORATIVE CONVERSATIONS CHECKLIST

GROUP	BEFORE THE CONVERSATION	DURING THE CONVERSATION	AFTER THE CONVERSATION
	☐ Jots down ideas to talk about ☐ Notes a specific part of the text or experience to share	☐ Active listening ☐ Adding on ideas ☐ Challenging ideas ☐ Referring to the text ☐ Sharing the "air time" ☐ Staying on topic	☐ Jots down new thinking from the conversation ☐ Makes a plan for what to do next
	☐ Jots down ideas to talk about ☐ Notes a specific part of the text or experience to share	☐ Active listening ☐ Adding on ideas ☐ Challenging ideas ☐ Referring to the text ☐ Sharing the "air time" ☐ Staying on topic	☐ Jots down new thinking from the conversation ☐ Makes a plan for what to do next
	☐ Jots down ideas to talk about ☐ Notes a specific part of the text or experience to share	☐ Active listening ☐ Adding on ideas ☐ Challenging ideas ☐ Referring to the text ☐ Sharing the "air time" ☐ Staying on topic	☐ Jots down new thinking from the conversation ☐ Makes a plan for what to do next
	☐ Jots down ideas to talk about ☐ Notes a specific part of the text or experience to share	☐ Active listening ☐ Adding on ideas ☐ Challenging ideas ☐ Referring to the text ☐ Sharing the "air time" ☐ Staying on topic	☐ Jots down new thinking from the conversation ☐ Makes a plan for what to do next

APPENDIX F

CONFERRING NOTES: INDIVIDUAL STUDENT FORM

Student _____   Unit _____

DATE	STRENGTHS	NEXT STEPS

226

Class _____   Unit _____

Student: Date: Strength: Next Step:	Student: Date: Strength: Next Step:	Student: Date: Strength: Next Step:	Student: Date: Strength: Next Step:	Student: Date: Strength: Next Step:
Student: Date: Strength: Next Step:	Student: Date: Strength: Next Step:	Student: Date: Strength: Next Step:	Student: Date: Strength: Next Step:	Student: Date: Strength: Next Step:
Student: Date: Strength: Next Step:	Student: Date: Strength: Next Step:	Student: Date: Strength: Next Step:	Student: Date: Strength: Next Step:	Student: Date: Strength: Next Step:

(Continued)

(Continued)

Student:	Student:	Student:	Student:	Student:
Date:	Date:	Date:	Date:	Date:
Strength:	Strength:	Strength:	Strength:	Strength:
Next Step:	Next Step:	Next Step:	Next Step:	Next Step:

Student:	Student:	Student:	Student:	Student:
Date:	Date:	Date:	Date:	Date:
Strength:	Strength:	Strength:	Strength:	Strength:
Next Step:	Next Step:	Next Step:	Next Step:	Next Step:

Student:	Student:	Student:	Student:	Student:
Date:	Date:	Date:	Date:	Date:
Strength:	Strength:	Strength:	Strength:	Strength:
Next Step:	Next Step:	Next Step:	Next Step:	Next Step:

REFERENCES

Achor, S. (2018). *Big potential: How transforming the pursuit of success raises our achievement, happiness, and well-being*. Crown.

Alden, C. (1999). Experience with scripted role play in environmental economics. *Journal of Economic Education, 30*(2), 127.

Allington, R. L., & McGill-Franzen, A. (2018). *Summer reading: Closing the rich/poor reading achievement gap* (2nd ed.). Teachers College Press.

Arter, J. A., & Spandel, V. (2005). Using portfolios of student work in instruction and assessment. *Educational Measurement: Issue and Practice, 11*(1), 36–44.

Bandura, A. (1997). *Self-efficacy: The exercise of control*. W. H. Freeman.

Bates, J. E., Almekdash, M. H., & Gilchrest-Dunnam, M. J. (2017). The flipped classroom: A brief, brief history. In L. S. Green, J. R. Banas, & R. A. Perkins (Eds.), *The flipped college classroom* (pp. 3–10). Springer.

Beck, I. L., McKeown, M. G., & Kucan, L. (2002). Choosing words to teach. In I. L. Beck, M. G. McKeown, & L. Kucan (Eds.), *Bringing words to life: Robust vocabulary instruction* (pp. 15–30). Guilford Press.

Beck, I. L., McKeown, M. G., & Kucan, L. (2013). *Bringing words to life: Robust vocabulary instruction* (2nd ed.). Guilford Press.

Beers, K., & Probst, B. (2012). *Notice and note*. Heinemann.

Beilock, S. (2015). *How the body knows its mind: The surprising power of the physical environment to influence how you think and feel*. Atria Books.

Bergmann, J., & Sams, A. (2012). *Flip your classroom: Reach every student in every class every day*. International Society for Technology in Education; ASCD.

Blank, S. C. (1985). Effectiveness of role playing, case study, and simulation games in teaching agricultural economics. *Western Journal of Agricultural Economics, 10*(1), 55–62.

Bonwell, C. (1995). Building a supportive climate for active learning. *The National Teaching and Learning Forum, 6*(1), 4–7.

Bronson, P., & Merryman, A. (2013). *Top dog: The science of winning and losing*. Twelve.

Brown, B. (2021). *Atlas of the heart: Mapping meaningful connection and the language of human experience*. Random House.

Burkins, J., & Yaris, K. (2016). *Who's doing the work? How to say less so readers can do more*. Stenhouse.

Cain, S. (2013). *Quiet: The power of introverts in a world that can't stop talking*. Broadway Books.

Calkins, L. (2000). *The art of teaching reading*. Prentice Hall.

Cambourne, B. (1988). *The whole story: Natural learning and the acquisition of literacy in the classroom*. Scholastic.

Carlson, S. M., & Moses, L. J. (2001). Individual differences in inhibitory control and children's theory of mind. *Child Development, 72*, 1032–1053.

Chaddock, L., Pontiflex, M. B., Hillman, C. H., & Kramer, A. F. (2011). A review of the relation of aerobic fitness and physical activity to brain structure and function in children. *Journal of the International Neurological Society, 17*(6), 975–985.

Chatfield, T. (2017). *Critical thinking: Your guide to effective argument, successful analysis, and independent study*. SAGE.

Chernikova, O., Heitzmann, N., Stadler, M., Holzberger, D., Seidel, T., & Fischer, F. (2020). Simulation-based learning in higher education: A meta-analysis. *Review of Educational Research, 90*(4), 499–541.

Cherry-Paul, S., & Johansen, D. (2019). *Breathing new life into book clubs*. Heinemann.

Chilcott, J. (1996). *Effective use of simulations in the classroom*. Creative Learning Exchange.

Chung, G. K. W. K., & Baker, E. L. (2003). An exploratory study to examine the feasibility of measuring problem-solving processes using a click-through interface. *Journal of Technology, Learning and Assessment, 2*(2). https://ejournals.bc.edu/index.php/jtla/article/view/1662

Corson, D. (1995). *Discourse and power in educational organizations*. Hampton.

Council of Chief State School Officers & National Governors Association. (2010). *Common Core State Standards for English language arts & literacy in history/social studies, science, and technical subjects*. https://learning.ccsso.org/wp-content/uploads/2022/11/ELA_Standards1.pdf

Cuddy, A. (2015). *Presence: Bringing your boldest self to your biggest challenges*. Little, Brown.

Cunningham, K. (2019). *Start with joy: Designing literacy learning for student happiness*. Stenhouse.

Darling-Hammond, L., & Adamson, F. (2010). *Beyond basic skills: The role of performance assessment in achieving 21st century standards of learning*. Stanford Center for Opportunity Policy in Education. https://edpolicy.stanford.edu/sites/default/files/publications/beyond-basic-skills-role-performance-assessment-achieving-21st-century-standards-learning_3.pdf

Delayed Gratification. (2022). *An answer for everything: 200 infographics to explain the world*. Bloomsbury.

DeNeve, K. M., & Heppner, M. J. (1997). Role play simulations: The assessment of an active learning technique and comparisons with traditional lectures. *Innovative Higher Education, 21*, 231–246.

Dorfman, L., & Cappelli, R. (2007). *Mentor texts: Teaching writing* through children's literature, K–6. Stenhouse.

Duncan, R. G., & Hmelo-Silver, C. E. (2009). Learning progressions: Aligning curriculum, instruction, and assessment. *Journal of Research in Science Teaching*, 46(6), 606–609.

Dutro, S., & Moran, C. (2003). *English learners: Reaching the highest level of English literacy.* International Reading Association.

Dweck, C. S. (2006). *Mindset: The new psychology of success.* Random House.

Effendi, A. (2017). The effectiveness of fishbowl technique towards students' self efficacy in speaking. *Journal of Languages and Language Teaching*, 5(2), 46.

Ericsson, K. A., & Pool, R. (2016). *Peak: Secrets from the new science of expertise.* Eamon Dolan/Houghton Mifflin Harcourt.

Faxon-Mills, S., Hamilton, L. S., Rudnick, M., & Stecher, B. M. (2013). *New assessments, better instruction? Designing assessment systems to promote instructional improvement.* RAND.

Fisher, D., & Frey, N. (2010). *Guided instruction: How to develop confident and successful learners.* ASCD.

Flipped Learning Network. (2014). *What is flipped learning?* https://flippedlearning.org/wp-content/uploads/2016/07/FLIP_handout_FNL_Web.pdf

Foote, C. J. (2005). The challenge and potential of high-need urban education. *Journal of Negro Education*, 74(4), 371–381.

Friend, M. P. (2013). *Co-teach! A handbook for creating and sustaining effective classroom partnerships in inclusive schools.* Marilyn Friend.

Fullman, J., Graham, I., Regan, S., & Thomas, I. (2014). *Talk nerdy to me: The world in facts, stats, and geeky graphics.* DK Publishing.

Gallagher, K. (2011). *Write like this: Teaching real-world writing through modeling and mentor texts.* Stenhouse.

Gelles-Watnick, R., & Perrin, A. (2021, September 21). *Who doesn't read books in America?* Pew Research Center. https://www.pewresearch.org/fact-tank/2021/09/21/who-doesnt-read-books-in-america/

Gilmore, B. (2006). *Speaking volumes: How to get students discussing books, and much more.* Heinemann.

Gladwell, M. (2008). *Outliers: The story of success.* Little, Brown.

Glenberg, A. M. (2011). How reading comprehension is embodied and why that matters. *International Electronic Journal of Elementary Education*, 4(1), 5–18.

Goldberg, G. (2015). *Mindsets and moves: Strategies that help readers take charge.* Corwin Literacy.

Goldberg, G., & Houser, R. (2017). *What do I teach readers tomorrow? Fiction.* Corwin Literacy.

Hall, T., & Strangman, N. (2002). *Graphic organizers.* National Center on Accessing the General Curriculum.

Hammond, Z. (2015). *Culturally responsive teaching and the brain.* Corwin.

Harvard Graduate School of Education. (n.d.). *Project Zero's thinking routine toolbox.* www.visiblethinkingpz.org

Hattie, J. (2012). *Visible learning for teachers: Maximizing impact on learning.* Routledge/Taylor & Francis Group.

Haystead, M. W., & Marzano, R. J. (2009). *Meta-analytic synthesis of studies conducted at Marzano Research Laboratory on instructional strategies.* Marzano Research Laboratory.

hooks, b. (2003). *Communion: The female search for love.* Perennial.

Institute of Education Sciences. (2016). *Teaching secondary students to write effectively.* https://ies.ed.gov/ncee/wwc/Docs/PracticeGuide/508_WWCPG_SecondaryWriting_122719.pdf

Jigsaw Classroom. (n.d.). *History of the jigsaw.* jigsaw.org/history

Judson, P. (2001). *Action research: How will direct instruction in prewriting strategies affect the quality of written products and student attitudes about their writing?* Minnesota Writing Project.

Kang, M. J., Hsu, M., Krajbich, I. M., Loewenstein, G., McClure, S. M., Wang, J. T., & Camerer, C. F. (2009). The wick in the candle of learning: Epistemic curiosity activates reward circuitry and enhances memory. *Psychological Science*, 20(8), 963–973.

Keene, E. O., & Zimmermann, S. (2007). *Mosaic of thought:*

Teaching comprehension in a reader's workshop (2nd ed.). Heinemann.

Lassonde, C., & Richards, J. (2013). Best practices in teaching planning for writing. In S. Graham, C. A. MacArthur, & J. Fitzgerald (Eds.), *Best practices in writing instruction* (2nd ed.). Guilford Press.

Lehman, C., & Roberts, K. (2014). *Falling in love with close reading.* Heinemann.

Lowry, L. (1993). *The giver.* Houghton Mifflin.

Lyman, F. (1981). The responsive classroom discussion. In A. S. Anderson (Ed.), *Mainstreaming digest* (pp. 109–113). University of Maryland College of Education.

MacKay, D. G., Shafto, M., Taylor, J. K., Marian, D. E., Abrams, L., & Dyer, J. R. (2004). Relations between emotion, memory, and attention: Evidence from taboo Stroop, lexical decision, and immediate memory tasks. *Memory & Cognition*, 32(3), 474–488.

Mazur, E. (1997). *Peer instruction: A user's manual.* Prentice Hall.

McCutchen, D. (2006). Cognitive factors in the development of children's writing. In C. A. MacArthur, S. Graham, & J. Fitzgerald (Eds.), *Handbook of writing research* (pp. 115–130). Guilford Press.

McTighe, J., & Wiggins, G. (2013). *Essential questions: Opening doors to student understanding.* ASCD.

Melton, A. W. (1963). Implications of short-term memory for a general theory of memory. *Journal of Verbal Learning and Verbal Behavior*, 2, 1–21.

Meyer, D. (n.d.). *Math class needs a makeover* [Video]. TEDxNYED. https://www.ted.com/talks/dan_meyer_math_class_needs_a_makeover

Mocko, M., Lesser, L. M., Wagler, A. E., & Francis, W. S. (2017). Assessing effectiveness of mnemonics for tertiary students in a hybrid introductory statistics course. *Journal of Statistics Education*, 25(1), 2–11.

Muhammad, G. (2020). *Cultivating genius: An equity framework for culturally and historically responsive literacy.* Scholastic.

Murawski, L. M. (2014). Critical thinking in the classroom . . . and beyond. *Journal of Learning in Higher Education*, 10(1), 25–30.

Nafisi, A. (2022, August 23). *An Iranian American writer makes a case against censorship and for Rushdie* [Interview]. NPR *Morning Edition*. https://www.npr.org/2022/08/23/1118959407/an-iranian-american-writer-makes-a-case-against-censorship-and-for-rushdie

Nasheed, J. (2019, December 16). Youth activist movements of the 2010s: A timeline and brief history of a decade of change. *Teen Vogue*. https://www.teenvogue.com/story/youth-activist-movements-2010s-brief-history-timeline-decade-of-change

National Center for Education Statistics. (2011–2012). *Schools and staffing survey (SASS)*. U.S. Department of Education. https://nces.ed.gov/surveys/sass/tables/sass1112_2013315_m1s_002.asp

Niedenthal, P. M. (2007). Embodying emotion. *Science*, *316*(5827), 1002–1005.

Niemi, D., Baker, E. L., & Sylvester, R. M. (2007). Scaling up, scaling down: Seven years of performance assessment development in the nation's second largest school district. *Educational Assessment*, *12*(3–4), 195–214.

Nimmo, K. (2020, July 23). 8 things creative thinkers do effortlessly. *On the Couch*. https://medium.com/on-the-couch/8-things-creative-thinkers-do-effortlessly-f9cdfecbf88d

November, A. (2012). *Who owns the learning? Preparing students for success in the digital age*. Solution Tree.

Oberhofer, T. (1999). Role playing in the history of economic thought. *Journal of Economic Education*, *30*(2), 112–118.

Paul, R. (2004, Fall). *The state of critical thinking today*. The Foundation for Critical Thinking. https://www.criticalthinking.org/pages/the-state-of-critical-thinking-today/523

PBS NewsHour & Newsela Staff. (2016, October 23). *Alaska villagers face dual threat of hungry polar bears, warmer weather*. Newsela. https://newsela.com/read/polar-bears-alaskan-natives/id/23211/

Pearson, P. D., & Gallagher, M. C. (1983). The instruction of reading comprehension. *Contemporary Educational Psychology*, *8*(3), 317–344.

Perry, B. D., & Winfrey, O. (2021). *What happened to you? Conversations on trauma, resilience, and healing*. Flatiron Books.

Poehler, A. (2014). *Yes, please!* Dey Street.

Popham, W. J. (2009). Assessment literacy for teachers: Faddish or fundamental? *Theory Into Practice*, *48*(1), 4–11.

Porter, J. (2017, March 21). Why you should make time for self-reflection (even if you hate doing it). *Harvard Business Review*. https://hbr.org/2017/03/why-you-should-make-time-for-self-reflection-even-if-you-hate-doing-it

Psychologist World. (n.d.). *Emotions and memory*. https://www.psychologistworld.com/emotion/emotion-memory-psychology

Ray, K. W. (1999). *Wondrous words: Writers and writing in the elementary classroom*. National Council of Teachers of English.

Richardson, W. (2011). Publishers, participants all. *Educational Leadership*, *68*(5). https://www.ascd.org/el/articles/publishers-participants-all

Rojas, M. A., & Villafuerte, J. S. (2018). The influence of implementing role-play as an educational technique on EFL speaking development. *Theory and Practice in Language Studies*, *8*(7), 726.

Rowe, M. B. (1986). Wait time: Slowing down may be a way of speeding up! *Journal of Teacher Education*, *37*(1), 43–50.

Ruggiero, V. R. (2012). *The art of thinking: A guide to critical and creative thought* (10th ed.). Longman.

Salmons, J. (2018). Two perspectives on critical thinking and research. *Methodspace*. https://www.methodspace.com/blog/critical-thinking-from-two-perspectives

Schulten, K. (2018, November 15). Writing for an audience beyond the teacher: 10 reasons to send student work out into the world. *The New York Times*. https://www.nytimes.com/2018/11/15/learning/writing-for-audience-beyond-teacher.html

Shirts, R. G. (n.d.). Ten secrets of successful simulations. *Learning Through Experience*. Simulation Training Systems. https://www.simulationtrainingsystems.com/ten-secrets-successful-simulations/

Stanier, M. B. (2016). *The coaching habit: Say less, ask more and change the way you lead forever*. Page Two Books.

Stewart, M., & Correia, M. (2021). *5 kinds of nonfiction: Enriching reading and writing instruction with children's books*. Stenhouse.

Stone, D., & Heen, S. (2014). *Thanks for the feedback: The science and art of receiving feedback well*. Penguin Random House.

Sutcliffe, M. (2002). Simulations, games and role-play. In P. Davies (Ed.), *The handbook for economic lecturers* (pp. 1–26). The Higher Education Academy Education Network.

TEDx Talks. (2014, March 11). *Creative thinking—how to get out of the box and generate ideas: Giovanni Corazza at TEDxRoma* [Video]. YouTube. https://www.youtube.com/watch?v=bEusrD8g-dM&ab_channel=TEDxTalks

Tomlinson, C. A. (2008, November 1). The goals of differentiation. *Educational Leadership*, *66*(3). https://www.ascd.org/el/articles/the-goals-of-differentiation

Tough, P. (2012). *How children succeed: Grit, curiosity, and the hidden power of character*. Mariner Books.

Trageser, C. (2020, April 1). *6 youth-led political movements to inspire you to vote*. Common Sense Media. https://www.commonsensemedia.org/blog/6-youth-led-political-movements-to-inspire-you-to-vote

Vogelsinger, B. (2023). *Poetry pauses: Teaching with poems to elevate student writing in all genres*. Corwin Literacy.

Vygotsky, L. S. (1978). *Mind in society: The development of higher psychological processes*. Harvard University Press.

Waack, S. (2018). Hattie ranking: 252 influences and effect sizes related to student achievement. *Visible Learning*. https://visible-learning.org/hattie-ranking-influences-effect-sizes-learning-achievement/

Waytz, A., & Mason, M. (2013). Your brain at work. *Harvard Business Review*.

Westerberg, T. R. (2009). *Becoming a great high school: 6 strategies and 1 attitude that make a difference*. ASCD.

Wiseman, T. (1996). A concept analysis of empathy. *Journal of Advanced Nursing*, *23*(6), 1162–1167.

Wong, A. (2016, July 14). Where books are all but nonexistent. *The Atlantic*. https://www.theatlantic.com/education/archive/2016/07/where-books-are-nonexistent/491282/

INDEX

Confident Teachers, *Inspired* Learners

JONATHAN ECKERT
Focus on feedback, engagement, and well-being to support comprehensive growth while elevating the essential work of educators.

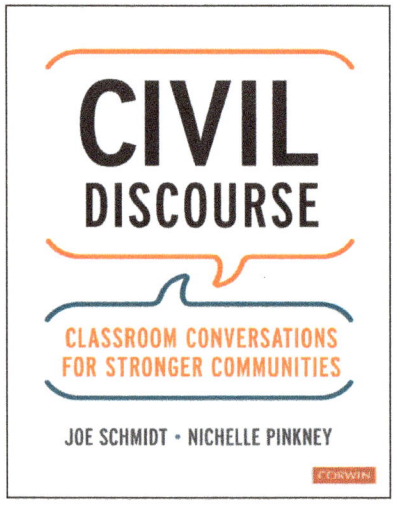

JOE SCHMIDT, NICHELLE PINKNEY
Facilitate contentious conversations by approaching civil discourse through the lenses of courage, understanding, belonging, and empathy.

CHASE NORDENGREN
Find actionable solutions to classroom management and culture, engaging lesson design, and effective communication.

JOHN HATTIE, DOUGLAS FISHER, NANCY FREY, SHIRLEY CLARKE
Discover how working with other people can be a powerful accelerator of student learning and a precursor to future success.

To order your copies, visit **corwin.com/teachingessentials**

No matter where you are in your professional journey, Corwin books provide accessible strategies that benefit ALL learners—and ease the many demands teachers face.

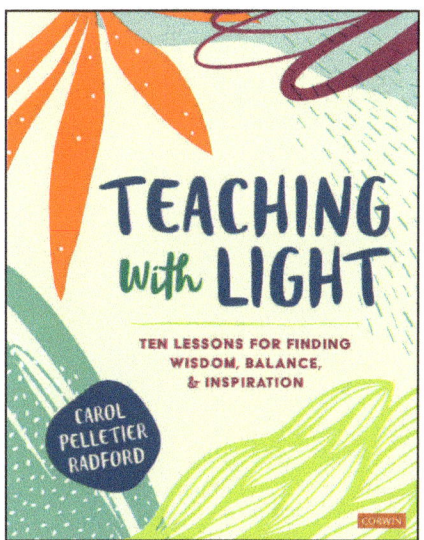

CAROL PELLETIER RADFORD

Equip teachers with the tools they need to take care of themselves so they can serve their students, step into leadership, and contribute to the education profession.

AMANDA BRUEGGEMAN

Develop student-centered approaches, promote collective efficacy, engage in coaching conversations, and prevent burnout while promoting student learning.

SERENA PARISER, VICTORIA LENTFER

Find actionable solutions to classroom management and culture, engaging lesson design, and effective communication.

STEPHANIE SMITH BUDHAI, KRISTINE S. LEWIS GRANT

Help teachers pivot instruction to ensure equitable, inclusive learning experiences in online and in-person settings.

CORWIN

A SAGE Publishing Company

Helping educators make the greatest impact

CORWIN HAS ONE MISSION: to enhance education through intentional professional learning.

We build long-term relationships with our authors, educators, clients, and associations who partner with us to develop and continuously improve the best evidence-based practices that establish and support lifelong learning.